WHEN TELEVISION WAS YOUNG

The Inside Story *with* Memories
by Legends *of the* Small Screen

ED McMAHON

and DAVID FISHER

THOMAS NELSON
Since 1798

NASHVILLE   DALLAS   MEXICO CITY   RIO DE JANEIRO   BEIJING

Published in Nashville, Tennessee, by Thomas Nelson. Thomas Nelson is a trademark of Thomas Nelson, Inc.

Thomas Nelson, Inc. titles may be purchased in bulk for educational, business, fund-raising, or sales promotional use. For information, please e-mail SpecialMarkets@thomasnelson.com.

Library of Congress Cataloging-in-Publication data
McMahon, Ed.
  When television was young : the inside story with memories by legends
of the small screen / Ed McMahon and David Fisher.
      p. cm.
  ISBN 10: 1-4016-0327-0
  ISBN 13: 978-1-4016-0327-4
  1. Television broadcasting--United States--History. I. Fisher, David,
1946- II. Title.
  PN1992.3.U5M295 2007
  384.550973--dc22
                                  2007023836

Printed in the United States of America
07 08 09 10 11   QW   7 6 5 4 3 2 1

interviews. The Archive preserves the history of TV by videotaping interviews with the people who made that history, from the inventors of electronic television to the biggest stars. It's an astonishing collection including more than 500 interviews, most of them available on the website—for free! The entire collection can be screened at the Archive's offices in Hollywood. Call 818-509-2260 for information.

And naturally, I want to thank our agent, the astonishing Bill Adler and our editor, Larry Stone, who knew just when to push a little harder to get this book completed.

My collaborator, David Fisher, would also like to thank Laura Stevens for her support and her continued efforts to make this book a reality.

ACKNOWLEDGMENTS

MANY PEOPLE GRACIOUSLY OFFERED THEIR TIME TO share their memories with me. I appreciate their contributions to this book and I hope that, together, we've captured some of the joy of the days when we invented television.

Among those many people are:

The remarkable pioneer Frances Buss, Barbara Barrie, Beverly Garland, Leslie Nielsen, Eli Wallach and Anne Jackson, Ed Reitan, the world's expert on the history of color television (visit his wonderful website at www.novia.net), David Wolper, Jerry Lewis, Dick Clark, Stanley Hubbard Jr., Ed Blier, Ron Seggie, Ward Qualls, George Schlatter, Jerry Zeitman, Dann Cann, Stanley Rubin, Sid Cooper of the sweetest notes ever heard on NBC, Penny Marshall, Herb Schlosser, Dick Shepherd, Woody Fraser, and Mike Wallace.

I also owe a great deal to Jane Klain and Rene Reyes at the Museum of Broadcasting, for their enthusiasm and their always good-natured support. The Museum of Television and Radio, with branches both in New York and Los Angeles, is an amazing repository of television history, and well worth visiting for hours of pure entertainment as well as serious research. The most difficult thing about a visit to the museum is leaving. Or take a look at the museum's website, www.mtr.org.

Also worth your time is a visit to the Academy of Television Arts & Sciences Foundation's Archive of American Television—online at www.emmysfoundation.org/archive. Our thanks to Karen Herman, who allowed us to utilize this resource and to quote from some of the

DEDICATION

I've spent my life working on television—but making every single moment possible were those people you rarely saw, the technical crew. From the cameramen to the grips to the make-up artists, I would like to dedicate this book to all of those people who really made television possible and received so little credit. Without their hard work, great skill, and relentless dedication, we would all still be watching test patterns.

—ED McMAHON

And I would like to dedicate this to all those people who were there when this great history was being made, but especially the Stone sisters of St. Louis, Missouri; Carol Stone Maune, Joanne Stone Curtis, and Mary Stone Colombo—who changed the history of my own life.

—DAVID FISHER

CONTENTS

WARM-UP

The elaborateness of the equipment
precludes the possibility of television
being available in homes or businesses generally.
What its practical use may be,
I leave to your imaginations.

—AT&T PRESIDENT WALTER GIFFORD, APRIL 7, 1927

GREETINGS! MY NAME IS ED MCMAHON, AND I WANT TO welcome you and thank you for coming to this book. We sure have some nice-looking readers here today! I know that many of you have traveled a lot of years to get here, and I want you to know how much I appreciate it. So just settle back in your seat and relax. In just a couple of pages the book is going to start, and we're going to tell you a really fascinating story. I know you're going to like it. But before I introduce Chapter 1, I want to take a few paragraphs to tell you a little about what you're going to read and get us all warmed up.

This book doesn't come with a band, but I do have some bad jokes.

Here, let me give you an example: a lot of people believe that kids today spend much too much time glued to the television set. Well, when I was growing up, believe it or not, we didn't even have television, so my parents had to glue me to the sofa.

See, that's a warm-up joke.

But there is some truth in it. I grew up before television existed. Instead we listened to a crystal set, which was a kind of homemade radio. I remember my grandfather, who lived in Lowell, Massachusetts, wrapping aerial wire around his house to try to catch the signal. Within a few years fancy radios were put inside beautiful wooden cabinets and became the central piece of furniture in a lot of living rooms, just as television sets are today. I remember I would lie on the floor in front of the radio for hours. When the wind was blowing just right, we could get as many as twenty stations. When people complained there was nothing to watch on the radio, that's exactly what they meant. We would sit and watch the radio set. Think of radio as television without the pictures.

In my house today we have eight television sets. I'm not kidding. The largest one is forty-eight inches, several of them are equipped to receive high definition, and each has cable and a DVD recorder. I don't have TiVo yet because I can record anything I want to see already, and I can watch it anytime I choose to. I can get about 425 stations.

The technology is unbelievable. In my lifetime we've gone from my grandfather wrapping wire around his house to pick up a distant radio signal, to bouncing signals off satellites so that we can watch live events taking place anywhere in the world. All that incredible technology, billions of dollars, and almost a century of research all enable me to turn on any one of my eight TV sets at any time, day or night, any day of the year, and find an episode of *Law & Order.*

What I'm going to do in this book is tell you how it all started.

Television is something we all take for granted now, but it wasn't always that way. There was a time when the concept of live pictures being sent through the air was science fiction. It was fantasy, magic. How could you send pictures through the air? Close your eyes and just think about that. Think about the wonder of the magic we take for granted. Pictures being sent through the air!

And once the magicians made it possible, the question became, what pictures would be shown on this magic box? Once the amazement had worn off, what pictures would capture the imagination? Would it be expensive? Who would pay for it? There were no answers to any of these questions. It all had to be imagined and created and discovered. The story I'm going to tell is how it all happened. I know the story because I lived through it.

I really was there at the beginning. The first public demonstration of television took place on the opening day of the 1939 World's Fair in Flushing Meadows, New York. And I was right there, standing among the thousands of people watching President Franklin Roosevelt announce that the fair was officially opened—on television. I don't really remember what I was thinking. I suspect I thought it was a very impressive gimmick. But I knew where my future was—I was going to be a radio announcer. Radio—that was my real love.

As it turned out, I hosted my own TV show even before I owned a TV set. Right after World War II, most of the TV sets were in bars. They were too expensive for people to have in their own homes. So people would go to a bar to watch a little twelve-inch, black-and-white flickering picture, and the longer you stayed in the bar, the better it seemed the TV picture got. Ah, yes, my friends, it's true. The occasional libation did enhance the viewing process.

Actually, I wasn't the first person in my family to be on television. That would have been my little cousin Sylvester. I'll never forget my mother looking at the TV and yelling, "Sylvester, get off the TV. You're going to fall and hurt yourself." That's another warm-up joke!

Now, obviously, you're much too young to remember those first TV sets. So let me tell you how they worked. In the late 1940s and early 1950s, you turned on the TV and had to wait a few seconds while it warmed up. You could smell the large tubes in the back of the set. It was kind of a pleasant aroma. You could hear it too. It made a sort of high-pitched sound that got louder as the picture came on. Then, after the picture appeared, you often had to play with an antenna on top of the set, moving the "rabbit ears" around, to get the picture to come in clearly. Finally, you would have to use the dials on the front of the set to adjust the vertical hold to get the picture to stop rolling, or the horizontal hold to straighten it out.

There was no such thing as a remote. If you wanted to change the channel, you had to turn a dial on the set. In those days the only remote control we had was my Aunt Mary. "Aunt Mary! Put on channel four, please." Young people find it hard to believe how difficult it was to watch TV in those days. I try to tell them how rough it was: "When I was your age, we were lucky if we got three channels. And if we wanted to change the channel, we had to get up, literally get up from the couch, and walk *all* the way across the entire living room to the TV. We learned how to change the channel for ourselves. But we survived."

Growing up, more than anything in the world, I wanted to be a radio announcer. I would stand in front of the radio with a copy of *Time* magazine, speaking into a flashlight, pretending it was a microphone, and practice reading the news—and the advertisements. Even then I knew who paid the bills.

Before going into the Marines, I was the night announcer on WLLH in Lowell, Massachusetts, "The Synchronized Voice of the Merrimack Valley." Not only did I read the news, but I also gave the time. "It's 12:17 a.m. Please, no applause."

But by the time I got out of the Marine Corps, everybody was talking about television. Nobody knew what it was, but we all knew it was coming. There were very few TVs in existence and almost nothing to watch. In the few cities that did have television, there was usually only one channel. And even on that one channel there was almost no programming. The eleven o'clock news was broadcast at nine o'clock. The entire TV schedule for the night usually consisted of something like: 8:00–9:00 p.m.: The Whatever-We-Can-Figure-Out-To-Put-On-That-Doesn't-Cost-Anything Show. Hosted by: To be announced.

To be announced? That was me! That was my future, and I knew it. I knew that one day, if I worked hard, I could be "To be announced"! At that point I had as much experience in television as just about everybody else in the world: exactly none.

Actually, a very few people had already been on television. One of them was a young kid named Jerry Lewis. Now listen to this one, because you're not going to believe it. In 1943, Jerry Lewis, the great tap dancer Bill "Bojangles" Robinson, and a woman named Arlene Woods performed on a very special broadcast. They were escorted by guards up to a secure studio in the RCA building at 30 Rockefeller Plaza, the same building where for so many years I had the privilege of working with Johnny Carson on *The Tonight Show*.

The way Jerry tells the story, this was one of the most exclusive broadcasts in history. The whole thing was a very big secret because NBC was developing its color television system and didn't want CBS to know anything about it. This show was broadcast from the RCA building in New York to Princeton, New Jersey, where Albert Einstein was watching it.

Think about that! Jerry Lewis performed for Albert Einstein on color television in 1943. I guess the good news was that it didn't matter how good or bad Jerry was, because Einstein couldn't change the channel.

After the broadcast, Jerry, Bill Robinson, and Arlene Woods were driven to Princeton to meet Albert Einstein. Now, my friend, that would have been some act: Einstein and Lewis! I asked Jerry what they talked about. He told me Einstein told him the story of how he had discovered the theory of relativity. "He said he was talking to one of his children on the telephone, and he was doodling on a pad. A little while later his houseman asked if he should throw away the pad, and Einstein looked and saw $E=mc^2$ and went to his lab, and the rest is history."

Who knew that Einstein was the comedian and Jerry was the straight man?

With just a few hours of programming a night, the only thing being broadcast most of the time was a test pattern. A test pattern was a black-and-white line drawing that looked a little like a very fancy hubcap. The test pattern meant that the local TV station was transmitting a signal, but there was no programming. The purpose was to allow viewers to adjust the sharpness and contrast of their TV sets. Sometimes the test pattern had a soundtrack, a high-pitched whine.

But people didn't care. It was television. People would watch the

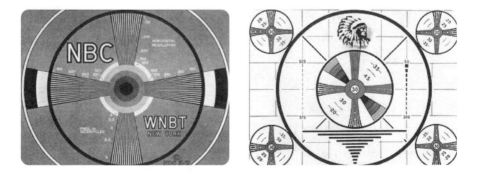

When a station broadcast programming for only part of a day, it would broadcast test patterns at other times to allow viewers—and technicians—to focus TV sets and broadcasting equipment. The NBC test pattern (left) dates back to when commercial broadcasts began. The most famous test pattern is the "Indian Head" pattern (right).

test pattern. Maybe they wouldn't talk about it around the water cooler at work the next day—"Boy, did you see that great test pattern on NBC last night?"—but they watched it. Just about the only good thing you could say about a test pattern was that it was broadcast without commercial interruption.

So that was the competition when I got into television. What would viewers rather watch, Ed McMahon or a test pattern?

I made my first appearance on television in 1947 when I was studying speech and the dramatic arts at Catholic University in Washington, D.C. My teacher was playwright Walter Kerr. I was married and paying my tuition by selling stainless-steel pots and pans door-to-door in the winter and working as a pitchman on the boardwalk in Atlantic City in the summer, selling the famous Morris Metric Vegetable Slicer. In my second year at Catholic, my class performed *Touch and Go*, a play Kerr had written. I was cast as a naval officer, obviously because I had a natural talent that Kerr was able to unearth—as well as the fact that I already had the naval officer's uniform. The play was such a big success that we were invited to perform it on television.

The fact that we couldn't see it, and that no one we knew could watch it, didn't matter. We were going to be on television! Even more exciting was that our play would be the first program broadcast on an experimental network. Somehow they had linked Washington to Baltimore, Philadelphia, and New York by coaxial cable. We all knew what that meant: it meant that *no one* would watch our play in *four* cities rather than just in Washington!

We turned the banquet room of the Wardman Park Hotel into a little television studio. We made all our own studio sets. I think we had one camera. No makeup. And that is how I made my dramatic debut on television.

The play eventually went to New York, and Walter Kerr became the most respected theater critic on Broadway. I went back to Atlantic

City and sold Metric Slicers—making me a star of television and boardwalk. But within two years I was doing thirteen hours of programming on WCAU in Philadelphia, everything from cohosting a cooking show to having my own late-night talk show. In Philadelphia, I was Mr. Television. I was on the cover of one of the first issues of *TV Digest* in 1949, which eventually became *TV Guide*.

TV had arrived. It was black-and-white and the screen was rarely larger than twelve inches, but it worked. It changed the world. It's hard to believe how very little people understood about television. I was in a supermarket one afternoon when an older woman stopped me and asked if I was "that nice Ed McMahon from the television." She seemed unusually suspicious that I could be me.

"Yes," I admitted. "That's me."

"My," the woman said. "You certainly are considerably taller than you look on my TV."

"Really? How tall did you think I was?"

She held up her thumb and forefinger to me. "Oh, about four inches."

But seriously, folks, it is a pleasure being on the same page with you. I hope you're all warmed up by now, but let me just tell you one more thing before I bring on Chapter 1.

The availability of television after World War II created a real paradox. Groucho Marx, on his quiz show *You Bet Your Life*, defined paradox as "two doctors," but that's not the kind of paradox I'm talking about. Television sets were very expensive, and people didn't buy them because there was very little programming. If there was something they really wanted to see, they could go to the corner bar or go downstairs to Mrs. McGillicuddy's apartment and watch through the open door like everybody else. However, because there were so few viewers, advertisers wouldn't pay very much to produce new shows, and so there was very limited programming.

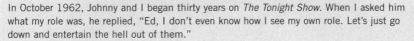

In October 1962, Johnny and I began thirty years on *The Tonight Show*. When I asked him what my role was, he replied, "Ed, I don't even know how I see my own role. Let's just go down and entertain the hell out of them."

A lot of smart people believed television was a novelty, a gimmick that would never catch on. In 1946 the legendary movie producer Darryl F. Zanuck told people confidently, "Television won't be able to hold on to any market it captures after the first six months. People will soon get tired of staring at a plywood box every night."

Even Lee de Forest, the inventor of the vacuum tube (which made radio and television possible), said, "While theoretically and technically television may be feasible, commercially and financially I consider it an impossibility, a development on which we need waste little time dreaming."

Finally, the two major radio networks, CBS and NBC, plus DuMont, a manufacturer of TV sets, and pioneering broadcasters in cities all around the country decided that if they made it, viewers would come. And they would buy TV sets. "It" was television. "It" was the forerunner of just about every television program on the air tonight. And what I'm going to tell you now—with a little help from my friends who were there—is the story of how it all happened.

So without further ado, I'd like to introduce you to the very first chapter. I hope you'll enjoy it. If I had a band it would start playing right now. But go ahead and hum the theme song of one of your favorite shows.

Let's get on with the book! Right here on this page today, I am very pleased to be able to write these words, *Heeeeeeerrrrrrre's Chapter One*!

Crosby Enterprises hopes to captivate televiewers
with a new series featuring a cast of chimpanzees
enacting Sherlock Holmes thrillers.

—*TIME* MAGAZINE, MARCH 6, 1950

T HE FIRST TELEVISION SHOW I EVER WATCHED WAS ED
Sullivan's Sunday night variety show, *Toast of the Town*, in 1949.
I was living in a suburb of Philadelphia, and our across-the-street
neighbor was the leader of a big band that played at the swanky
Warwick Hotel. That was a pretty prestigious job, but what really
impressed people in the neighborhood was that he had his own television set. Having a TV set was a big status symbol in those days.
Because of Pennsylvania's blue laws, which prohibited most businesses from being open on Sundays, our neighbor couldn't work
Sunday nights, and so he would take his wife out for dinner. Being
the big-hearted person that I am, I volunteered to babysit.

11

Although, truthfully, the only sitting I wanted to do was right in front of his television set.

If you ask people younger than forty years old when it was they first saw television, they will look at you as if you had come from . . . 1950. If you are under forty, you grew up with television. It was always there. It was always everywhere. You were practically raised on *Sesame Street*. But if you ask the Greatest Generation or Baby Boomers, they will remember the first time they saw television. Believe me, it was a big deal. Penny Marshall, Laverne on *Laverne & Shirley* and the director of movies like *Big* and *A League of Their Own*, grew up in an apartment building in the Bronx. "The Altmans had the only television in our building," she told me. "They lived on the first floor, near the incinerator. They were nice people. When their TV was on, they would keep their door open so the neighbors could watch. When you took the garbage to the incinerator, everybody would be standing outside watching the Altmans' television.

"We finally got our own TV. I think we had a Hoffman; then we got a Zenith. I got woken up anytime there was dancing on television, particularly tap dancing. I had a blind grandmother who would sit in front of the TV in the living room, and every once in a while she would suddenly shout, 'Babe, come in quick! There's dancing.' That meant we all had to stop whatever we were doing and run in to watch. The problem was that sometimes it was just somebody typing. I think she just wanted the company. I mean, who was going to come running into the living room if she shouted, 'There's typing'?"

Like a lot of other people, the first thing Carl Reiner ever saw on TV was a boxing match. "We went to a friend of my brother-in-law's house to watch Kid Gavilan fight. There were eighteen people there, piled into his living room. We didn't even say hello. We just sat around the house while they banged on the TV set because the picture was rolling."

Jim McKay, host of *Wide World of Sports*, had a similar experience. He remembers walking into a bar with a college friend, "and up there on the shelf in the corner was this box that looked like a radio, except in the top right-hand corner there was a screen and two guys were hitting each other. It was dazzling; it was mind-boggling. I kept thinking, *This is happening right now, just as we're looking at it.* I couldn't believe it. I'd heard about television. You know, people kept saying, 'It's coming, it's coming. There are going to be pictures through the air.'"

"Pictures through the air" was a perfect way to describe television. We all knew it was coming, just like we knew rocket ships were coming, and cars that ran on alcohol, and gigantic airplanes that could carry hundreds of passengers, and wrist radios like the one Dick Tracy wore—they were all coming. Television was going to appear in some distant future. We knew that companies were experimenting with various types of radios with pictures, but I don't think anybody really expected it to be available so soon.

Now you would think that the first thing to be televised from one American city to another would be something majestic, something meaningful, something historic. Actually, it was Secretary of Commerce Herbert Hoover's forehead. The transmission took place on April 7, 1927, and was the highest-rated show in history to that point. I would tell you that this broadcast made . . . headlines—but even I wouldn't stoop to a joke that bad.

Actually, Secretary Hoover's image wasn't really transmitted through the air. The thing he was on was known as "radio vision," a mechanical process that transformed light into electrical impulses that could be transmitted over telephone wires. He was in Washington, D.C., speaking to an audience gathered in the office of AT&T president Walter Gifford in Whippany, New Jersey. The problem was that Hoover was sitting much too close to the camera. It wasn't really his fault. Nobody had ever been on camera before, so who knew? But after backing up, Hoover delivered his prepared speech, telling the audience, "It is a matter of pride to just have a part in this historic occasion . . . the transmission of sight, for the first time in the world's history."

A telephone operator named Edna Mae Horner helped set up the connection, making her the first woman to appear on American TV.

Hoover was followed by a vaudeville comedian named A. Dolan, who performed first as an Irishman, wearing whiskers and telling his jokes in a brogue. Dolan then changed into blackface and told old minstrel show jokes. His performance was compared favorably by a local newspaper to *Fred Ott's Sneeze*, which was a moving picture Thomas Edison had made for his kinetoscope.

That was the whole show: Hoover, the telephone operator, and a comedian. Better than a sneeze, critics claimed. That was also the highlight of the radio vision process, because it never took off.

But here's how the television system we use was invented. When most people look at a potato field, they see potatoes. But one day in 1920, an Idaho teenager named Philo Farnsworth—what a great name for an inventor; it sounds like a name W. C. Fields might have made up!—was tilling his family's potato field into neat parallel furrows when it occurred to him that a picture might be broken down into similar parallel lines or dots and sent electronically through the air and reassembled at its destination. Don't expect me to explain the technology. At least Philo knew what he was doing. He worked out his concept with his high school science teacher. "This is my idea for electronic television," he told him.

"What's television?" his teacher asked.

To develop his invention, Farnsworth moved to Hollywood and set up his lab in his kitchen. It took him seven years to make it actually work. The first television picture ever transmitted electronically over the airwaves without a wire was a sheet of glass with a horizontal black line painted on it. This was the first straight line delivered in television history. How could I not love the man?

Apparently Philo Farnsworth had a sense of humor. A few years later, when he was trying to develop his invention, one of his investors wondered, "When are we going to see some dollars in this thing?" Farnsworth responded by broadcasting a picture of a dollar sign.

About twenty-five years later Philo Farnsworth appeared as the "mystery guest" on the game

In 1862 the first still image was transmitted over wires. Twenty years later Alexander Graham Bell and Thomas Edison theorized about telephones that could transmit pictures. But it wasn't until 1927 that Philo Farnsworth (above) filed a patent for his "Image Dissector," the first true electronic TV system.

Courtesy of Stephen Cox Collection

show *What's My Line?* The object of the game was for panelists to guess the profession of ordinary guests. For the final segment panelists put on blindfolds, and a mystery guest, someone so well-known that panelists would instantly recognize him, appeared. Since the voices of these stars might also be recognizable, they disguised them in a variety of ways, or the host, John Daly, answered the questions for them. The biggest stars in show business appeared on the show, people like Johnny Carson, Lucille Ball, Sophia Loren, and Mickey Mantle.

Anyway, after the panel managed to establish the fact that Philo Farnsworth was an inventor, one of them asked, "Have you invented some sort of machine that might be painful when used?"

"Oh yes," Farnsworth responded. "Sometimes it's most painful." Farnsworth, it turned out, wasn't particularly proud of his invention. He didn't let his own kids watch TV, telling them, "There's nothing on it worthwhile. We're not going to watch it in this household, and I don't want it in your intellectual diet."

Television really began only a couple of years after the broadcast of Farnsworth's line. In 1931 Don Lee, the owner of several radio stations and Cadillac dealerships in Los Angeles, began broadcasting an hour of programming a day—except Sundays. Supposedly he went into TV because he thought it would help him sell more cars than his competitor—a Packard dealer. His main problem was that absolutely nobody in Los Angeles had a television set, and so he gave away plans for do-it-yourself TV receivers so that people could make their own. TV kits were also for sale from major radio set dealers.

Don Lee didn't even have a station. All he had was a transmitter, W6XAO, and it broadcast mostly action clips and close-ups of movie stars. Believe it or not, in 1932 Don Lee successfully broadcast a movie to an airplane in flight. In 1932! That's pretty impressive. A year later a movie clip of the Los Angeles earthquake was broadcast only a few hours after it took place, which was arguably the beginning of TV news. That same year Don Lee broadcast the first movie ever shown on TV, *The Crooked Circle*. By that time it was estimated that as many as five people had TV sets and could have watched the movie at home.

In 1935, only eight years after the broadcast of Herbert Hoover's forehead, RCA, the owner of NBC, gave away 150 TV sets in New York City and became the first company to follow a broadcasting schedule. It put a transmitter on top of the new Empire State Building and built a television studio in Radio City, Rockefeller Center. The first regularly scheduled program in American history was . . .

Imagine a drum roll, please.

The first regularly scheduled program in American history was *Felix the Cat*, a cartoon. In those days there was almost no original programming, with the exception of politicians' speeches. You can

The legendary RCA executive David Sarnoff demonstrates color television technology to the press in October 1946. RCA and CBS had a long and bitter battle over which company would receive permission from the FCC to sell color television sets first. CBS won the battle in 1951, only to have to stop one month later because of the Korean War.

make your own joke about that! But there just weren't enough viewers to justify any investment.

The year 1939 was a pivotal one in the history of television. TV really got started that year. The first public demonstration of television took place in 1939 at the New York World's Fair. David Sarnoff, the head of RCA, said, "Now we add sight to sound," and President Franklin Roosevelt became the first president to appear on TV. I would like to think that as I watched, I became one of the first people to say those magic words, "Let's see what else is on"—but I didn't.

In 1939, nobody was making any money from TV and there were a lot of smart people who doubted it would ever be financially successful. There were some people willing to gamble that it would be profitable, but even among those people, the belief was that the real profit would come from manufacturing and selling TV sets. The programming was just the come-on to get you to buy the set.

In 1951 Milton Berle signed a thirty-year contract with NBC that paid him $200,000 a year—whether he worked or not, demonstrating that there was real money to be made from programming. During a live performance of Berle's show one Tuesday night, an NBC executive mentioned to an agent that Berle looked about ten pounds heavier on television. The agent agreed, but pointed out, "Most of it's in his wallet."

There were other people in 1939 who believed television could be just as successful as radio. Well, maybe not *as* successful . . . because who was going to waste time watching nothing on television when you could listen to Jack Benny, George and Gracie, *Amos 'n' Andy*, the scary *Inner Sanctum*, all the soap operas and the dramas, the big bands with Sinatra and Rosemary Clooney, and all the great singers of the Metropolitan Opera—all for free?

But there were a few dreamers who believed television could be profitable. One of those people in 1939 was Stanley Hubbard, who is now a member of the TV Hall of Fame. As a pioneer in radio, Hubbard had gone on the air in Minneapolis in 1923 with the first station in radio history to be completely supported by advertising. His son, another broadcasting pioneer named Stanley S. Hubbard, told me, "Other radio stations had some advertising, but they were actually supported by the company that owned them. My father's thought was, 'If I put some popular music on the radio rather than a fat lady singing opera, maybe I can get enough listeners to sell advertising.' In those days the technology didn't exist to play records on the radio, and so he made a deal with the Marigold Ballroom in Minneapolis that if they gave him a little studio, he would broadcast their band live five nights a week. That was the beginning of advertiser-supported broadcasting." Stanley Hubbard was also the first person to broadcast a fifteen-minute daily news show.

When television came along, Hubbard was already doing very well, but he saw the possibilities. After the 1939 World's Fair ended, he bought the first TV camera, the only one RCA was selling, and seven TV sets. Those TV sets were consoles with a top that flipped up. A mirror on the bottom side of the flip top reflected a small TV screen. The picture tube was vertical. Those TV sets cost as much as $600 each, which was just about the price of a new automobile.

Hubbard set up a demonstration in the lobby of the Radisson Hotel in Minneapolis and then talked the local American Legion into putting on a parade. He broadcast that parade to his seven TV sets. Thousands of people stood in line for hours to see the parade on TV. That was a pretty impressive display of the interest in this new thing. All those people were willing to wait in line to watch the parade on television instead of simply going outside and watching the parade itself.

In 1939 nobody really knew how the television industry was going to work, who was going to own or run the stations, whether television stations would rely on advertising or be self-sustaining, what kind of programming they would telecast, if there would be networks as there were in radio or if stations would be independent. There just weren't any rules.

The stations that were on the air were considered experimental, meaning they didn't have any commercials. No commercials? Let me just pause while we consider television without commercials. It's a good thing that didn't catch on. Just imagine a world without Tony the Tiger or Speedy Alka-Seltzer or Mr. Clean or Ed McMahon!

Less than two decades earlier, radio had started in a very similar way—without commercials. David Sarnoff, an RCA vice president, had started the National Broadcasting Corporation (NBC) radio network because RCA controlled most of the important radio patents, and so RCA received a royalty payment on just about every radio sold in America, no matter who manufactured it. Sarnoff wasn't a broadcaster. He was a manufacturer, and he started NBC to attract listeners who would then go out and buy radio sets. He thought that the real profit was in selling the equipment. In the late 1930s and early 1940s, RCA invested millions of dollars in the development of television because its radio patents were about to run out, and the only way it and other manufacturers could sell TV sets was to put on programming that people wanted to see.

In 1939 a lot of these experimental stations began broadcasting outside the studio, which was sort of necessary because there were almost no television studios. TV cameras covered the gala premiere of *Gone With the Wind* in Atlanta in 1939. The first musical was broadcast that year, Gilbert and Sullivan's *Pirates of Penzance*. In the first heavyweight fight ever shown on TV, Lou Nova beat Max Baer at Yankee Stadium. The few people who viewed it were impressed— there was the great Max Baer bleeding real black-and-white blood! In May, the first baseball game was broadcast, a college game between Columbia and Princeton from Baker Field in New York. There was only one camera, and the announcer was the legendary Bill Stern. "Welcome to the first telecast of a sporting event," he said. "I'm not sure what it is we're doing here, but I certainly hope it turns out well for you people who are watching."

Stern was probably radio's most famous sports broadcaster, but he had a reputation for being . . . now, my friends, let me be charitable here . . . less than 100 percent accurate. One time when he was broadcasting a Notre Dame football game, he told listeners that running back Jack Zilly had broken loose. "He's at the fifty, the forty, the thirty-five, the thirty, the twenty . . ." It was about that time that Stern realized that he had the wrong guy carrying the ball. It wasn't Zilly; it was

Emil "Six Yard" Sitko. But that didn't faze Stern at all. "He's at the five . . . and he laterals the ball to Sitko who takes it in for the touchdown!"

So adjusting to TV wasn't going to be that easy for him. Just before Bill Stern was about to announce his first horse race, from Belmont Park, he asked another sports legend, Ted Husing, for advice. Supposedly Husing explained the essence of TV sports broadcasting to Stern in two sentences, telling him, "I can't help you, Bill. On TV there's no way to lateral a horse."

A few weeks after the college game, the first major-league game, a doubleheader between the Brooklyn Dodgers and Cincinnati Reds, was telecast by station W2XBS, which later became WNBC. Two cameras were used, and newspaper reports about the broadcast were mixed. Apparently the players were easy to see, but it was almost impossible to see the ball. Well, you could see that might be a problem; it was going to be tough to attract viewers for a baseball game if they couldn't see the baseball.

In April 1941 the U.S. government's National Television Systems Committee (NTSC) announced that commercial TV would begin on July 1. There were fewer than seven thousand television sets in America, most of them in bars. The committee issued licenses to ten stations, three of them in New York City, which became the capital of the television world. W2XBS in New York City changed its name to WNBT, which eventually became WNBC, and went on the air a day early, broadcasting two hours of amateur boxing. Among the shows telecast on the first day of commercial television were *Excerpts from The Bottlenecks of 1941*, a military training film, the game show *Truth or Consequences* with Ralph Edwards, which was simulcast on radio, and the first quiz show, *Words on the Wing, a Spelling Bee*.

Definitely more importantly, at the beginning of a Dodgers–Phillies game that first day, the first commercial in history was broadcast. And so the world was changed forever. That was the start of television as we know it. With the transmission of that commercial, television broadcasting had become a business. The commercial was for Bulova watches, and it cost the company nine bucks for the ten-second ad. Among the other sponsors that first day were Sun Oil, Lever Brothers, and Procter & Gamble. Some things just never change, do they?

WCBW, which later would become WCBS, went on the air in the afternoon with a fifteen-minute news telecast, followed by an illustrated version of *Jack and the Beanstalk*. A third New York station, W2XWV, which eventually became DuMont's New York station, also went on the air.

Five months after commercial television began, America entered World War II and television went to war. Commercial TV pretty much ended for the duration, but technical development continued. The military developed television-guided bombs, an early ancestor of the so-called smart bombs.

One of the secret experiments the army conducted turned old B-24s into remote-controlled bombs designed to destroy the Nazis' heavily protected V-l and V-2 missile launching sites. Project Aphrodite was one of those big hush-hush deals. The old bombers were stripped down and loaded with ten tons of explosives, enough power to penetrate the cement walls of German launching sites and submarine pens. The way it worked was that after a pilot got the plane airborne, a second plane flying behind it took over by remote control, using a TV camera in the B-24's nose to guide it to its target. Once the plane switched to remote control, the pilot was supposed to bail out because he was riding a bomb. It was on one of these missions that pilot Joseph Kennedy Jr., JFK's older brother, was killed. Eventually the army realized that this plan wasn't going to work and shut it down.

A lot of people saw television for the first time during the war. Herb Schlosser, who later became the president of NBC, was trained by the Navy as an electronic technician. One afternoon in 1944 his instructor

boasted, "Now we're really going to show you something!" A TV camera was trained at the street, showing every person who walked by.
Schlosser remembers just looking out the window, then at the black-
and-white TV set, then out the window again, with absolute wonder.
That was the magic of television in those days; it didn't matter what
was on, just the fact that pictures were being sent through the air.

As soon as the war ended in 1945, television and I both returned
to civilian life, and I tried to figure out how to get into television. It
was sort of like trying to grab hold of a fistful of cotton candy.
Television was there, it was real, and if you played with the antenna,
you could watch it, but everything about it seemed experimental or
temporary. By 1946 the NTSC was issuing licenses to stations all over
the country. The licenses were absolutely free, and the number of stations licensed in each city depended on the size of the city—TV
broadcast towers had to be a certain distance apart to make sure the
signal was clear. In most major cities there was competition for the
licenses, but the requirements in smaller locales were relatively
simple: you had to ask for it. In some places they literally could not
give away a license. People still didn't believe TV would work, and
the initial investment to build a station and buy broadcasting equipment was substantial, with absolutely no guarantee that it would ever
be successful. In smaller areas you could get a broadcast license
pretty much just by sending in a postcard asking for one.

In Minneapolis, Stanley Hubbard really wanted to get into the
television business, but he had a lot of difficulty raising the money
he needed. Most banks wouldn't loan him money because they didn't
think TV was a safe investment. Finally a New York stock speculator
named Tom Bragg, who owned New York Shipbuilding, bought an
interest in the company. "I asked Mr. Bragg how he happened to
invest in our company," Hubbard remembered. "He said, 'Because
Jack Warner [one of the Warner brothers] told me not to.'

"Tom Bragg said, 'I was having dinner with Jack Warner at his brownstone on Park Avenue, and I asked him about television. He told me television will never work. "Can you imagine," he said to me, "trying to produce a new movie for every night of the week? It's not possible." Jack Warner's vision was movies. That's all he saw.

"'After dinner I went back into the kitchen to thank the cook for the fine dinner. The whole staff was gathered around a small TV set. I knew right then and there that TV was going to be a big deal. That's why I invested.'"

Those people who owned stations were desperate for any programming that would attract viewers and didn't cost too much. "Too much" meaning, pretty much anything. Basically, stations broadcast live sports events, old newsreels, and PTA meetings. The movie industry didn't want any part of television. Not only did the Hollywood executives refuse to sell their old movies to TV, but they prohibited all the actors under contract from appearing on TV. They figured that if people saw their stars on TV for free, they wouldn't pay to see them in the movies. And they also thought that without movie stars to draw viewers, nobody would be interested in watching TV. Well, we all know how well that one worked out!

But at that time it wasn't just the movie studios that were afraid of television. The head of the Musicians' Union, James Petrillo, refused to allow any live music on television. Producers could use prerecorded music or play the ukulele because the ukulele was not considered a musical instrument. Petrillo was holding out for a good deal for his union members. But, as he said when testifying in front of Congress about this ban on live music, "We have asked the [TV] industry what is the future of television. They tell me, 'Jim, we don't know.'" When Petrillo finally made his deal with the networks in 1948, NBC celebrated by broadcasting a concert featuring the NBC Symphony Orchestra led by Arturo Toscanini.

Every aspect of television was new. You couldn't do anything wrong because there was no right. There was no established structure. Everyone was just making up the rules as they broadcast. The networks didn't even know how long a program should be. Radio shows were either fifteen minutes or half an hour, but nobody knew how long a viewer would sit in front of the box before becoming bored. NBC decided that twenty minutes was a good length for a drama and in 1948 ordered what was supposed to be the first filmed drama made for TV, a series called *Public Prosecutor*. By the time the producers had filmed twenty-six episodes, the three networks had decided that shows should be thirty minutes long—twenty-six and a half minutes of programming with the remainder for commercials. *Public Prosecutor* had to be completely reedited to fit the new requirements.

Stan Rubin and Lou Lantz, two screenwriters whose contracts had been dropped by Columbia, created an anthology series for television that would dramatize famous short stories in the public domain. That meant they wouldn't have to pay for any rights, and viewers would be familiar with the stories. For continuity they added a host, a bookshop proprietor who would introduce each week's story and fill in gaps that were too expensive to film. The story that they picked for the pilot was "The Diamond Necklace" by Guy de Maupassant.

They were able to raise enough money to make a pilot to try to sell the series, they hired Arthur Shields as host, and they made a deal with Hal Roach Studios in which they guaranteed to film the whole series there if they could sell it.

Two weeks after finishing the pilot, they sold the show, not to a network but to a sponsor, the American Tobacco Company. In the early days, sponsors completely controlled programming. They bought airtime from a network and put on pretty much whatever show they wanted to. American Tobacco ordered twenty-six half-hour episodes of *Your Show Time* with an option for a second season. But Stanley

Rubin added one more clause to the contract: after the show had been run twice, the rights reverted to Rubin's company. American Tobacco didn't object, figuring that after viewers had seen them twice these shows would have very little value.

Rubin and Lantz's problem was that it cost more money to shoot the shows than American Tobacco was paying for them. Television was turning out to be a tough business. The more shows they made, the more money they lost. Being successful was going to bankrupt them. They tried to borrow the money from banks, offering to put up the residual value of the shows for collateral. Great, the banks asked, what's residual value? Nobody knew what "residuals," "pilots," or "syndication" meant. This was all new stuff. The banks turned down their request.

In what might be the first case of television censorship, American Tobacco told Rubin and Lantz they could not produce any stories by Russian writers, including Tolstoy, Turgenev, and Chekhov. The Cold War had just begun, and American Tobacco didn't want anything to do with communism. "I argued and I argued and I argued," Rubin remembered. "But that was their final answer. No Red writers!"

The actors were each paid the Screen Actors Guild minimum, fifty-five dollars a day. If there was one thing easy to find in Hollywood, it was actors willing to work. For the part of a beautiful young woman in the third show, the film editor, Dann Cahn, recommended a young woman he was dating. Rubin auditioned her and turned her down because she didn't have enough experience. Coincidently, I met the same young woman several years later, after the Marines had recalled me and ordered me to Korea. But by the time I met her on the set of a movie called *How to Marry A Millionaire*, Marilyn Monroe had become the biggest star in the world. After we spoke for a while, she suggested we have our picture taken together. I went outside her trailer, and a few minutes later she joined me, wearing a beautiful fur coat. As the photographer focused on us she kind of moved in next to me and whispered, "You know, Ed, I don't have anything on under this."

Now imagine me smiling.

Just how much do you think the residual value of that show would have been if Rubin had cast Marilyn Monroe?

Your Show Time, also known as *Lucky Strike Time* and hosted by Arthur Shields looking book-store-ownerish and smoking a Lucky, of course, went on the air on the East Coast in September 1948. This was the first spon-

From the Author's Collection

After being called back into service by the Marines in 1952, I got ready to go to Korea. But first I stopped by the set of the movie *How to Marry A Millionaire* and received this reminder of what we were fighting for.

sored filmed series in television history. The East and West Coasts weren't connected by coaxial cable, and after being shown in the east, the film was flown to California and went on the air in the west in late January 1949.

ABC had a live anthology series called *The Actor's Studio* that was done in New York. Like movie actors, stage actors were thrilled to get the extra work. A lot of young stars like Julie Harris and Cloris Leachman appeared in this series. In 1949 Marlon Brando made the only television guest appearance of his career in a play called *I'm No Hero*.

The same week "The Necklace" was broadcast in California, the very first Emmy Awards were held at the Hollywood Athletic Club. The people in the TV industry—all seven or eight of them—thought it would be prestigious to give their version of the Oscar. The name *Emmy* is a variation of the nickname for the Image Orthicon Camera, which was used on most shows and was called the "Immy." For those people who haven't seen it—or like me, haven't won *one*, ever, not one, even though I have been on TV almost sixty years—the statue is a female with lightning bolt wings, holding what looks like a ball. Actually, Emmy is holding an electron to remind people that television is made possible by electricity.

In 1949 the very first Emmy was given . . . the envelope please . . . (I have always wanted to say that) to "'The Necklace,' written and produced by Stanley Rubin and Lou Lantz, for the best film made in Hollywood for television." Stan Rubin still has that Emmy sitting on

Courtesy of Stephen Cox Collection

The proud winners of television's first Emmy Awards in 1949 included (3rd from right) Shirley Dinsdale holding Judy Splinters. To her right is Stanley Rubin and, at the far right, technical and programming pioneer Klaus Landsberg, who helped invent the kinescope.

a shelf in his office. The new Television Academy gave two other awards that night. The Most Popular Program was *Pantomime Quiz*, a charades show, and The Most Outstanding TV Personality of 1948 was given to Shirley Dinsdale and her puppet, Judy Splinters.

Just to give you some idea of the state of the TV industry in 1949, the first Emmy Awards for excellence on television were not broadcast on television.

But television was catching on, probably much more quickly than anyone had ever imagined. In September 1947, almost four million people watched the Yankees beat the Dodgers in the first World Series ever telecast. The TV rights went for $65,000—but the radio rights went for $175,000. It was the largest TV audience so far, and the series was broadcast by all three New York networks.

To give you some idea of how fast TV was growing, there had been only six thousand sets in use in the whole country in 1946. Within five years more than twelve million sets had been sold. "Televendors" were lowering their prices. Tele-Tone, one of more than one hundred TV manufacturers, sold its almost six-inch-by-four-and-a-half-inch set for *only* $149; an RCA seven-inch "teleset" cost $140. Philco's *Ensemble* model was $219. Of course, that was still a lot more than I could afford, and for most people a TV set cost at least a week's pay. Some manufacturers were still selling make-it-yourself TV kits without cabinets. There were all kinds of gimmicks available, too; some people would buy the smallest possible set and then put a TV screen magnifier that hooked onto the cabinet right in front of it.

TV was also starting to make an impact on American society. I can't tell you how many women would come up to me years later and tell me, "I go to bed with Johnny and you every night." Well, we both knew they meant watching *The Tonight Show* before they went to sleep was a regular part of their everyday life. In 1948 television was just starting to have that kind of impact. On Tuesday nights, for example, the movie theaters and the restaurants were empty because people were staying home, or going to a friend's house, to watch Milton Berle's show. The same kind of brash comedy that really had not worked very well for him on radio made him television's first superstar. On radio, for example, you couldn't start the show by coming out dressed as a woman, and not a particularly attractive woman either. But the TV audience loved it. "Uncle Miltie" brought the best of his stage act to TV.

People started to wonder how television would affect the country. CBS vice president Adrian Murphy sounded a lot like Professor Harold Hill selling trombones when he said, "It will recement family life. I talked with a man who had seen his teenage daughter for the first time in two months. He bought a set, and now she brings her boyfriends home."

Time wrote that "TV enthusiasts are sure that it will eventually make radio as obsolete as the horse—and empty all the nation's movie houses. Children will go to school in their own living rooms, presidential candidates will win elections from a television studio. Housewives will see on the screen the dresses and groceries they want and shop by phone." And then the magazine quoted a Manhattan mother who had already figured out how valuable it was: "Now I know where the kids are. The television set is the best babysitter in the world."

Fred Allen claimed to *Time* that television would "change Americans into creatures with eyeballs as big as cantaloupes and no brain at all."

In the same article, David Sarnoff said that some day "political candidates may have to adopt new techniques . . . Their dress, their smiles and gestures [which] may determine, to an appreciable extent, their popularity."

Now, that's a pretty impressive look into the future.

Of course, the president of Boston University warned, "If the [television] craze continues with the present level of programs, we are destined to have a nation of morons."

The president of the Television Broadcasters Association was a little more hopeful, explaining, "Television holds the key to enlightenment which may unlock the door to world understanding."

Nobody really knew. Anything was possible. Television was so new, so exciting, and a mystery to so many people. Beverly Garland, who has probably worked on as many different shows as any actress in history and was the first woman to star in a detective series (the syndicated show *Decoy*), remembers getting a telephone call from the son of a friend, who told her his mother was very upset. "She says she knows that the TV signal is coming through her window, but she doesn't understand why a friend of hers is getting something different on her screen than she's getting on hers."

For people like me, television offered a tremendous opportunity. It was the greatest thing you could imagine for a young guy. A whole industry was in the process of being created, and nobody could turn you down for a job because you didn't have any experience. People got into the business just by being in the right place.

The barber at the Beverly Hills Hotel, a man named Irving Steinberg, was cutting the hair of the young director John Frankenheimer and told him, "I've always had a dream that I wanted to be on television." Frankenheimer liked the way the man cut his hair. "OK," he said, "Want to be an actor? Just come on down."

Frankenheimer cast Steinberg as an extra in a *Playhouse 90* show he was doing. It went well, and he continued to cast Steinberg—in more than sixty shows. "I took him back to New York with me," Frankenheimer remembered. "He played twenty different roles when we did *For Whom the Bell Tolls*. That show was on tape. There is one point that if you watch carefully enough you can see he shoots himself; in one scene he fires a gun, and then we cut to him falling dead. When he fired he had a mustache; when he got shot he didn't. The CBS business affairs people looked at the paychecks going out and said, 'Who's this guy Irving Steinberg? We're paying Jason Robards, Maria Schell, and Irving Steinberg.' Irving Steinberg had a hell of a career."

Sid Caesar had done a single guest appearance on Milton Berle's *Texaco Star Theater*, but didn't have any real experience on TV when an NBC vice president invited him and the legendary producer Max Leiberman out for lunch at a restaurant on Fifty-Second Street. Caesar was trying to decide what to order when the executive asked him, "You want a half hour, an hour, or an hour and a half?"

As Caesar told the story, "I'm looking at the menu and I'm thinking, *Who's going to wait an hour for food*? So I asked, 'You gotta wait an hour and a half before your order comes?'

"'No, no, no,' the guy said. 'What kind of show do you want? Do you want a half-hour show? An hour show?' I looked at Max and I said, 'Let's go for the hour and a half.' That's the way it worked in 1948." A couple of months later, the *Admiral Broadway Revue*, starring Sid Caesar and Imogene Coca, was on the air—broadcast simultaneously on both NBC and the DuMont networks.

I GRADUATED FROM CATHOLIC UNIVERSITY IN 1949 WITH my degree in drama. To pay my way through school and support my young family, I had become a very good Atlantic City Boardwalk pitchman. Although I probably could have made as much as six thousand dollars that summer selling slicers and dicers on the Boardwalk, instead I applied for a job at the new TV station in Philadelphia, WCAU. WCAU Radio had been founded in the 1920s by the Levy brothers, who had eventually asked their brother-in-law to quit his job at his father's cigar business and invest in their radio station. This was a pretty famous story at WCAU. The brother-in-law, Bill Paley, eventually ran CBS Radio and knit together a network of local stations to carry CBS's television programming that would become the Columbia Broadcasting System Television Network.

Paley was competing with General Sarnoff at NBC and less so with ABC and DuMont for local affiliates in major cities all over the country. That's why big shows like Milton Berle's *Texaco Star Theater*, Ed Sullivan's *Toast of the Town*, Jackie Gleason's *Cavalcade of Stars*, and Sid Caesar's *Admiral Broadway Revue* were so important. Local stations would want to join a network that guaranteed the most viewers.

From 1948 until 1971, newspaper entertainment columnist Ed Sullivan hosted television's most successful variety show, presenting everything from South American plate-spinners to Elvis Presley and The Beatles. Here he poses with actress Gina Lollobrigida, who was called the world's most beautiful woman.

However, the networks filled very few hours in the programming day, and local stations had to fill the rest of the time with their own programming. That's where I came in. I was a graduate of a major university, and I also had experience selling pots and pans. That made me perfect for television.

I also had a very strong work ethic, unlimited enthusiasm, and—perhaps most important of all—my father knew a guy working at the station. Many years earlier my father had been partners in an Atlantic City game of chance with a man named John McClay. This particular endeavor is probably more accurately described as a game of very little chance. But what was important was that people believed they could win; of course, at one time they had also believed in Santa Claus. When a patron of this particular art form actually did win, which somehow managed to happen despite all precautions, my father and McClay would stage a phony argument to manipulate the winner into choosing a cheap prize—and then walk away happy, convinced he had managed to outsmart those purveyors of pleasure, McMahon and McClay. John McClay Jr. was the program manager at WCAU.

I had applied for a job at WCAU just before my graduation, and in August 1949, John McClay told me that the station had decided to begin afternoon programming, and he was looking for someone just like me to cohost the show.

Even though I had never been on commercial TV before, they offered me the job as cohost of WCAU's first afternoon show. The show was to be three hours long, and they knew exactly what they wanted it to be: cheap. I was allowed to do pretty much anything I wanted to do as long as it didn't embarrass the station or cost anything—not necessarily in that order. Can you imagine that? I'm out of college a few months with no real experience, and they offered me the opportunity to create and star in my own show!

It was a vote of confidence. They recognized my appeal: I worked cheap. They offered me seventy-five dollars a week, which was considerably less than I could have made on the boardwalk. But I didn't care. This was an opportunity to . . . starve. Actually I cared a lot because I had a family and I had rent on our apartment to pay. But I also had confidence in myself and a belief that this new television thing was going to be big, and I wanted to be part of it. I saw how people were responding to it. They were mesmerized. Crowds would stand in front of a store and watch television through the front win-

Courtesy of Stephen Cox Collection

An early TV production in which there were lights, cameras, and very little action! One of the things that anyone who worked in early TV remembers is how hot the lights were.

dow. The fact that they couldn't even hear the audio didn't matter. It was a movie theater you could bring into your own home.

The first few weeks I was on the air nobody even knew my name. I was just this guy who showed up on your TV screen three hours a day and did the show. My cohost, a nightclub and vaudeville comedian named Bob Russell, took me aside one day and explained that I didn't have the personality to be successful on TV because I didn't have the charisma a person needed. I listened to him respectfully because he was a veteran of TV—he had been in it a few hours longer than I had. But the truth was, he didn't understand that TV wasn't a nightclub, and it wasn't vaudeville; it wasn't like any medium that had ever come along before. He thought you had to be *big* on the screen, just as you had to be big on stage or in the clubs. You had to project. But that wasn't true at all on TV; what you had to be was genuine. The screen, as small as it was, exposed phonies. It was like a lie detector. The viewing audience liked me, perhaps because it was so obvious I loved what I was doing.

After several months the station split up Bob and me and gave me my own hour-long show, *The Take Ten Show*—WACU was channel ten in Philadelphia—which started at 5:30 in the afternoon. On that show I interviewed Girl Scouts selling cookies; I hosted cooking segments; I had animal acts and singers and comedians and ventriloquists. As we used to joke about ventriloquists, "I was interviewing a dummy one day, and in the middle of the interview, he dropped his puppet!"

We did the show in a converted radio studio on Sixteenth and Chestnut. You don't realize how long three hours is until you have to fill it every day. We did everything that didn't cost anything. It became immediately obvious that TV was the greatest selling tool in history, and so anybody who had anything to sell would come on our show. On one of my later shows I had the Clooney Sisters, one of the top singing acts in the business. I was thrilled that big stars would come on my little show until I realized they weren't doing me a favor; they were selling tickets to their performance. When Ringling Brothers came to Philly, we had clowns and elephants, dogs that balanced plates, and trained bears. We had book authors. I interviewed a tree surgeon as we both sat out on a limb—which he proceeded to cut off, enabling us to fall into an unseen mattress. We had models showing clothes sold in the local department stores. We had a handsome young singing bricklayer named Al Martino, who would sing while building a brick wall. And when we got really desperate, I would go out into the street and interview people as they walked by the studio.

All of us who were there at the very beginning—the performers, the technicians, the producers, the stagehands—made up television as we went along. We were creating what television would become. Every day was an experiment. We had the luxury of making mistakes because we had so few viewers. Everything was live, and there was no kinescope, videotape, or Internet to immortalize those mistakes and make sure everyone in the world could see them. And believe me, we took advantage of that luxury.

One of the first CBS shows was *What's It Worth*, in which people would bring in personal items and have them appraised. Sound familiar? It was exactly the same show as the now-popular *Antiques Roadshow*, but we were doing it half a century ago. Frances Buss, the director, wanted to be able to show close-ups of some of the items, but the technology didn't exist for close-up shots, and so an engineer machine-made a lens extension for extreme close-ups of the details. He invented it on the spot. That kind of thing was happening almost every day.

I had no writers and no producers, although I had one assistant. We had two cameras, and they were gigantic. TV cameras today are lightweight and remote controlled and have remarkable zoom lenses. The cameras we used were big boxes with four lenses, connected with thick cables. Operating them required at least two men—one to work the camera and one to move the heavy cables and push the camera dolly. The camera director in the control booth would tell the cameraman which of his four rotating lenses to use—a close-up, a wide-angle, a 135-millimeter, or a 90-millimeter on a turret—and the cameraman would have to rotate them by hand.

We didn't have any makeup artists because we didn't wear makeup. The cameras required intense bright lighting, so the studios were always unbelievably hot. At times the whole crew worked in undershirts. Color cameras required even brighter light, and when CBS experimented with color in 1951, the floor of the studio buckled. Because of the light, cameras had difficulty with certain colors. To look natural you either had to use black or brown lipstick and kind of a greenish rouge or no makeup at all.

In addition to doing *The Take Ten Show*, I did most of the local commercials on WCAU. Just about all of them were done live, and they were mostly straight stand-up spots. I would stand in front of the camera holding up the product in my right hand, making very certain the label faced the camera, and extol its virtues. If there was a competitive product, I would assure viewers my product was much better than Brand X—they could take my word for it, even if they didn't know my name. I was a pitchman again, and I could do that very well. The first product I pitched on TV was a do-it-yourself pants presser. "Forget about ironing! Just insert this miracle frame inside your pants like this, hang your pants in your closet, and forget all about it. And presto! The wrinkles have disappeared . . . ."

Talent, as anyone who appeared on air was called (even if they didn't have any), worked for the station and often appeared on several different shows. Like staff announcers on radio, we were paid a straight salary, and stations used talent as much as possible. Within a year of my first appearance on TV, I was hosting thirteen shows a week. I was honored as Philadelphia's "Mr. Television" and had my own fan club with almost one hundred active members.

I was a TV star—and I still didn't own a TV set. And because what I did was local programming, it wasn't kinescoped, which was the only means we had of making copies of a show, so I had never seen myself on TV. None of that mattered; I was too busy working on TV to watch it. I hosted just about every type of program WCAU could create. Five mornings a week I produced, wrote, and starred in *Strictly for the Girls*, which was probably the first breakfast show in TV history. I sang, I interviewed little children and celebrities, and I sold everything from cereal to Chevrolets. At noon I became Aunt Molly's mischievous nephew on *Home Highlights*. One of the sponsors wanted me to wear a chef's toque. I turned them down. What did they think I was—a clown? Actually the clown came later. Aunt Molly was played by a lovely actress named Jean Corbett. My job was to sample Aunt Molly's cooking, to put in too much sugar when she wasn't looking, and to ask our guests silly questions. The amazing thing was that I worked not only for CBS, but on Sunday nights I hosted an anthology show about World War II submariners called *The Silent Service* on WFIL, Philadelphia's ABC station. Several nights a week I hosted *The Million Dollar Movie*. I hosted one of the first game shows, *Cold Cash,* sponsored by Birds Eye Frozen Foods. We had a supermarket freezer on the set and kept cash in it. Our cash really was cold. There was no job description for what I did. I was an announcer; I was a host; on some of the shows I was an entertainer, meaning I sang a couple of songs or told jokes. I was a pretty unique species, a television personality.

In 1950 my boss at the station, Charlie Vanda, created *The Big Top*, a weekly circus variety show for the CBS network. Originally I was to be the ringmaster. "Laaaadiesss and gentlemen, and children of allllllllll ages . . . ." But even before we began rehearsing, I was replaced in the center ring by a very popular New York radio person- ality, Jack Sterling. In order to ensure he stayed with the radio station, they gave him a job on television. So I made my national TV debut as Ed the Clown, the leader of Ed McMahon and his Merry Band of Clowns. I was the guy whose red nose blinked HELLO! HELLO! My foil was a wonderful man named Chris Kegan; everything happened to him. If I was standing by a pool and somebody jumped in—Chris, who was standing twenty feet away, got soaked.

It's quite possible that I appeared on television more than anyone else in the country in those early years. I don't know for sure because television programming was so local. In Philadelphia I was sort of the living test pattern. If you turned on your TV, you were going to see me.

The only thing that stopped me was that I was recalled by the Marines for the Korean War. By the time I got back to Philadelphia, the station was on the air the entire day, and all of my old shows except *The Sealtest Big Top* were off the air. So WCAU created a five-minute commentary following the eleven o'clock news entitled *Five Minutes More with Ed McMahon*. The station gave me five minutes to do or say anything of my choosing, from telling a long joke to doing a tribute to blind pianist George Shearing. I started a campaign to outlaw the lyrics to "The Muskrat Ramble," raised funds for charity, and even shared the occasional horse-racing tip.

It was great fun, but it wasn't enough for me. I needed more to do. I had plans. I didn't know exactly what those plans were yet, but whatever I was going to do, I was going to do it on TV. So as explorers had done for centuries, I began to look to the great north. In my case, the great north was about 120 miles up the brand-new New Jersey Turnpike to a place where adventure and the center of the television world in America lay—New York City.

Eva Marie Saint was doing a show with, I believe,
Larry Blyden. Larry was a very fine actor, but he
hadn't done a lot of TV. In this scene the two of them
were passengers on an airplane. They were in the air,
you could see the sky and the clouds racing by
through the window. Eva said her line and Larry went
blank, he just completely forgot what he was
supposed to say. We didn't have cue cards or a
teleprompter in those days. He turned pale, he didn't
know what to do. Finally, he just stood up and said,
"I'm sorry, but this is where I get off." And he walked
off the plane.

—ANNE JACKSON, AMERICAN ACTRESS

NEW YORK WAS WHERE TELEVISION WAS HAPPENING.
And more of it was happening every day. As the future mayor
of New York, then city council president Vincent Impellitteri, wrote
in 1947, "Everything television needs is located in our wonderful
town—writers, designers, cameramen, engineers, producers, directors,
all are here in abundance. The only living theater left in America is
supported in New York and theater is a wellspring for television. The

In the early 1950s almost all TV was live and most of the network shows were broadcast from New York, like this 1949 Philco Television Playhouse production of Sylvia Dee's *And Never Been Kissed*, starring Broadway actress Patricia Kirkland.

national headquarters of the networks, talent agencies, program packages, transcription companies, and, most important, the advertising agencies through which the huge national companies sponsor TV shows are all here. We hope to see a great television city established in New York."

Did you read that? "Most important, the advertising agencies"? Now that was a guy who understood television. In those days the big corporations controlled television through the major advertising agencies. The most important names in TV were J. Walter Thompson, BBDO; N. W. Ayer, Grey Advertising; Doyle Dane Bernbach, Young & Rubicam—the great advertising agencies, all of whom had their headquarters in the East Fifties. The networks or local stations sold their airtime to the agencies, who bought or created the programming for their major clients, and the networks would broadcast it.

For example, General Foods bought an hour of airtime on CBS on Monday nights at eight o'clock. General Foods decided what programs went on the air, not CBS. All the network did was to provide the vehicle to broadcast the programming. So rather than having commercials for several different products during the same show, the show was brought to viewers by a single sponsor. That's why so many programs were named after corporations; *Texaco Star Theater, Armstrong Circle Theatre, The United States Steel Hour, General Electric Theater, Lux Video Theatre, Alcoa Hour, Schlitz Playhouse, Chevrolet Tele-Theatre, Ford Theatre, Hallmark Hall of Fame, Philco Television Playhouse, Colgate Comedy Hour, Kraft Television Theatre, The Hazel Bishop Show* (for Hazel Bishop Lipstick), even *20 Mule Team Borax Presents Death Valley Days*. Almost every one of the major advertising agencies was headquartered in New York City, and that was a major reason why New York was the center of early television.

America's second city, Chicago, was also second in importance in television. In addition to a very large viewing audience that couldn't be reached from the East Coast, it had creative talent readily available from theater and radio. The few major ad agencies that didn't have their main offices in New York City were in Chicago. A long time before Oprah and Jerry Springer started broadcasting from Chicago, great programming was coming from the Windy City. The first great children's show, *Kukla, Fran and Ollie*, started in Chicago; *Garroway at Large* started waking up America in Chicago. Even Mike Wallace started in Chicago, hosting beauty contests between televised pro wrestling bouts.

Los Angeles lagged behind because the movie studios wanted to destroy TV, not help it grow. The studios would not allow TV stations to broadcast old movies, and they would not allow the actors they had under contract to appear on TV. That was fine with the TV network executives. New York was live TV, L.A. was film, and at first the television executives were against filming TV shows. They thought that if shows were on film, local stations would broadcast them anytime it suited their needs, rather than when the network wanted them to, which would hurt the credibility of the network.

So it was obvious to me—and to just about everybody else trying to make it in TV—that we had to be in New York. All of us—the announcers, the actors, the young directors—all shared the belief that we were just one audition away from success. We knew it could happen; we had seen it happen to people we knew and worked with. Television was being created, and we were right in the middle of it all. There was a tremendous amount of airtime to be filled—a TV executive described television as "an eater of hours"—and there were very few people with experience to fill it. Opportunity was definitely there.

I figured the best way for me to break into network television was to come in the back door—by doing commercials. In radio, the announcers were stars, but some announcers, men with great voices, couldn't make the transition to television because they weren't comfortable gesturing with their hands while reading copy. It came very easy to me because I had worked on the boardwalk and had learned how to demonstrate the slicer-dicer, the potato peeler, the pen that will write underwater just in case you get a good idea while you're in the swimming pool . . . while continuing my spiel. If you could sell in Atlantic City, you could make it on TV.

I began commuting to New York. Every morning I would put a five-dollar roll of dimes in my pocket and take the 8:00 a.m. train from Philly along with all the *schmatta* boys going to Seventh Avenue. I hired an answering service, Radio Registry, and as soon as I got into Penn Station, I would get on the phone with my roll of dimes, calling advertising agencies and people I had met, trying to get an audition for a commercial. The phone booth was my office. Sometimes I would walk by the NBC studio on Forty-ninth Street. Even then *The Today Show* had a window in the studio. I would stand there and watch Dave Garroway and Jack Lescoulie and the famous monkey, J. Fred Muggs. I especially admired Garroway. I studied him and used him as a role model. As I watched, I knew that one day I could be on the other side of that window.

In a good week I would get between five and eight auditions; in a bad week I would be lucky to get one. But I wasn't alone. There were a lot of talented men competing with me for those jobs, and we all got to know each other. There were Frank Simms, Pat Herndon, and Fred Collins (that's the Fred Collins who informs you that "more people watch ABC than any other news organization in the world"). Bill Wendell was part of that group. The great sports broadcaster Jack Whittaker, who was doing the weather in Philadelphia, also took the morning train to New York. Don Pardo was an NBC staff announcer, and so he had real status. Dick Stark, who did the Chesterfield ads on *Perry Como*, and I came out of an audition one day into the pouring rain. Dick had a car and driver waiting for him, while I had to fight for a cab. By the time I got to the next audition, Dick already had the job. I decided that's what I needed, so I got a driver with a beat-up old car. Bob Delaney worked all the time; one time Ted Bates hired him to deliver a good "Ho ho ho." Let's be honest, you can't really louse up "Ho ho ho." But the agency executives spent the entire day arguing whether it should be, "HO ho ho," or "ho ho HO!" I wasn't the best of this group, but I was considered competitive. I was solid. And among that competition, that was very good.

New York was the big leagues of announcers. "We all had a clock in our head," my Philadelphia neighbor Dick Clark once explained. "They would tell us, 'This is a thirty-second spot,' meaning it has to run 29.4 seconds. We would read it and it would be 29.4 seconds. We were almost infallible. If they wanted it three-tenths of a second shorter, that's what they got. Any member of that group was able to read a spot and then tell the person timing it exactly how long it was, to the tenth of a second."

If there was a potential client I wanted to cultivate, maybe a casting director for one of the big ad agencies, I might take him or her to lunch at 21, which was expensive. The next day I would have a ham sandwich and coffee at the Horn & Hardart Automat for thirty-five cents. Maybe I'd go over to Schrafft's for a piece of pie for dessert. To kill time between auditions, the announcers hung out at a restaurant named Michael's Pub, while the technicians hung out at places like Hurley's on Sixth Avenue and Jim Downey's over on Eighth, and the actors hung out in the coffee shop on the ground floor of the NBC building. We all had our places. New York City had a tempo and a style and a history. Just being there was exciting, but more than that, you could walk down the street and feel the possibilities.

Television depended on established stage actors, on young actors who had come to New York to make it on Broadway, on nightclub performers, on the best-known radio broadcasters, and on B-movie actors. TV was perfect because it let all of them earn a living without interfering with their real jobs. They could work on daytime shows from the Sunday morning religious programs to the afternoon soap operas and still appear on Broadway or in a club or do a radio show at night. And they could earn a good living from TV while auditioning for stage roles or a B-movie or waiting for their next booking.

Good actors, singers, and comedians worked all the time. During Leslie Nielsen's first year in New York, he appeared in more than forty different live shows—while at the same time learning his craft at the Actors Studio. "I hardly had time to stop," he remembers. "I would rehearse one show in the morning for four hours and another one in the afternoon. As long as they had different camera days—the day they were broadcast—you could do that."

Most actors didn't consider working on TV an art or craft; it was a paying job. "Serious actors looked down on television," Beverly Garland said. "It was considered the bottom of the food chain. But I had bills to pay. My theory was, I needed to work, whether it was television or radio or a play. My theory was that if somebody is going to pay you for your talent, work."

Some of the great actors began their careers on live TV: Paul Newman and Joanne Woodward, Charlton Heston, Natalie Wood, Eli Wallach, and Anne Jackson. The director Richard Lester started as the musical director on WCAU's live daily western called *Action in the Afternoon* while I was flying in the Korean War. Marlon Brando's first job was on *The Actor's Studio.* Jack Lemmon hosted and performed in comedy sketches on the *Toni Twin Time,* a variety show in which viewers had to try to figure out which of the Terry twins, Lemmon's cohosts, had the Toni home permanent and which one had spent a lot of money getting her permanent at a salon.

Television was unlike anything else the actors had ever done. It wasn't as confining as the stage or as expansive as motion pictures. You couldn't play it as broadly as a play or as tightly as a movie. As the great Barbara Barrie, who worked on TV for more than four decades, remembers, "The question came up the first series I ever did. We were all sitting around the table, and I asked, 'For whom are we playing? Are we playing for the audience in the theater, or are we playing for the camera?' We decided it's going to go on a small box in a living room, so we couldn't play for the audience in the theater. The live audience was here to see how a show is filmed, and they were fascinated by TV, but they weren't particularly interested in our performance, so we couldn't play for them. We finally decided that we were playing for our fellow actors. We had to figure it out from scratch."

For actors, everything was different. The fact that TV was broadcast live to millions of people was a big factor in that difference, especially when animals—who did not know how to follow a script—were involved. And censorship was never an issue in the theater as it was in television.

Barbara Barrie learned right away just how different live television could be. "I was getting ready to do my very first show, and I went to my dressing room. What I didn't know was that they locked the studio door at airtime, and I got locked out. The show was going on the air, and I was in the first scene and the door was locked. That really is the actor's nightmare. I started banging on the door. Dan O'Connor, the stage manager, opened it and literally picked me up and carried me across the set. 'You're on,' he said, and like that we were on the air live."

With a few exceptions, television was live. Unbelievably, gloriously, incredibly live. What you saw was what you got, mistakes included. There were no second chances. Today it's almost impossible to imagine the magnitude of the pressure it put on all of us. For the first time in history not hundreds, not thousands, but millions of people watched the same thing at the same time. As it happened. Live.

The great director John Frankenheimer told about a young actor making his debut on *Playhouse 90* in a cast led by Mary Astor, who was a major star of early television. An hour before the show the actor was a complete wreck, but when the show went on, he was terrific. As Frankenheimer told the story, "I went to him after the show and said, 'You were wonderful. What happened? You were so nervous.'

"'I was dying,' he said. 'I didn't know what to do. I didn't think I could stand it. I walked behind the sets, and every nerve in my body was just screaming. There was Mary. I said to her, "Mary, you've done 180 shows. How do you do it?" She looked at me and she said, "There's nothing to it." And then she turned around and threw up. From that moment I was fine.'"

Things really could go wrong, and often did. And you were on the air live and completely vulnerable. Careers really were at stake. There were no options. Videotape didn't exist, and kinescopes were simply a filmed version of the live show. Sid Caesar summed it up perfectly: "This thing has to go on the air at nine o'clock Saturday night come hell or high water." The only option was a test pattern.

George Schlatter, the legendary producer and creator of *Laugh-In*, was booking guest stars for Judy Garland's variety show. One week he booked the popular singers Louis Prima and Keely Smith. He paid the top salary, $7,500. But a few hours before the show was going on the air their manager, a woman named Barbara Bell, approached him. "Let's just say Barbara was unpleasant," said George. "She came up to me and said, 'Maybe you didn't understand, that was $7,500 *each*.'

"OK, I understood. She was holding us up. There was nothing we could do. The clock was ticking. I raced around and got a check for $7,500 for Louis and $7,500 for Keely. When I handed them to her, she looked at them and said, 'I said *each*. Where's mine?' She got it. We were going on the air live."

Caesar had it right, "Nine o'clock Saturday night, come hell or high water."

When something went wrong on live TV or somebody made a mistake, the only thing to do was just keep going. In 1947 they began referring to those mistakes as bloopers. A *blooper* actually was a word used in radio to describe a popping or howling sound, a transmission problem, that sounded like *bloop*.

When Johnny Carson and I were doing the game show *Who Do You Trust?* some days I had to do three live commercials in a half hour, in addition to giving him the questions and helping with the setups. One afternoon I was doing a spot for Stay Puff fabric softener, which made diapers fluffier. Now this was back when mothers still had to be careful not to stick the safety pin in the baby while fastening the diaper. I had two piles of diapers in front of me, fluffy diapers washed with Stay Puff and not fluffy diapers washed with Brand X. I was supposed to try to stick a pin through Brand X but have some difficulty, and then easily stick it through a diaper washed with Stay Puff while explaining, "See how easy it is to pin."

Go ahead, say it out loud: "See how easy it is to pin." That's not hard, is it? I would get it right nine hundred and ninety-nine times out of a thousand. Unfortunately, I was on live TV when the thousandth time came along. I put my hand confidently on the fluffy pile and said earnestly, "See how easy it is to pee." On national TV. Johnny laughed so hard that he had to leave the stage. I corrected myself almost immediately, "Pin, I mean pin," but it was too late and my correction only made it worse.

That was embarrassing for me, but it wasn't nearly as painful as what happened to Sid Caesar. One night on *Caesar's Hour* they were doing a parody of the movie *High Noon*. Caesar played the sheriff—the role played by Gary Cooper in the movie—whose three deputies run away when they find out an outlaw gang is on its way to town to kill the sheriff. "The deputies were supposed to take off their badges, and one by one they were supposed to pin them on me. I was supposed to act like they were actually sticking their badges in my chest. I was supposed to be in agony," Sid remembered. "The pin on the badge was about an inch long. When I did my costume change before the sketch started, I had to put on boots and a gun belt and a rubber sponge under my shirt to take the pins. But as I'm walking out to do the introduction to the sketch, I look over on the side and there's the sponge just laying there. I had forgotten it. I had no protection.

"There was nothing I could do. We were on the air. So the first deputy comes in and says, 'Sorry, Sheriff, my wife isn't feeling well. I gotta get going.' I tried to take the badge and run, but he pinned it right into my chest. Right through the skin.

"Then the second deputy came in, 'Well, Sheriff, I'm sorry. See, my wife wants to go to a dance tonight.'

"I go, 'No, no,' but it didn't matter. He pinned it right to my chest. I'm in such pain, tears are coming from my eyes. The writers backstage think this is hysterical. The third guy comes in, the same thing. That's three pins in me. After the show the writers were thrilled that the skit had gone so well. 'Gee, Sid, we know you do great pain takes, but boy, these were sensational.'

"'Yeah,' I told them. 'Because they were real!' I had to go get tetanus shots right after the show."

When actors or announcers had to work with a prop or a set or demonstrate a product, there was always the chance it wasn't going to work. That was the announcer's nightmare. In 1954, in one of the historic moments in TV history, June Graham, substituting for Betty Furness, who was the Westinghouse spokeswoman, was supposed to demonstrate an electronically activated refrigerator door that popped open if you nudged it. The idea was that if you were carrying something in both hands you could still open the door. The problem was that before the commercial started a stagehand had accidentally knocked the plug out of the wall, so June was banging away at a door that wouldn't open, reading lines describing the inside of the refrigerator. The director was smart enough to go to a close-up while a stagehand plugged the refrigerator back in.

I had something like that happen to me one night in Philadelphia on *The Million Dollar Movie*. Each night I was supposed to walk into the WCAU "vault" and pick out a movie. One night I went down into the vault to get a really terrible film, *Butch Minds the Baby*. And somebody closed the vault door behind me. I had no choice, I had to walk around the entire set and come out from the side. It was like Ed McMahon's Magic Show; one second I was locked in the vault, and suddenly I reappeared—without one word of explanation.

Believe me that the motion pictures I got out of the vault on WCAU's *Million Dollar Movie* were not stored there for safe-keeping. The major studios refused to allow TV to broadcast quality pictures, and so maybe the show should have been called *The $2.98 Movie.*

There were always doors that wouldn't open. Leslie Nielsen remembers performing in a drama called *My Eyes Have a Wet Nose*, which was about a Seeing Eye dog. "We did the show from Morristown, New Jersey, which was the first time I had been on location. That was a big deal because it meant you were important enough to shoot a show out of town. I was doing the show with a fine actor named Ralph Meeker. He was playing the blind man. In the scene I introduced him to the Seeing Eye dog, and finally the time came for me to leave. I said, 'I'll come back and see you this afternoon.' I turned and tried to open the door.

"The door didn't work. I could turn the knob, but it wouldn't unlatch the door. I have to make an exit, so I was pulling on the door, and supposedly Ralph Meeker couldn't see what was going on. Finally he heard me struggling and said, 'What's going on, Bob?'

"'Well,' I said, 'the door seems to be stuck.'

"And Ralph, he was such a professional, without even pausing he said, 'Oh yes, I wanted to mention that to you. That began first thing this morning. Why don't you use the *other* door?'

"The only *other* door had already been established as the closet. At the beginning of the scene, I'd opened it up and hung my coat there. But I didn't have any options. I opened the closet door and walked out."

A similar thing happened to the respected German actor Helmut Dantine on a DuMont show one night. DuMont was the fourth network, but it was a distant fourth. If they could do a show for five cents, they would try to cut it to four cents. In the climactic scene of this drama, Helmut Dantine had a confrontation with another actor and, to defend himself, pulled a small dagger out of the cane he was carrying. Using the dagger to keep his enemy away from him, he was supposed to open the door and make his escape. However, the door wouldn't open. He pulled harder and began to panic. So he pulled even harder. What he didn't realize was that the door opened outward, and he had to push it open instead of pulling. It was such a flimsy set that after a couple of really strong pulls, the whole set fell over on top of the actors. The audience could see the walls moving up and down, and then suddenly the second actor, desperately trying to save the show, said loudly, "Oh my God! I've been stabbed!"

Mike Wallace is now one of the most respected journalists in television history, but when he was starting his career in Chicago, he was just like me and took every job he could get. Mike was once the pitchman for Peter Pan Peanut Butter on Claude Kirchner's *Super Circus* and had to dress up in the straw hat and cane. But that wasn't the worst of it. "On that show," he remembers, "a very young, attractive woman in a short skirt, named Mary Hartline, was a drum majorette for the band. One Sunday afternoon they had an elephant act with baby elephants. As I learned, they shine a bright light in the elephant's eyes, and he drops his load. Obviously you do this offstage, not onstage. But in the dress rehearsal, they had forgotten to do that. Out came the elephants, and out came these huge elephant turds. The smell was unbelievable. But we had to rehearse. So the music went on, and Mary Hartline was dancing around the stage getting elephant debris all over her beautiful legs.

"Finally the rehearsal was over and we had about twenty minutes before we were going to do a live show. There was a jurisdictional dispute between stagehands and electricians, and the stagehands said they were not going to clean up the stage. The electricians said they weren't going to clean it up. Greg Garrison was the director; his associate director and I were shoveling elephant turds off the stage when the studio doors opened. Kids came running about halfway down the aisle and began to smell it. We had to persuade them to sit in the front. And about a half hour later the elephant act came on. All of this is on live television, no tapes.

"Finally the time came for me to do the commercial for Peter Pan Peanut Butter. Thank God I was off camera. They had a youngster on camera, and I was saying, 'See little Johnny? See how he spreads his bread with Peter Pan Chunky? Now watch little Johnny take a bite.' The poor kid, who was close to nauseated from the stench of the elephant turds, took one bite, and you could see this saliva hanging from the corner of his mouth, and he started to cry in the middle of the commercial. There really was nothing they could do about it.

"That was the last time Peter Pan sponsored *Super Circus.*"

A very common mistake on live television was people walking into a set not knowing the camera was on them. That kind of thing happened a lot, and when it did, it usually ruined whatever illusion the set had created. There was an early women's talk show called *Vanity Fair,* hosted by a woman named Dorothy Doan. The show supposedly took place in a New York apartment on a very high floor. The set had a large window, and through the window you could see the tops of buildings. It was an effective illusion—effective until a carpenter casually walked past the window while the show was on the air.

Illusions could also be destroyed on live television when people walked off the set. Beverly Garland costarred with Joseph Cotten and Maureen O'Sullivan in a 1957 *Playhouse 90* entitled "The Edge of Innocence." "In the final scene a young man died," she remembered.

"In the last minute he was lying on the floor, and we all stood over his body unraveling the mystery. We rehearsed the show for about a week, and each time, after dying, this young actor would just crawl off and go back to his dressing room. There was no need for him to lie there in the rehearsal. He wasn't needed. He was dead.

"On the night of the broadcast, we were on the air and everything was moving along perfectly. He died, collapsing onto the floor and we were just about to reveal who had killed him and why. Unfortunately, he forgot this was the performance. He was visible on camera—but he got up onto his hands and knees and crawled off the set. We just stopped. We stood there watching him sneak off camera in absolute astonishment.

"There was nothing we could do. We just went to black. That was it. We were done."

"The Edge of Innocence" wasn't the only time dead men walked on live TV. The sets in dramas were right next to each other so that the cameras could move quickly from one scene to the next. Actress Peggy Webber, who appeared on just about all the great dramatic shows, remembers working in a play in which an actor named Lou Krugman was shot to death. He stayed dead as long as the camera was on him. "But when the red light went out," Webber recalled, "he stood up and started brushing himself off—and walked through a door right into the next set where the camera was on, muttering to himself, 'Thank God that one's over.'"

The problem with using animals on live TV was that they were animals. Animals rarely followed the script. They were totally un-predictable. In 1953 WCAU ran a live, five-day-a-week, hour-long black-and-white western called *Action in the Afternoon*. A live western? Just imagine how tough that was to do. They built the fronts of three or four buildings from the town of Huberle, Montana, in the parking lot at the back of the studio. The problem was that on occasion viewers would see cars or trucks driving past in the background or hear horns honking. Occasionally a plane would fly overhead. The set was as cleverly done as you can build an Old West town in a parking lot near a highway in Philadelphia. The telephone pole was disguised as a totem pole, and the mikes were hidden all over the set, in hitching posts, tree stumps, rocks. Actors on this show included people like Jack Whittaker and John Zacherley, who played the town mortician.

The problem was the horses. These weren't stunt horses; these horses were rented from a nearby riding academy. When they weren't starring on TV, they took little kids for pony rides. TV wasn't their real job, and so they did whatever they felt like doing. One afternoon while the show was on the air, there was this terrible crunching sound that drowned out all the actors. The technicians couldn't figure out what was causing it—until they saw a horse eating one of the mikes. The horses just wouldn't take direction. They did a hanging scene once in which the outlaw being hanged was sitting on the horse when something spooked it. The horse took off, leaving the actor literally hanging. Fortunately the director cut to another shot while the technicians raced in and quickly cut down the actor.

In another action scene a posse was supposed to race out of town to stop a stagecoach robbery. But this time one of the horses wouldn't move. The sheriff, Jack Valentine, who had replaced me on *Strictly for the Girls* when I was recalled by the Marines, kicked the horse, pulled on its reins, probably threatened to report the horse to the Screen Actors Guild, but that horse didn't care that the bandits were robbing the stage. It just stood there. Finally, Valentine shouted, "Ben, I'll catch up with you," and the posse raced away.

The smartest animal on TV was *The Today Show* chimpanzee, J. Fred Muggs. NBC executive Pat Weaver created *The Today Show*, *Home* (shown at noon), and *The Tonight Show*. *Today*'s ratings got a big boost when Muggs became a regular in 1953. The problem was that eventually he figured out that when the red light was lit on the camera, meaning he was on the air, he could do just about anything he wanted to do and wouldn't be punished. He turned out to be a mean monkey, who took complete advantage of being on live TV. He would hit Dave Garroway and guests on the show—and when the light went off, he ran for cover. They finally got rid of him when he bit the great comedienne Martha Raye. So that was one of the few rules of early TV: you're not allowed to bite your guests.

A couple of years later, Muggs actually sued Dave Garroway. This is absolutely true, so help me Judge Judy. Muggs's owners sued Garroway, claiming he had destroyed Muggs's career by saying J. Fred Muggs had bitten him.

Courtesy of Stephen Cox Collection

Most of the monkey business on TV in 1953 featured superstar chimpanzee J. Fred Muggs, whose unpredictable antics practically single-pawedly saved Dave Garroway's *Today Show*.

The things that they were able to do on live TV were amazing. And none of that magic of early TV could possibly have been done without incredibly creative technicians. Cameramen and sound people and stagehands invented techniques that enabled them to create visual illusions. Producer Woody Fraser, who created shows like *The Mike Douglas Show* and *Good Morning America,* began his career with a children's show entitled *Commander Five.* "This was in Chicago, and we got all the stagehands who had worked at the opera, so they knew how to rig the stuff we needed. The main set was the interior of a spaceship, but we were supposed to be in outer space, so we had to create outer space. I remember we wanted to have a chase scene. The stagehands built all the planets and hung them with wire. Then they built the rocket ships and put fishing line through them to keep them on a path. They moved them along the path by putting on a black glove, which was invisible against a black background, and moving them by hand. Then they stuck matches in the back of the rockets, and when we wanted to show the rockets taking off, they would light the match, and flame would appear to be shooting out of the back of the rocket, and they would just whip it along the fishing line. It was very crude, but it looked great on camera."

In those days when a mistake happened, there really was nothing anybody could do about it—including the censors. The censor's job was to protect viewers from . . . from whatever it was that he felt they needed protection from. The censors knew what words or ideas or actions were "dangerous." Both radio and motion pictures had a very strict code of conduct, a list of words you weren't allowed to say, and a list of the things you couldn't show. Basically, the FCC prohibited "obscene or indecent" material, although "indecent" material was permitted on late-night TV.

Believe it or not, when Johnny and I started on *The Tonight Show* we weren't allowed to use the word *pregnant.* We could say, "She's with child" or "She's expecting." She could even be thinking about it, but on TV she couldn't be pregnant. The strangest memo I ever got from Standards and Practices—that's what they called the censor—warned me to stop using the word *query*. Query? A query is a question. What could be wrong with that?

The first couple of years we did *The Tonight Show,* we did a sketch on occasion called "The Homework School of the Air" in which Johnny put on a mortarboard and answered questions that had been submitted by kids. Very big kids. My role was to read the questions. But I found myself saying the same thing over and over: "Here's a question from . . ." "Here's another question from . . ." "Here's a good question from . . ." Just to change things a little, I said, "Here's a query from . . ."

Standards and Practices informed me that I couldn't use the word *query* because "it might sound like *queer*." Homosexuality just didn't exist in TV land. In 1954, pianist Liberace appeared on the cover of *TV Guide,* decked out in his usual sequins, and the headline asked "When Will Liberace Marry?"

I think every censor had words he didn't want used, especially if he didn't know what it meant. On a variety show one night, Danny Thomas urged the Russians to "tear down that *facacta* Berlin Wall." *Facacta* is a Yiddish word that means *lousy, ridiculous.* It's used as an adjective, as in "What could the *facacta* censor have been thinking?" When Thomas' producer asked the censor why it had to be cut, the censor said it sounded too much like the dreaded *F* word.

The way people got around censors was to find ways of sneaking in words or actions, reminiscent of what performers did in the old burlesque theater. Johnny Carson was the master of the double entendre, saying one thing while looking completely innocent—and making it obvious to the audience that it referred to something else entirely. That's one of the reasons people loved him so much.

George Schlatter remembers when the sitcom *F Troop* came very close to beating the censor. In one episode the enemy was the Fukawi Indian tribe. Larry Storch's F Troop was out in the desert, and this Indian tribe could be heard roaming around in the dark of the night yelling, "Where the Fukawi? Where the Fukawi?"

The whole show was filmed before it was discovered. Eventually Standards and Practices forced them to change the name of the tribe to the Heckawi. Where the Heckawi?

At a 1949 meeting of the Television Producers Association, a committee was appointed to examine such potentially controversial matters as cleavage, the length of time a kiss could last—and a proposal to edit professional wrestling matches to eliminate "suggestive positions."

One of the biggest stars of early TV was Arthur Godfrey. He had a morning show, a talent show, and he did a variety show at night. Once he filled in for Johnny on *The Tonight Show* for a week. Arthur Godfrey was one of my idols; I tried to model myself after him, and eventually we became friends. What I remember most about him is each night after *The Tonight Show* we would go out together for dinner. He had his chauffeured Rolls Royce waiting outside, but he liked to drive it. We would get in the front, his driver would get in the back, and we would go to Danny's Hideaway or sometimes to 21.

One day on *Arthur Godfrey and His Friends*, he and two guests were dressed as street cleaners and were pushing brooms. "Well," Godfrey said, "we've dished a lot of it out. Let's clean some of it up."

What could he have been referring to? Whatever it might have been, please imagine a meaningful cough here, a lot of people got very upset. The manager of CBS's Milwaukee affiliate claimed, "Godfrey's remarks were the most obnoxious and filthy ever inflicted on a television audience." *Variety* headlined, "CBS Out on a Godfrey Limb" and warned that he might be responsible for "industry-wide censorship." It wasn't just words that could get you in trouble with the censors—both official and unofficial—in those days. Sometimes it was innuendo.

Getting used to any new technology created new problems for the censors. Under the bright lights certain shades of red became translucent, so women were not allowed to wear negligees, nightgowns, or what were then known as "foundation garments." It wasn't just real women who couldn't wear these clothes; they couldn't even be shown on mannequins.

Courtesy of Stephen Cox Collection

Garry Moore and Johnny Carson both hosted quiz shows broadcast from New York theaters converted into television studios. They are shown here appearing on Johnny's show *Who Do You Trust?*

When Elvis Presley made his first appearance on Ed Sullivan's show, he got a lot of people upset because he moved his hips when he sang. This rock-and-roll stuff was considered potentially dangerous to teenagers. The CBS censor solved this problem by allowing Presley to be shown only from his waist up. Elvis actually had made his first TV appearance on the famous bandleader Tommy Dorsey's show, and he had also appeared with Steve Allen on his Sunday night variety show. Steve Allen dressed him in a tuxedo and had him sing "Love Me Tender" to a basset hound so that the censor didn't have to worry about those gyrating hips.

Eight years before Presley's appearance on Ed Sullivan's show, the famous stripper, Gypsy Rose Lee, appeared in a variety show televised from Madison Square Garden. She started singing a little ditty entitled "Psychology of A Stripteaser," and within a few bars CBS was showing its initials. Apparently the audio was still on though, because the men in the audience could be heard suggesting, "Take it off! Take it off!"

At least they permitted Gypsy to appear. When Donald O'Connor hosted *The Colgate Comedy Hour*, he wanted to have as a guest America's most famous madam, Polly Adler, who had written the big best seller, *A House Is Not A Home*. Polly Adler was the Mayflower Madam of the Forties—but NBC wouldn't let her be on the show.

A few really old motion pictures were available to TV, most of them made before the government began censoring movies. So they had to be edited before they could be shown on TV. Both Rudolph Valentino's 1921 classic, *The Sheik,* and its sequel made five years later, *Son of the Sheik,* included love scenes that were considered acceptable when the films were made, but had to be cut before they were allowed to be shown on TV decades later.

Broadcasters were worried about violence on television right from the beginning. NBC was accused of "outdoing Edgar Allen Poe" by televising *The Fall of the House of Usher*. For a while, just about any kind of violence was prohibited from being dramatized on live TV. Even Hanna-Barbera's *Tom and Jerry* cartoons had to be edited to eliminate most of the violence! By nature, a cat and a mouse are not going to get along, but by the time the censor got done, they were practically dancing, although definitely not suggestive dancing.

All violence had to be suggested. During the big climax of *Kraft Suspense Theatre's* serial killer story, "The Creeper," a woman making a phone call was interrupted by a man's voice, telling her, "What nice lipstick you have . . ." She looked at the man—who was never seen—and was stunned. Her mouth opened in shock, the phone fell from her hand, the dramatic music reached a crescendo, and the camera focused on the phone dangling while she screamed. The end. Except the viewers had absolutely no idea who the serial killer was. Generally, after watching an entire show, viewers like to have that kind of information. Not knowing who the killer was sort of defeats the entire purpose of watching the show. Thousands of people called CBS to find out the identity of the killer.

Without question, the best-known example of censorship took place on *The Tonight Show* on February 10, 1960, when Jack Paar was supposed to tell a joke about a woman who confused the meaning of W.C.—the British expression for a water closet, or toilet—and thought it meant Wayside Chapel. Here's the joke:

An English lady, while visiting Switzerland, was looking for a room, and she asked the schoolmaster if he could recommend any to her. He took her to see several rooms, and when everything was settled, the lady returned to her home to make the final preparations to move. When she arrived home, the thought suddenly occurred to her that she had not seen a W.C. [water closet, a euphemism for bathroom] around the place. So she immediately wrote a note to the schoolmaster asking him if there was a W.C. around. The schoolmaster was a very poor student of English, so he asked the parish priest if he could help in the matter. Together they tried to discover the meaning of the letters *W.C.*, and the only solution they could find for the letters was a Wayside Chapel. The schoolmaster then wrote the following note to the English lady:

Dear Madam: I take great pleasure in informing you that the W.C. is situated nine miles from the house you occupy, in the center of a beautiful grove of pine trees surrounded by lovely grounds. It is capable of holding 229 people, and it is open on Sunday and Thursday only. As a great number of people are expected during the summer months, I would suggest that you come early, although there is plenty of standing room as a rule. You will no doubt be glad to hear that a good number of people bring their lunch and make a day of it, while others who can afford to go by car arrive just in time. I would especially recommend that your ladyship go on Thursday when there is a musical accompaniment. It may interest you to know that my daughter was married in the W.C. and it was there she met her husband. I can remember the rush there was for seats. There were ten people to a seat normally occupied by one. It was wonderful to see the expression on their faces. The newest attraction is a bell donated by a wealthy resident of the district. It rings every time a person enters. A bazaar is to be held to provide plush seats for all the people, since they feel it is a long-felt need. My wife is rather delicate, so she can't attend regularly. I shall be delighted to reserve the best seat for you if you wish, where you will be seen by all. For the children, there is a special time and place so that they will not disturb the elders. Hoping to have been of service to you, I remain, sincerely, The Schoolmaster.

That was it. The censor cut the joke out of the show, and Paar got so angry he quit in mid-show, on live TV. Believe me when I tell you that Jack Paar's walking off the show was one of the biggest news stories of the whole year because Paar was the "King of Late-Night TV." He created *The Tonight Show*. Less than a month after quitting, he returned, telling the audience, "As I was saying . . . before I was interrupted . . . When I walked off, I said there must be a better way to make a living. Well, I've looked—and there isn't."

As I've said so many times through so many years, you are correct, sir.

Eyestrain and eye fatigue can result from viewing
television. To enhance visual comfort, viewers should
be aware that if the picture is turned up before the
sound, it may become unsteady and distorted while
the sound is being adjusted. This annoys the eyes.

Don't sacrifice balance and steadiness for extra
brilliance.

Use a filter to neutralize snow.

Don't wear sunglasses (they tend to make the
eyes more sensitive to light).

Oldsters, whose eye muscles are less flexible,
may need special eyeglasses for middle-distance
television viewing.

—NEW YORK STATE OPTOMETRIC
ASSOCIATION, JANUARY 1949

B Y THE EARLY 1950s TV SETS WERE SELLING LIKE HOT-
cakes. Well, maybe not quite as fast. Remember that the original purpose of programming was to sell TV sets. RCA and others
thought the profit would be in "the furniture," not in selling airtime
to advertisers—and in the early 1950s, it seemed that they were
right. Everybody had accepted the fact that TV was here to stay. Stay?

People were crazy about TV. The American Medical Association issued a warning about "television legs," blood clots that formed when people sat still in front of the TV set for too long. (It was never just "the TV"; it was always "the TV set.") But whatever it was called, everybody wanted one of their own.

There were more than twelve million sets in use in 1952. Three years later that number had more than doubled. In some smaller cities there were months-long waiting lists to buy a new TV set. More than one hundred different manufacturers were selling them in all sizes and qualities, although most of those companies were losing money. Among the most profitable manufacturers, DuMont claimed to be "First with the Finest in Television." And RCA was selling "rotomatic tuning," a round tuner that promised "less dialing. Just click and view your program pretuned." Philco countered with "deep dimension—the greatest advance since the miracle of television. A giant-sized twenty-four-inch screen. Now you're seeing not just part of the picture, but all of the picture with pinpoint detail." Zenith's twenty-one-inch came with a "SuperAutomatic Station Selector and a built-in Picturemagnet antenna" and sold for $199—less trade-in. That is correct; you could trade in your old set and get credit toward a new one.

In 1951, after a long and bitter battle with RCA, CBS received FCC permission to sell color TV sets, which were expected to revolutionize TV. There was almost no color programming, but that didn't seem to matter too much; the test pattern would be in color. As the respected TV historian Ed Reitan explained, "The CBS color system was not compatible with existing black-and-white sets. The sale of CBS sets started in September 1951, and one month later the U.S. government asked CBS to stop manufacturing them to preserve materials for the Korean War. CBS sold approximately one hundred sets in that one month, and only twenty-five sets could receive CBS's first color broadcast. Frank Stanton, the president of CBS, said, 'It is our patriotic duty to follow this order. We're stopping manufacturing of the sets, we are recalling all the sets that have been sold, and the others have been destroyed. We are stopping broadcasting as of tomorrow.'"

CBS waited a day before following the order, Reitan discovered, because in Detroit and Chicago the network had been advertising heavily that it was broadcasting the first professional football game in color, and hundreds of people were expecting to watch the game in TV showrooms. But let me ask you, how happy would you have been telling those hundreds of football fans the game wasn't being broadcast? Me neither. That game marked the end of color TV until after the Korean War.

People finally began to understand that the TV waves didn't come into their houses through the window, but they still had questions about how it worked. Newspapers and magazines ran advice columns. "Should I turn my channel selector in only one direction?" a reader asked *TV Guide*. "No," was the response. "Your channel selector is made to turn in any direction, but the continuous changing of your selector will wear out the contacts."

And just like any new development, some people took advantage of the situation. Ahhh yes, my good friend, there were indeed some scoundrels lurking out there in TV land. TV repairmen were considered to be the auto mechanics of the time. The business of repairing television sets was created mostly by returning World War II radiomen, and while the majority of them were honest, there were some who, I daresay, lacked virtue. There were fifty thousand TV repairmen, and they weren't exactly loved and respected. How could they be when *The TV Technician's Handbook on Customer Relations* included such helpful tips for the novice repairman as, "There will be occasions when, in order to make time, you may inadvertently have a few small screws left over after repairing a TV set. Solution: either put them in your pocket when the customer is not looking or mingle them with other items of the same type you may have in your tool kit."

Probably the most common scam used by repairmen was selling used tubes as new ones. They would buy used tubes for about three cents each, shine them up, give them an electrical jolt to temporarily rejuvenate them, and then install them and charge new tube prices. By the time the tubes failed, the repairman was long gone. The district attorney in the Bronx, New York, broke up a hot tube racket that had installed more than six hundred thousand defective tubes.

All kinds of gimmicky products were available too. One company in Peoria, Illinois, sold 3D glasses it called "genoscopes." What a great name for something that did nothing! These glasses consisted of a series of filters on a pair of optically perfect lenses "that turned an ordinary picture into 3D." Supposedly they worked best on TV shows with a lot of motion. They came with a money-back guarantee: if you sent them your money, you were guaranteed not to get it back.

By 1954 Swanson was selling frozen TV dinners—which could be heated easily and eaten on a folding TV tray table, sitting right in front of the TV set. The novelty of television had pretty much worn off.

As more stations began broadcasting and the coaxial cable spread across the country, viewers suddenly had a lot of choices, and they expected to be entertained by more than a test pattern. What's really interesting is that most of the programs that are popular right now were being produced half a century ago. Makeover shows? In 1953 *Glamour Girls* transformed the winner through modeling lessons, a new wardrobe, and personalized makeup. Courtroom shows? *They Stand Accused* was based on real cases in 1954. Dance contests, talent shows, and morning, noon, and nighttime talk shows were all on television half a century ago. The Food Network? Every local station had at least one cooking show and usually several. Sports programming?

About a third of all TV programming in the late 1940s was sports. There was more reality on live TV than there appears to be on reality shows now. DuMont was doing a true reality show in 1949. It pointed a camera at Madison Avenue and just panned up and down the street, calling it *Window on the World*. There's no more reality than that!

But there was at least one significant programming difference in the first decade after World War II. At that time the networks produced extraordinary dramas. They brought great theater to a mass audience. I love TV today, but fifty years ago the networks were putting on full-length dramas every week. They presented Broadway shows with incredible casts. They produced original plays by brilliant writers. They dramatized great literature. And they did it live. In 1955, fourteen live drama series were on the air weekly or monthly.

Ed Bleier, an ABC and Warner executive for more than forty years, pointed out that the reason good dramatic programming was so important was that the first two or three million people to own television sets lived in the big cities and were upscale, so programming was aimed directly at their interests.

Obviously this was pre-pre-*Gilligan's Island*. In a typical week of programming in October 1949, viewers could watch the NBC Symphony Orchestra, the New York Philharmonic, a Boston Symphony Orchestra dress rehearsal, *The Bell Telephone Hour* with legendary violinist Jascha Heifetz, *Crusade in Europe* (derived from the book by and including an interview with General Dwight Eisenhower, this was the first documentary series), and a lot of theater. Live plays were broadcast on *Ford Theatre, NBC Theatre, Theater Guild on the Air,* the *Chicago Theater of the Air* performing *The Mikado,* and *Studio One.* It was because of these dramas that TV's first decade has become known as "The Golden Age of Television."

The advantage of being in New York City was that television networks had easy access to theater, to the Broadway shows, and to off-

Broadway. More live theater was probably being done in New York than anywhere else in the world. Television offered exposure for new plays, as well as steady work for the stage actors. The first program broadcast by the brand-new CBS Television Network was *Tonight on Broadway,* which featured selected scenes and some backstage glimpses from the big Broadway hit *Mister Roberts,* starring Henry Fonda.

Initially the networks could not afford to put on full stage productions, so they produced abbreviated "televersions." *Mister Roberts,* for example, was done on tiny sets with only a few actors. The late-night show *Monodrama Theater,* which DuMont broadcast from a tiny studio at 515 Madison Avenue, featured one actor who stood in front of a curtain and performed a monologue or read a play.

One of the first great TV dramas was an adaptation of a really suspenseful radio play, *Sorry, Wrong Number,* which CBS had broadcast in 1946. A bedridden woman picks up the phone—they had party lines back then with several people sharing a common phone line—and overhears two men plotting a murder. Her murder, as it turns out. And nobody believes her. What made this show absolutely perfect for TV was that it required one actor, one set, and two cameras. "It was just the bedroom, the wall behind the bed, and, perhaps, a doorway," remembered the camera director, Frances Buss. "What made it so exciting for all of us was that the great film director John Houseman supposedly was coming to New York to direct it. That a man of such stature in movies would deign to direct a television program was a very big thing. That didn't happen very often. The reviews credited Houseman as the producer and director, but as far as I can recall he was never there. I don't think he had any interest in doing a television show. He had an assistant named Nicholas Ray who came and stood behind me when I put the show on the air."

Sorry, Wrong Number, like almost all of these shows, was one hour long, but by 1952 the networks were doing several half-hour filmed

Courtesy of Stephen Cox Collection

The beginning of the end of "The Golden Era of Live TV" came in 1956, when the networks began using Ampex videotape recorders to record and edit programs. Videotape made the most significant difference on the West Coast where many national television shows had been broadcast from grainy kinescopes. This room-sized machine did the same thing in 1956 as home systems available inexpensively to anyone today.

dramas. *Playhouse 90*, which went on the air in 1956, was ninety minutes long, and *Matinee Theatre* did hour-long live dramas five days a week at noon. All of this was done with the limits of 1950s technology. The shows were shot with big, bulky cameras dragging thick cables across multiple sets, and it was important to make sure the cables didn't get crossed when the cameras moved. There was no videotape, so everything had to be perfect the one time it was shown on the air. Costume changes had to be made on the run. There were no teleprompters, so scripts had to be memorized. Doing it in that one take was like putting together pieces of a complex puzzle. Each production had to be completely choreographed; every move had to be planned so actors could get to their next scene and the cameras could be rolled into position as fast as possible. Getting that done was always tricky and sometimes almost impossible. The things they accomplished with props and stagecraft and creativity were absolutely incredible.

In 1956 *Kraft Television Theatre* did a dramatized version of Walter Lord's book about the sinking of the Titanic, *A Night To Remember.* They built thirty-one different sets, including authentic reproductions of the Titanic's bridge, the engine room, and several decks. The grand staircase included the ornate details of the original ship. Some of the sets were built at an angle to create the illusion that the ship was listing, and a fireplace was built to collapse in the finale. The cast included 107 actors, and the producers had built a three thousand-gallon water tank right in the studio. And all the props had to work. There's nothing, absolutely nothing, on TV today that is even close in complexity to the productions that were being done fifty years ago.

But we took it all for granted because we did that kind of stuff all the time. In 1949 Charlton Heston and Leslie Nielsen both made their major TV debuts in the *Studio One* production of "Battleship Bismarck," the story of how the British Navy hunted down and sank the legendary Nazi warship. To re-create the havoc aboard the ship as it was sinking, they lined the entire floor of the studio, which was above Grand Central Station, with waterproofing about three-feet-high around the ends and made a gigantic pool. They constructed ramps so the three cameras could move around. This entire set was built for one live performance.

In later years, some shows were taped, but what they accomplished was no less amazing. The great director John Frankenheimer created a raging Mississippi River in a studio for his *Playhouse 90* production of Faulkner's novella *Old Man*. Sterling Hayden starred with Geraldine Page in the story of an escaped convict who rescues a pregnant woman from a great flood. As Hayden recalled the show, "They had to build a tank that would hold two hundred tons of water at CBS. The building engineer said if Frankenheimer put that tank in the studio, the whole building would fall down. But Frankenheimer insisted, and so they shored it up with twelve-by-twelve timbers and put in the tank."

During the actual production Hayden had to deal with special effects—produced tidal waves, fog, rain, wind, parts of horses floating by, large trees and telephone poles, cows and chickens, and a mob trying to beat him to death. Hayden was so nervous about doing *Playhouse 90* that he fasted for a couple of days before the show, and then Frankenheimer kept him awake for the three full days they were in production so that he would appear to be exhausted.

"Frankenheimer loved to move the camera fast," Hayden said. "It was wild. I was so scared, but I roared through that whole thing. I went into one set to do a scene and there were no cameras! Then, racing around the corner like an old San Francisco fire truck, came a camera on a dolly. And a guy came along, put up a light, and *Bang!* We go!"

Respected network executive Charles Cappleman remembered *Old Man* well. "Frankenheimer wouldn't tell the actors it was time for a break. Instead he kept them out in the rain on the set because he wanted them as ticked off as they could be and exhausted looking. And he got it. We had a scene with a cockroach in it, so we had to have a cockroach wrangler. That's what he was called, local 399 Teamster's Union, a cockroach wrangler."

Frankenheimer was one of a group of brilliant young directors who grew up in live television: Sidney Lumet, Sidney Pollack, Arthur Penn, George Roy Hill, Robert Altman, Franklin Schaffner. Even Yul Brynner got his start directing a children's show called *Mr. I. Magination.* These were the kind of optimistic guys who believed they could do anything—and then they went ahead and did it. All of us who were starting our careers in television knew that our only limitation was our creativity.

Frankenheimer remembers directing *No Passport for Death* with John Cassavetes. "It was about a young Puerto Rican who illegally came into the country and, unknown to him, he was carrying small-pox. The police were after him, and he didn't know why and felt as if he were a fugitive and had to escape. The script was terrible."

In the big finale, Cassavetes was supposed to try to escape by jumping off a roof. Today, that's a very simple stunt. They could drop *me* from the space shuttle and make it look real, but jumping off a roof and making it look real on live TV at that time was almost impossible. But Frankenheimer came up with the solution. "We cut to Cassavetes on the roof. Then we cut to Leo Penn on the ground screaming, 'Don't jump!' Then we throw a dummy off the roof and in the meantime Cassavetes runs down the stairs and jumps into the net. I mean, in my crazed head at twenty-four years old, that was going to work fine.

"I had never seen it done before. So we did it. For it to work, Cassavetes had to run down five flights of stairs and jump in the net. The problem was that the people who lived in the apartment house were out on the stairs blocking him, so in dress rehearsal he never made it into the net. Also when we threw the dummy off the roof in the dress rehearsal, it hit a clothesline. We broadcast live without this ever having worked.

"Just before we went on the air, it started to snow. We had put production assistants on each landing of the building to keep people from getting in Cassavetes' way. Finally at the climax of the show, Cassavetes stood on the edge of the roof and looked down. Leo Penn came into the alley, and we were intercutting them. We cut to Cassavetes up there with a close-up. Viewers could see it was him.

We cut down to Penn. Then Cassavetes took off down the steps. We were committed to it now.

"We had a double standing on the edge of the roof, and from a distance he looked like Cassavetes. We cut to Penn, who yelled, 'No!' And we cut back to the roof and threw the dummy. It looked fabulous coming through the air. Through the second monitor, the camera we were to go to, I saw Cassavetes steaming down the alley, and I saw the dummy in the air, and I said, 'Kill him.'

"Cassavetes took off; I cut to camera three just as he landed in the net. Perfect. The only time we ever made it was the air show. And when you stop to think of everything that could have gone wrong, realize he could have turned his ankle, somebody could have blocked him, he could have tripped. He had to go at breakneck speed to make it down five flights, run through an alley in the snow and jump in that net.

"And then we got a few letters saying, 'When are they going to stop using that phony snow on television?'"

Not only were directors challenged by the planning required by the constraints of live television, but the writers also had to plan carefully in order to work within the physical limitations of live television. While telling their stories, the great writers like Rod Serling, Paddy Chayevsky, Reginald Rose, Tad Mosel, and Gore Vidal had to find ways of including the time the actors needed to make a costume change or move from one set to the next. They used thirty-second or one-minute commercials, or they plotted the story so actors wouldn't appear in two consecutive scenes, or they inserted transition shots. Directors planned their shots to give actors an extra few seconds, and actors wore one costume over another.

"We never had enough time to make all the changes," Leslie Neilsen remembers. "We all became quick-change artists, but when it was necessary, we also used to underdress, we called it. We would

wear one costume on top of another and another and another. I did a *Hallmark Hall of Fame* entitled "Skipper of the Skies" and I wore eight different costumes all at the same time. I played a pilot shot down over France, and between the first two scenes I had to take off my flying clothes and peel down to my pajamas because I was supposed to be in the hospital. In the next scene I was out of the hospital, and underneath my pajamas I had on an Air Force uniform, and under that I was wearing casual slacks and a shirt. I remember doing a *Studio One* drama, which opened with a party sequence. I had to open a bottle of champagne. This champagne had not been stored in a refrigerator, so it was warm. When I opened it, it looked like a geyser at Yellowstone Park. I got completely soaked. While I had several planned costume changes, the shirt was the foundation, and I had to leave it on. I was in a sequence of scenes, so the days changed and the scenes changed, but I didn't have time to change that shirt. It took several months of TV drama time for that shirt to dry."

A lot of the problems could have been solved by using the new magnetic tape, kind of a very basic videotape, which was demonstrated by RCA in late 1953. In announcing this new development, David Sarnoff said black-and-white programming with sound could be recorded and played back immediately, adding, "One possibility this opens is viewers being able to record TV programs at home." This was in 1953. You couldn't tape anything very long, but the technology existed, and it worked, and it could have been used.

It turned out that the television executives really didn't want to use videotape because it would have allowed a shoot to be stretched out over several days, and it would have made it easy to do a lot of remotes, meaning their production costs would increase substantially. They would have to pay the whole crew for several days' shooting. It would make television more like a movie than a stage play.

In 1955 Lee Marvin was doing an episode of *Studio One,* directed by Franklin Schaffner, called "Shakedown Cruise." His costar was a lovely young actress named Constance Ford. The show was shot in Studio 105, which, naturally, was on 105th Street and Fifth Avenue. It was an old movie theater that had been converted into a TV studio. The seats had been taken out, and all the lights and equipment had been installed. But like all movie theaters, the floor sloped toward the screen, and putting in a new level floor was much too expensive. And usually it didn't make any difference.

Lee Marvin was playing a cop. In one sequence he had to move from a living room to a phone booth to make a call. The way Schaffner planned the transition, Marvin would be smoking a cigarette in the living room. At the conclusion of that scene he would put the cigarette down in an ashtray; the camera would hold on the burning cigarette long enough for Marvin to race into the phone booth. The only way to make it work was to put the phone booth on a dolly and roll it into position right next to the living room set. Marvin could just step out of the living room into the booth. Most of the time in rehearsals he didn't make it. That wasn't unusual. Somehow when a show was on the air, adrenaline kicked in and a shot got done.

Before the broadcast, the producer asked Marvin if he was going to be able to make it. "Watch me, baby," he said. "Just watch me."

Here's what happened on the air. Lee Marvin casually put his cigarette into the ashtray, the camera panned down on it and held the shot as the smoke curled into the air, and Marvin took off. Lee Marvin was a Marine. He was a big man. He was very powerful—and he was running full speed when he hit that phone booth—which, unfortunately, was still sitting on a dolly.

Marvin's momentum caused the phone booth to start rolling down the sloping floor. Marvin was great—he picked up the telephone and did his scene. He didn't even react. The cameraman was great too—when that phone booth started rolling he moved with it. As it picked up speed, he stayed right with his shot. The phone booth rolled right past Constance Ford, who was standing in the background changing her costume and was almost totally naked. She kept changing; she didn't even notice a phone booth and camera rolling by. Finally the phone booth crashed into the studio wall and stopped.

I'll tell you the definition of a true professional. Lee Marvin was still talking on that phone. Come hell or high water!

WHILE THE ADVERTISING AGENCIES WERE ALL WITHIN A few blocks of each other, actual production was spread all over New York. From the rehearsal space above Rattner's Kosher Restaurant on Sixth Street and Second Avenue in the East Village to the 105th Street studio in Harlem, pretty much any large empty space became a rehearsal hall or was converted into a studio. New York's first TV studio, DuMont's Studio A, was a converted auditorium in Wanamaker's Department Store. CBS transformed the tennis courts above Grand Central Station on Vanderbilt Place into studio space, and it was there that some of the original color TV experiments took place. An indoor horse-riding ring on West Sixty-sixth Street was still being used for riding while TV shows were broadcast from the back—and that's where ABC still is today. Liederkranz Hall was an old German singing hall on Fifty-ninth Street that supposedly had the best acoustics in the city, but its acoustic superiority was lost when the hall was divided into four TV studios. Radio studios generally were much too small to be used for television, but almost every theater in New York that wasn't in regular use for stage productions or concerts got converted.

Sid Caesar's *Your Show of Shows*, for example, was first broadcast from the International Theater on Fifty-eighth Street. After a couple of years, that theater was torn down and Caesar's show moved to the

Center Theater, on Fiftieth Street and Sixth Avenue. The Center, originally called the RKO Roxy, was right in the heart of Manhattan and was a smaller version of the Radio City Music Hall. It seated 3,700 people and had three huge stage elevators and one of those magnificent chandeliers hanging over the orchestra. Originally it was supposed to be the home of the Metropolitan Opera, but when it opened in 1933, it was used for big stage productions and movies. *King Kong* had its world premiere there and at Radio City. But by 1950 the theater wasn't used too much, so Milton Berle began broadcasting his show from there. Ethel Merman and Mary Martin did one of TV's first spectaculars from there in 1953. The problem with the Center Theater was that it was only four stories high, so it was demolished in 1954 and replaced by the Radio City parking garage.

Then Caesar moved to the Al Jolson Theater at Fifty-ninth Street and Seventh Avenue. That theater seated 2,770 people, and by the time it was torn down a few years later to be replaced by an apartment building, Caesar was off the air. DuMont opened its state-of-the-art, five-million-dollar Tele-Center on East Sixty-seventh Street in 1954, just as TV production started to move to Los Angeles.

But the biggest theater in New York was New York itself. From the observation tower on the Empire State Building to the cosmetics counters at Macy's, the whole city was there to be used. It was bigger and better than the greatest set designer could have envisioned. The actors' unions even signed waivers permitting ordinary New Yorkers—bakers, cobblers, and shoe-shine men—to appear on shows. Air travel had not yet become common, so most Americans had never been to New York City. TV brought the city—all the things that were good and that were bad—to the entire country.

The first remote TV broadcast took place in 1928, long before anybody could really see it, when a station in Schenectady, New York, broadcast New York governor Al Smith's speech accepting the

Democratic nomination for president simultaneously on radio and TV. Remote broadcasting wasn't as technically difficult as you might think it would be. All that was needed was a mobile unit—basically a truck carrying transmission equipment, a camera, and long cables—and a clear visual line to a transmission antenna. In New York, you could broadcast from pretty much anywhere as long as the transmitter on top of the mobile unit had a direct visual line to the antenna on top of the Chrysler Building. In 1944, while its Grand Central Terminal studio was being renovated, CBS broadcast shows from all over New York.

That year Frances Buss directed a game show called *Missus Goes A-Shopping*. "It had been very popular on radio," she explained. "It was broadcast locally and hosted by John Reed King. He asked the contestants silly questions, things that would make them laugh and maybe embarrass them a little. The prizes were mostly products. We did the show from supermarkets all over the New York area, and as long as we could get a sight line to the Chrysler tower, it would work. I think we were sponsored by Mother's Macaroni. The trouble was that great crowds of people would come to the supermarket to be on television, and the stores would lose a lot of merchandise to people who shoplifted while everyone else was watching the show."

Even subway cars could become studios. There is nothing that better represents New York than the subway. In 1950, *Ford Theatre* filmed establishing shots for its production of "Subway Express" in the IRT between Chambers Street and Grand Central Station, and then moved the whole crew—the actors and technicians, more than one hundred people—up to the Bronx where the rest of the show was done live from a subway car in an otherwise deserted rail yard. Years later I starred in a theatrical movie entitled *The Incident*, and we filmed in a specially built prop subway car on rockers to give the appearance of reality. In 1950, however, they used actual subway cars.

Broadcasting from a location was toughest on the actors and crew.

The hundreds of TV shows and movies produced in New York every year now have first-rate facilities. The dressing rooms, makeup facilities, food wagons, all the power and equipment, everything they need to be comfortable, are in huge trailers. It's all self-contained. Like a gypsy caravan, the production company just sets up shop for a day anywhere they need to be. That's not the way it used to be when TV first began shooting in New York. "It was hard," Barbara Barrie said. "Very, very hard. We didn't have any facilities. We used to change in telephone booths—that was before they were all glass, obviously. If we needed to use the ladies' room, we would go into Schrafft's. When we were shooting in the winter, we would run into the nearest store to get warm. For lunch we would all go to a local diner. We would just make do. Nobody had their own car, so when we had to move to a different location, we'd all take cabs or sometimes go on the subway."

"It seemed like it was always too cold or too hot when we were filming," remembers Beverly Garland. "We were filming *Decoy* in Central Park late one freezing-cold night in the middle of winter, and the cameraman came up to me and said, 'Beverly, it's almost midnight. I'd like to get this shot of you running down this path, but the camera is frozen. What I want you to do is run as fast as you can, but do it in slow motion. I think I can make it work.' And that's what we did."

The show that relied the most on the excitement of New York was *Naked City,* my favorite show. It was a half-hour filmed—not live— detective series that went on the air in 1958. What made it different from anything that had been done before was that it was shot almost entirely on location. They would use as many as forty different locations in a single show. I mean, they shot everywhere—Wall Street at rush hour, Yankee Stadium during a ballgame. They even shot in a tiny stateroom in the passenger liner *Liberté* when it was in port. Because they were using film, they could shoot in a moving subway car—although the city made them rent a car which was then hooked onto the regular train. One time the producer discovered the dreary vaults underneath the Whitestone Bridge and was thrilled, telling people, "What a good place for a murder."

Naked City was the first of the cop shows that stressed realism, and at the end of each show viewers were reminded, "There are eight million stories in the Naked City. This has been one of them." When one of the leading actors, John McIntire, had a dispute with the producer, he became the first continuing major character on a network TV show to be killed. A mob hit man forced his car into a gas tanker—blowing him right out of the series. Eventually McIntire was replaced by Horace McMahon—no relation to me—and the show was extended to an hour.

Getting that realism on film required some pretty creative work. When they were filming a scene in which a car raced down the East Side Drive, for example, they put a sound man with all his equipment in the trunk of the car and a second sound man, the lighting director, and a cameraman with a handheld camera in the backseat, and they shot the scene as the car raced down the East Side Drive.

Naked City also filmed outside all winter. In one show that was set in January, the bad guy was caught by a mob on the docks, suspended from a crane by his feet, and dunked into the freezing Hudson River. The producers really did suspend a stunt man from a crane by his feet and actually dipped him in the river. Unfortunately for the stunt man, they had to shoot the scene several times. As he explained afterwards, "A-b-b-b-b-b-b-b-o-o-o-o-u-u-t-t-t-a-a-a-d-d-doz-en t-t-t-t-imes." OK, maybe he didn't actually say that.

When *Naked City* was shooting a scene down on the Bowery one time, several of the derelicts living there crowded around the set, started shouting, "Cut" and "Roll 'em," and refused to leave when asked. In order to clear the set, a production assistant gave each of them a few dollars to leave the area. Yes, it was a bribe, but it worked very well for at least an hour. Or just long enough for the word to spread all over the Bowery that a TV production company was paying people just to leave. Maybe a thousand people descended on the set, and many of them got paid to leave—in fact, some of them got paid to leave two or three times!

Television and movie productions were still a rarity in New York in those days, and New Yorkers had not grown accustomed to seeing the big trailers on every corner. So in 1958, when a dark Ford sedan turned onto Lenox Avenue in Harlem and someone stuck a machine gun out the rear window, the NYPD went into action. Two detectives drew their guns and raced toward the car. But before anyone could get hurt, a man leaned out the car window and started screaming, "Don't shoot! Don't shoot!"

New Yorkers were constantly mistaking the *Naked City's* two police cruisers for NYPD squad cars. Beverly Garland had the same problem when she was on the street dressed as a police officer. "*Decoy* was a syndicated series and wasn't on the air in New York, so absolutely nobody knew who I was. They thought I was a real police officer. I had one woman come up to me and ask me what time it was. I said, 'I'm sorry, I don't wear a watch.' She gave me this really nasty look and said, 'You're a policewoman and you don't wear a watch?' When I explained, she didn't believe I wasn't a policewoman."

Eventually *Naked City's* producers had to paint the show's two police cruisers a bright red, yellow, and black, making them the weirdest-looking police cars in NYPD history. Coming down the street, they could not be mistaken for real police cars—but in black-and-white on the show, they looked just like the regular police cars.

You know, a funny thing happened over the years. New Yorkers got so accustomed to movies and TV programs being filmed in the city that they stopped paying attention. Several years ago a detective I've known for many years became part of a special joint bank-robbery task force the NYPD formed with the FBI. One afternoon they broke up a bank robbery in progress, arresting three thieves. While waiting for assistance, the task force held the robbers at gunpoint against the wall. You've seen how they do that—on TV—a thousand times, both hands against the wall, feet spread-eagled, nose to the bricks. My detective friend was holding a machine gun on them, standing on the sidewalk about five feet away. Let me repeat that: the man was holding a *machine gun*! And New Yorkers didn't even hesitate. They just walked right between him and the robbers. Of course it was understandable; they were New Yorkers. They had things to do. If those crazy movie people wanted to make their movie, fine, but don't get in my way. Not only were they not bothered by a man standing there holding a machine gun, but most of them didn't even acknowledge his presence. They had seen it all before. On television.

ONE OF THE REASONS THE TV INDUSTRY DEVELOPED IN NEW York was because a vast reservoir of actors was there for the theater, but within a few years, actors were going to New York not just for theater, but because TV was there. There was so much work in New York City that once actors got known, they didn't even have to audition.

"Actors wanted to be in New York," Barbara Barrie explained. "They didn't think it was good to go to California. They complained about doing television, but at least the material had some substance to it. When I started out, there were no casting directors. The first thing I auditioned for was a *Kraft Television Theatre* drama, and I got that audition because I had met the director of the play at a party. After I got that part, directors would just call me and ask me to meet the person who was casting the show. The whole thing was very informal. If somebody wanted me, they wanted me."

The wonderful Nanette Fabray remembers being very surprised when a producer offered her a leading role in the serious drama *Arms and the Man*. She was surprised because all of her experience had been in musical comedy. She had never done a drama in her life. "It wasn't until I was well into rehearsals that they realized their mistake. I had been hired because I had starred in *Arms and the Girl* for the Theatre Guild, which was a musical version of a play called *The Pursuit of Happiness*." In that show Fabray had sung the less-than-classic song, "A Plough, A Cow, and A Frau." "When they found out I wasn't actually a dramatic actor, they put me down a bit. But that was all right; I held my own."

Hallmark Hall of Fame, which went on the air in 1951, was the first show produced by a major corporation to promote its product. Presenting both classic programs like *Arsenic and Old Lace,* starring Tony Randall, Tom Bosley, and Boris Karloff, as well as original programming, it became the longest running anthology show in television history.

Many of these young actors were studying their craft in places like The Actors Studio and the Herbert Berghof Studio, where they did Chekov and Shakespeare. Lee Strasberg was teaching Stanislavsky's "The Method," in which you became your role. The goal was to experience the emotions of the role as they would be felt by the character you were playing. Supposedly John Barrymore Jr. was working on a *Hallmark Hall of Fame* when someone asked him about method acting. He told them, "My method involves talent, whiskey, and ice."

Much of the excitement and the energy of live TV came from the fact that nobody knew how an actor was going to perform for the camera. For the first few years, there was no teleprompter or cue cards, and actors were constantly *going up*—that's actor talk meaning forgetting—on their lines. When that happened, the other actors had to cover it up. Sometimes an actor would suddenly remember he or she had to go make a phone call and get his or her lines from the stage manager. At other times cast members would give the actor a cue: "You know what I think? I think you really believe you couldn't have committed the murder because you spent the night with your wife!" If Jackie Gleason forgot a line when he was doing *The Honeymooners*, he would rub his stomach—meaning he needed to be fed his line. Leslie Neilsen remembers the night he was supposed to stand up and reveal, in great dramatic fashion, "The killer was Sidney Kidd!" But the effect of that dramatic revelation was somewhat diminished when he said, "The killer was Kidney Sidd!"

In 1950 the great character actor Brian Donlevy was called in at the last minute to replace a sick cast member in "The Pharmacist's Mate" on *Pulitzer Prize Playhouse*. He was playing a naval officer. Donlevy didn't have enough time to learn his lines, so they were written all over the set. There were lines written on the ceiling, on the backs of cabinets, on the sides of cups, everywhere. But just to make sure he had all the help he needed, a stage manager dressed in a sailor's uniform and, carrying a clipboard, followed him throughout the whole play. When Donlevy hesitated, the stage manager would say, "Sir, would you suggest we tell the Admiral that . . ."

"Yes," Donlevy would agree, "yes, let's tell him that right away."

While a show was on the air, the actors had to be ready to respond to anything, and I mean anything. One afternoon on *Captain Video and His Video Rangers* an elephant that was going to be used on another show later that day began trumpeting loudly. I don't care how good an actor is, in that situation he can't act like he didn't hear the elephant. Captain Video stood up straight and said, "What the hell was that?"

To which Ranger Craig replied quickly, "I don't know either, Captain, but you'd better get down. It might be dangerous!"

One of the greatest original programs in TV history was Rod Serling's *Playhouse 90* drama *Requiem for a Heavyweight.* One of the leads was given to Ed Wynn, who had been a popular vaudeville and radio comedian and was one of television's first big stars. In 1949 *The Ed Wynn Show* won the Emmy as the Best Live Show, and he won a second Emmy as TV's Most Outstanding Personality, succeeding Shirley Dinsdale and her puppet, Judy Splinters! In

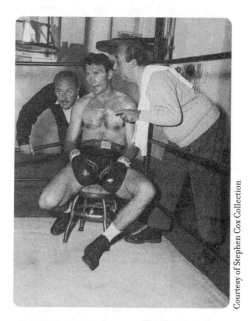

Courtesy of Stephen Cox Collection

Playhouse 90 presented live, often original, and usually brilliant programming week after week, while discovering great writers like Rod Serling. His *Requiem For A Heavyweight,* seen here, won six Emmy Awards and was later made into a successful motion picture. Left to right: Keenan Wynn, Jack Palance, and Ed Wynn.

Requiem, Wynn was cast in the first really serious role of his life. All during the rehearsals he kept playing with his lines, trying to make people laugh—because that's what he knew—or simply forgetting them completely. Charlie Cappleman, a CBS executive for more than four decades, remembers the concern about Wynn. "During the week of rehearsals, somebody came to producer Marty Manulis and said, 'I don't think Ed Wynn's going to make it. I don't think he's capable of doing this show. He doesn't have the stamina; he doesn't seem to be able to remember his lines.'

"This was only the second week *Playhouse 90* was on the air, and there was tremendous pressure to get it right. On Friday there was a run-through, and several network executives came down to the rehearsal hall to watch it. What Ed Wynn didn't know was that they had secretly hired another actor and had been rehearsing him to step in and replace Wynn. The star, Jack Palance, stood up for Ed Wynn, threatening to walk off if Wynn was fired. And Manulis insisted, 'I think Wynn's going to make it.'

"They stayed with him through rehearsals, and finally Manulis had to make the decision. 'Yes, we'll go with him.' Wynn did a magnificent job. He somehow got himself up to do the job and was nominated for an Emmy as Best Supporting Actor. But you had to have the guts of a burglar to be a producer for live television."

The availability of videotape beginning in 1957 changed everything. For Johnny and me, on *Who Do You Trust?*, it was great. It made our jobs easier. We were live Tuesday through Friday, and on Friday we did two shows so that we could have Mondays off. But for the producers of the dramatic shows, it meant much more was possible—and that meant different problems to deal with.

All of a sudden actors could be . . . temperamental actors. When the great director George Schaefer was taping *Playhouse 90*, he had finished a scene and was about to go to lunch when the stage manager told him that a famous actor starring in the show wasn't happy with the scene and wanted to do it again. Schaefer confronted him. "I want to do it again," the actor demanded.

Schaefer looked right at him. "You were magnificent," he said. "Trust me."

Now, what was the actor going to say, "You're wrong, I was terrible"?

My friends, those are words no actor has ever spoken. And they certainly weren't spoken this time. Instead the actor smiled, agreed, and walked away. Magnificently.

Videotape made it possible to do much larger productions, the biggest being *Playhouse 90*'s "For Whom the Bell Tolls," starring Jason Robards, Maria Schell, Maureen Stapleton, and Eli Wallach in 1959. It was a really ambitious project because they had to re-create the whole Spanish Civil War in a TV studio. It was the most expensive show in TV history to that point, with a budget of almost half a million dollars. It was the first TV drama to be presented in two parts. They rehearsed four weeks, and it was shot over ten days. To make the production even more difficult, most of the actors were working in Broadway shows at night, so they were exhausted during rehearsals. But as Eli Wallach, who played the gypsy Rafael, remembers, right in the middle of shooting, the whole production almost fell apart. "It was a great piece. All these wonderful actors. Maureen Stapleton had a scene in which she was supposed to fire a machine gun, but she hated guns. She was afraid of them. Maureen was afraid of everything—horses and guns and airplanes. She told our producer, Fred Coe, 'I'm not coming back. I'm too tired and I'm terrified of guns. I can't do it.'

"The studio was on Fifty-fifth and Ninth. The morning we were taping her scene everybody was there, the actors, the extras, the crew, but not Maureen. She wasn't joking. She didn't want to do the scene with the guns. So she just didn't show up.

"She lived somewhere up on Riverside Drive. Coe grabbed a few people, and they all jumped in a taxi and went to her building. She was holding up the Spanish Civil War. They walked right past the doorman and went up in the elevator to her apartment. Her boyfriend opened the door. 'Where is she?' Fred Coe asked. She was in the bedroom. There was nothing going to stop Coe. He went into the bedroom, and she was in bed, naked. He tore the covers right off the bed, put her over his shoulder, put a blanket over her, and carried her downstairs, into a cab, and right to the studio. He told her, 'Get your ass into makeup and get out here.'

"I think she was more terrified of him than she was of machine guns. She did what he told her to do, and the scene was shot."

In just one decade TV had gone from a live broadcast of an actor standing in front of a curtain acting out a monologue, to re-creating the Spanish Civil War. In the 1950s, TV introduced the great plays and literature to the whole world. When NBC did a three-hour-long adaptation of *Richard III* starring Laurence Olivier in 1956, more people saw it in one night than all the people who had ever seen it since Shakespeare wrote it. You could turn on the TV pretty much any night of the week and see the greatest stage actors in the world performing the greatest plays. For free.

But even after that first decade, there were people who still didn't quite understand live TV. "I was always a big boxing fan," Eli Wallach said. "Loved it. When there was a fight on the radio, my father and I would be glued to the radio, and then when they started showing boxing on TV, we would watch all the time. After every fight they would stick the microphone in front of the winning fighter, and he'd say breathlessly, 'Hello, Ma. Hello, Pa, I won.' Just like they do now.

"I was cast as a boxer in 1955 in *Shadow of a Champ* on the *Philco Television Playhouse*. Tony Canzoneri, who won world championships in three weight classes, was in the cast. We did it live upstairs at

Radio City. In the show I boxed three rounds. When the show was over, I went right to the phone and called my father. I was out of breath, and I said, 'Well, Pop, what'd you think?'

In an era of 60" flat screens, HDTV, LCDs, plasma, digital, satellite and cable, TiVo, surround sound, and programs on demand, it's nice to remember that in 1950 TV sets came in black and white and the screen could be as huge as 16"!

"My father, who was always criticizing me, didn't answer, so I asked the question again.

"He was silent for a few more seconds; then finally he said, 'You couldn't say hello?'"

Ernie Kovacs and I would have endless arguments about the need for a punch line. I would tell him, "Ernie, you're so close to a joke. Do two more lines and you're there."

But he didn't want to. "That's selling out," he told me.

He was a delightful, wonderful man. One day he called my wife and said, "Tell George to come over to the studio. I want to show him something."

When I got to the studio he was standing on a large set, next to a car. It looked like they were going to do a car commercial. He had this big smile on his face. I'll never forget it. "Watch this." He leaned on the front fender and the whole car fell through the floor. "There," he said. "Is that enough of a punch line for you?"

—GEORGE SCHLATTER,
AMERICAN TELEVISION PRODUCER

A S I MAY HAVE MENTIONED TWO OR TEN TIMES, money was just about the only thing that mattered to the networks. Putting popular radio and nightclub comedians and singers on television was very appealing because they had name recognition, and they didn't require elaborate sets and crews. And some of the old vaudeville, burlesque, and nightclub comedians were perfect for television, particularly those physical comedians who couldn't work on radio, and entertainers whose acts you had to see to appreciate.

Nobody knew what type of humor would work on television, and some of what was tried didn't. Take Olsen and Johnson. Please, take them. They were major vaudeville and Broadway stars. Their act consisted of . . . everything. Their Broadway show, *Hellzapoppin'*, ran a record 1,400 performances and was two hours of nonstop activity during which anything they thought of happened. It is easy to understand why they flopped on radio. The radio audience couldn't see the stuffed cows, the dead birds, the baboons, the midgets, the dried peas and pin feathers, the clowns, the stooges, the rubber snakes and spiders, the eggs and bananas, the seltzer bottles, the pies and more pies, the piglets, the blocks of ice, the skirt blowers, the chorus girls and cakes, and every member of the audience who might be assaulted in any possible way that was an essential part of their act. But would it work on television?

Fireball Fun-for-All went on the air in October 1949. Ole Olsen and Chic Johnson were confident television was the perfect medium for their act because "all of our gags are ocular." To make sure the audience didn't miss a thing, they insisted on using five cameras. Five cameras! I think the most I ever had in all the shows I did were two cameras. But the real problem they faced, Chic Johnson explained, was "we had to figure a way of jumping out of the TV set and into people's parlors. It may take time, but we'll do it." That was the problem. You can't jump out of a TV set! It's impossible, except in Stephen King's stories. The show turned out to be more of a fun-for-a-few and lasted only four months.

Another of vaudeville and radio's most popular comedians, Ed Wynn, brought his act to TV in 1949. *The Ed Wynn Show* was the first major network program to be produced in Hollywood; it was broadcast live on the West Coast, and two weeks later a kinescope of the show was shown in the east. Ed Wynn was a shtick figure, a true rubber-faced clown. Coincidently, my mother had once dated Ed Wynn, long before I was born, obviously. My great-grandmother ran a boarding house for actors, and Wynn stayed there for a brief time. Growing up, that was pretty much my connection to show business.

On stage Wynn wore outlandish costumes, funny hats, and huge shoes and was known for his instantly recognizable falsetto laugh. His show was a collection of old gags, corny jokes, and funny faces. It was the same kind of act Ed Wynn had been doing successfully for decades because it was hard for him to adjust to the new technology. In December 1949, he introduced Lucille Ball and Desi Arnaz to television; the first time they appeared on TV was as guests on *The Ed Wynn Show*. The critics liked his show and they gave him Emmy awards, but he never attracted a large enough audience, perhaps because the show was on kinescope in the east. Kinescopes were films of live TV shows made of the broadcast, not of the performance itself. A camera would be set up in front of a TV set, and the show would be filmed as it was being broadcast. The quality was poor, and kinescopes were gray and grainy —and more than anything, what people wanted from television were shows that were new and fresh.

Fred Allen had the longest-

One of television's first stars was vaudeville and radio comedian Ed Wynn, who won an Emmy in 1949 as host of his own variety show. Seven years later he proved he could be a dramatic actor by starring in *Requiem For A Heavyweight* on *Playhouse 90*.

Courtesy of Stephen Cox Collection

Some radio stars, like George Burns and Gracie Allen, made the transition to TV with their own shows—George would often interrupt the show to speak directly to the audience and then return to the plot.

running hour-long comedy show in radio history, but his witty, topical humor just didn't work on TV. "Television is called a new medium," he complained. "And I've discovered why they call it a medium—because nothing is well-done." After failing with three different types of shows, he decided that TV permitted "people who haven't anything to do to watch people who can't do anything." But his real bitterness was reserved for network executives. "Television is a triumph of equipment over people, and the minds that control it are so small you could put them in the navel of a flea and still have enough room beside them for the heart of a network vice president."

However, a number of the great radio stars were able to make the transition to television with only minor adjustments. If their characters were firmly established in listeners' minds, the shows were successful as long as they were faithful to the character. For example, Jack Benny was just as cheap on television as he had been on radio, but now viewers could actually see the pay phone in his living room. And Gracie Allen was just as confused on TV as she was on radio. In fact, at the end of every *George Burns and Gracie Allen Show*, George and Gracie stood in front of the stage curtain and talked to the audience—just as if they were still on radio. "Gracie," George would say, "is it true your maid dropped you on your head when you were a child?"

"Oh, don't be silly, George," Gracie would reply. "We couldn't afford a maid. My mother had to do it."

Courtesy of Stephen Cox Collection

Milton Berle dressed for success in a great variety of wild costumes. Mostly, though, he proved that with the right make-up and special effects, a man in a woman's clothes could look exactly like a man in a woman's clothes.

The veteran comedian who was most successful on TV was Milton Berle. *Milton Berle.* Say it loud and there's music blaring. Say it soft and it's almost . . . well, actually you can't say it softly. He would never have permitted it. Nothing about Berle was soft and easy; he was loud and outrageous and . . . Milton Berle. Or "Uncle Miltie," as millions of people referred to him. Or "Mr. Television" as he called himself. What can I possibly say about Milton Berle that he hasn't already said about himself? Historians have written that Milton Berle was responsible for millions of TV sets being sold, or as the joke was told, "Berle helped sell millions of TV sets because when he was on television my uncle sold his, my aunt sold hers . . ."

Milton Berle had been successful in vaudeville and nightclubs—he was the highest-paid nightclub performer in America—and people used to say he would appear at the opening of an envelope. But his kind of gag-a-second comedy didn't really work on radio or in the movies.

"I remember my first appearance on the radio. I had them rolling in the aisles. Then the usher came in and took away the dice. And then the second time . . ."

Thank you, Milton. Thank you for appearing in my book today.

"Did I tell you I reached millions of people? Fortunately, they couldn't reach me!"

That was Milton Berle, ladies and gentlemen. Milton Berle. Thanks, Milton.

Before Berle went on the air, the TV networks weren't convinced one performer could do a new show every week. A single performer could do a weekly program on radio because radio was easy. The actors stood in front of the microphones and read their scripts. As long as you had writers, you could do radio. But doing a new TV show every week meant new material, new sets, new costumes. You needed makeup artists and grips and electricians and a lot of props every single week. People didn't know if it was possible to do it all over again, brand-new and live, for an hour every week.

Texaco Star Theater went on the air in June 1948. Because it was pretty much accepted that one person just could not do a whole new show weekly, Berle was supposed to rotate as host with comedians Henny Youngman, Morey Amsterdam, and Jack Carter. But Berle just took over. His guests on his first show were Pearl Bailey and Señor Wences, a ventriloquist. Milton's show was so popular that

Some of the many, many, many faces of Uncle Miltie

almost immediately he became the permanent host. *Texaco Star Theater* became a reflection of everything Berle had learned in his career, anything that would get a laugh. His entrances were legendary. He would come onstage in a dog sled, on a donkey, in a horse and buggy or kiddie car, or even drop from the rafters as if by parachute. When he made his entrance, it would always be in some sort of unexpected costume. One night he opened his show wearing only a barrel, explaining that he had just finished paying his taxes. He might be Li'l Abner, Superman, Santa Claus, a caveman, or a cop, but most often he was in drag. He loved dressing as a woman. Believe me, I know women, and Milton did not look like a woman. Even with a dress that didn't fit, makeup, a silly wig, and carrying a handbag, he definitely did not look like a woman. One night he wore a dress with a long train, which got caught in the curtain as it rolled up, lifting him into the air—and causing him to explain, "I feel high tonight."

The audience loved everything Berle did. Except maybe for the woman he warned, "Don't laugh, lady; you and I go to the same plastic surgeon."

So much for the statement I made in Chapter 3 that TV programming was initially high class because most TV sets were bought by affluent people. Those people had the Metropolitan Opera and Alistair Cooke's *Omnibus*. Everybody else had Milton Berle.

Uncle Miltie would play with his audience as if he were in a nightclub, rather than on TV. "Good evening, ladies and germs," he would say. As the camera focused on a completely bald man in the front row, he would start in, "I want to tell you how happy I am that this gentleman is shining right in my eye. For a minute, I thought he was sitting upside down. I'm only kidding, sir; you haven't got a bald head—you just shaved too high. No, no, really, I'd like to put my finger in your ear and go bowling . . ."

The rest of the show was modeled on vaudeville. Within a few months his Hooper rating was 86.7 percent, meaning eight and a half out of ten TV sets . . .

"What is this? An audience or an oil painting?"
Thank you again, Milton.

As I was saying, the Hooper rating meant that 8.6 out of every ten TV sets in America were tuned to his show. Very few entertainers ever dominated any medium the way Milton Berle dominated television. On Tuesday nights at 8:00 p.m., most of the country stopped to watch Uncle Miltie. *Texaco Star Theater* was the most popular show in the entire history of television. OK, admittedly there wasn't that much history, but no TV show had ever come close to attracting this kind of attention. Theaters would delay their opening until nine o'clock. Some businesses would shut down, and restaurants would be empty. Supposedly there was a noticeable drop in the level of Detroit's reservoirs right after nine o'clock because everyone in the city waited until the show ended to go to the bathroom. However, bars with TV sets did very well.

When I was in Philadelphia, I had to do everything on my own shows, from booking my guests to writing my own script. And it was a lot of work. But that was nothing compared to what Milton Berle did. He had absolute control. He was the star, the director, a writer, a cameraman, and the editor. He laid out the show schedule, directed the acts, planned the camera shots, and supervised the lighting, costumes, the sets, and the musical arrangements. During rehearsals he would even lead the band. I know how busy I had been, and he was doing it all on national television!

His control of the stage was absolute. When he was onstage other performers weren't allowed to speak until "The Berle Light" went off. The Berle Light was connected to a rudimentary laugh track he created before other shows started using canned laughter. When a show played before a live audience, it didn't need canned laughter, but when shows went to tape, they couldn't keep the audience there for hours. The Berle Light consisted of a reel-to-reel tape recorder and . . .

"Did I tell you about that poor man who was hit by a car crossing West Fifty-second Street? A woman rushed to help him, and put his head in her lap. 'Are you comfortable?' she asked him. In a weak voice he answered, 'I make a nice living.'"

Thank you, Milton, but if you'll just let me finish here.

The Berle Light was a reel-to-reel tape recorder on which his assistant, Hal Collins, had recorded laughter. When the tape recorder was running, a light under the camera was lit so that other performers knew not to say a word. When the light dimmed, they could speak.

After his opening routine Berle would introduce his guests, who ranged from stars of the Metropolitan Opera to plate spinners. Then he would appear in wacky skits, tell some jokes, maybe do a few pratfalls, and change costumes, and change costumes again. Costumes were his big thing. He would change at the drop of a purse, at least five times each program, each costume more outrageous than the last one. Milton was particularly adept at using high heels and black teeth to get laughs. The shows were raucous and rowdy. He constantly interrupted his guests' performances, and he convinced them to dress in silly outfits and participate in wild skits. He even had the great opera tenor Lauritz Melchior dress in blackface. But he was also one of the very first hosts on television to insist that African Americans be permitted to appear on his show.

A lot of comedians in those days had running character gags. Jack Benny was cheap, Fred Allen was acerbic, and Milton Berle? He was, as columnist Walter Winchell called him, "The Thief of Bad Gags!" Berle had a reputation for stealing material from other comics, and although he always claimed it was part of his act, Bob Hope said, "I want to get into television before Berle uses all my material." Fred Allen called him "a parrot with skin on."

Berle objected to those complaints. "I don't mind personal insults, but when you insult the jokes I tell, you're insulting some of the best comedians in the world." There were people who said a comedian's career was pretty much over when Berle stopped stealing material from him. Actually, those people were mostly Milton.

After serving with the Marines in Korea I came home in 1953 to discover what I had been fighting for—so that Jack Benny could have Marilyn Monroe on his great TV show.

But seriously, folks, I was listening to Jack Benny on the radio last night, and I have to tell you he was so funny that I dropped my pad and pencil. Now, honestly I don't steal other people's material; I just find it before it's lost, that's all. Come on, folks, those are the jokes.

As TV expanded outside the cities, Milton Berle's popularity faded. That was no surprise; it would have been nearly impossible to maintain the level of popularity he attained for more than a few years. In

1953 Texaco dropped its sponsorship of the show and was replaced by Buick. Three years later his show was cancelled—although one of his guests his last season was Elvis Presley. Milton Berle began appearing in dramatic shows, but by 1960 he was hosting the game show *Jackpot Bowling*, telling jokes between the attempts by contestants.

What Berle did was bring the best of vaudeville, burlesque, night-clubs, and even radio to television. It was big, broad comedy—and at least once each show Milton was that big broad! *Da dum bump!* But while he was recycling vaudeville, young comedians like Sid Caesar, Ernie Kovacs, Steve Allen, and Jackie Gleason were inventing tele-vision comedy. Let Caesar explain it:

"One of the skits we did was called 'The Fur Coat Episode.' Nanette [Fabray] walks down the street and sees a fur coat in the store win-dow and goes in. 'How much is it?' 'It's reduced down to $750.' So she buys the coat.

"I come home from work, and I go, 'Hello, dear.' I sit down, and she says, 'Hi sweetheart, how are you doing?' Then she comes over and gives me a kiss that's almost two minutes long. I keep looking. What could this be? I said, 'Is this a love kiss?' Then she comes in and serves me dinner. She almost chews it for me, and when the meal is over, she lights my cigar—and then she comes out with the coat on and doesn't say a word. I look at it, and the camera closes in on my face and just holds the close-up for more than a minute. And slowly, very slowly, I begin to cry."

Television allowed for a new kind of visual comedy, the comedy of reaction. I wasn't a comedian, but even I would do visual material. I did an entire show standing in front of a huge stuffed elephant—with-out ever mentioning the elephant or even acknowledging that I was standing in front of a stuffed elephant. I did an interview with a singer right outside our studio—and as I asked my questions, an elaborate faked shoot-out took place behind us. "So why did you decide to become a singer?" I asked as people were ducking behind cars, racing around, shooting, right behind us—and I never noticed. Hey, if you don't notice an elephant, surely you're not going to notice a shoot-out.

Five Minutes More with Ed McMahon was broadcast in Philadelphia at the end of the eleven o'clock news. I would often get back from a day in New York City about eight o'clock and rush to the studio. I could do anything I wanted to do. One night I began the show with the camera doing a long, slow pan of a photograph of the entire famed Mummers band. As a recording of the band played in the background, I announced, "This is the Mummers marching band, and this will make the tenth consecutive year this incredible group has marched in the Thanksgiving Day parade. . . ."

As I began relating the history of the Mummers marching band, my stage manager, a wonderful man named John Heatherton, interrupted me. "Ed," he said loudly. "What do you want me to do with the band that's waiting out in the hall?"

"John," I said, placing a gentle hand on his shoulder. "How long have you been in television?" Four years, he told me. I nodded, understanding, "You see, John, I know that what you saw on the monitor made it look as if there was a band right here in the studio, but actually it was a photograph and a recording."

He agreed that it was just a photograph and a recording. "That was great the way you did that. But what do you want me to do with the band that's waiting out there in the hall?"

I explained it to him again, maybe raising my voice a little. "There is no band in the hallway. Look around, John. Do you see them?"

He didn't, he admitted.

"Of course you don't. . . ."

"Because they're out there in the hall," he said.

I took a deep breath. "OK, John, have it your way. The entire Mummers band is here. . . ."

The great Sid Caesar and the great Imogene Coca were among the first comics to use the unique capabilities of television to create a new form of comedy. But their creativity was inspired by the unique challenges of live television. When videotape was introduced it changed the dynamics by making everything more rehearsed.

"So you want me to send them home?"

Send them home, I told him. I turned and looked into the camera. "Excuse me, ladies and gentlemen, but sometimes as we do this program, there is some confusion." Meanwhile, all two hundred members of the entire Mummers band, in full regalia, marched across the stage right in front of me playing loudly.

You could not do that joke on radio. Or in a nightclub. It would not have worked in the movies. It was a gag made for television.

Sid Caesar pioneered the art of television comedy. Unlike Milton Berle or Jack Benny or Fred Allen, Caesar had not served his time as a stand-up comedian. He didn't really tell jokes. Instead, he delivered funny lines both verbally and physically. He hadn't faced vaudeville audiences in small towns. He wasn't a graduate of radio—although he had appeared on Broadway for producer Max Leibman. The first real success of his career came on TV.

Caesar was a skilled performer, a comic actor capable of doing everything from physical humor to mime. He could play any role from a Freudian psychiatrist to a slot machine. He was a talented ad-libber, he could do all the usual dialects, but he was especially great at doing double-talk in foreign languages. He could say nothing in more languages than almost any performer before. The listener could identify the language without understanding a single made-up word. For his TV shows, beginning with the Leibman-produced *Admiral Broadway Revue* in 1949 and followed by the classic *Your Show of Shows*, Sid Caesar created his own repertory company, including comedienne Imogene Coca, Carl Reiner, and Howie Morris. But much more than Berle, Caesar depended on his writers, and he put together what undoubtedly was the greatest writing staff in show-business history.

If there were a writer's hall of fame, Sid Caesar's team would take up an entire wing. Among them were Larry Gelbart, Danny and Neil Simon, Mel Tolkin, Selma Diamond, and Carl Reiner. Woody Allen would join the writing staff later. Mel Brooks once described his experience this way: "I should have been impressed, but I wasn't because I was a cocky kid filled with hubris and a marvelous ego. I thought I was God's gift to creative writing—and it turned out I was!"

Caesar's shows consisted of monologues and pantomimes, blackouts, guest performances, skits, large production numbers, sketches in which he played familiar characters like jazz musician Progress Hornsby (whose band had a musician who played radar—"he's the one who would warn us in case we approached the melody"), and parodies of movies and plays. In addition to doing parodies of the most popular films, the whole company would also parody obscure foreign films and Italian operas. They did a lot of very funny operas. And these weren't just brief skits; some of them lasted a half hour or longer; sometimes they would last the whole show. And unlike Berle, in many of those bits Caesar played a supporting role. This was the kind of comedy that led to . . .

"You know, that reminds me of the company accountant. He's shy and retiring. He's shy a quarter of a million dollars. That's why he's retiring!"
Come on, Milton! Please. That's enough, OK?

The comedy Sid Caesar and friends were doing in the early 1950s led directly to the great comedy shows like *Rowan & Martin's Laugh-In* and *Saturday Night Live*. Once they did a complete skit without speaking, in which they played the characters from a beautiful German clock. To mark the hour, Sid Caesar, dressed in lederhosen, would hit an anvil, Carl Reiner would hit Caesar's hammer, Howie Morris pumped the bellows, and Imogene Coca would cool the hammer with a stream of water.

At least that's the way the clock was supposed to work. But the springs of this particular clock had supposedly given out, knocking off the timing, so as each hour passed, this once perfectly tuned operation became more and more chaotic. By the end of the skit, the characters were being hit with the hammers, water was spraying all over them, and the whole thing was a disaster. It is what might have happened if the Marx Brothers had been Swiss.

In the early years when all the shows were live, Caesar was able to show off his comic brilliance. Comedies had the same problems on live TV that every other show experienced. Caesar explained, "There were many times when a door wouldn't open, so you had to come in through the window—but you had to be prepared to accept the situation and have some fun with it." On one show, the opera *Pagliacci* was done as a twenty-minute-long musical, which included classic arias like "Take Me Out to the Ballgame" and "Yellow Rosa Texas" sung in pseudo-Italian. During that show Caesar demonstrated his legendary ability to ad-lib. "I was at the makeup table and I got the pencil and I was going to draw a tear and the pencil breaks and it makes a straight line. So I took the makeup brush and I continued the line. And then I drew another straight line while I'm singing, and then—I put a line across those two lines and then another line across. From nowhere I started to play tic-tac-toe. When the pencil broke it was 'What do I do?' Oh heck, I'll follow the line. That was the spark that happened."

Another time Caesar was playing the great defense attorney Clarence Darrow. As the skit began Caesar made a loud summation proving why his client was innocent! The jury was supposed to find Caesar's client guilty, and he would spend the next ten minutes lambasting the jury. But instead of asking the jury if they found the defendant *innocent,* the judge asked the jury, "Do you find the defendant *guilty*?"

The foreman of the jury had one word, which he was supposed to pronounce when asked if the defendant was innocent. But the wrong question had been asked. "No," the foreman said firmly, thereby blowing the entire skit.

Caesar didn't even flinch. He jumped up, screaming, "You're wrong! My client is guilty, and I'll prove it!" Then he proceeded to ad-lib the entire rest of the sketch.

Saturday nights belonged to Caesar's *Your Show of Shows* until 1954, and he continued on the air until 1958 with *Caesar's Hour* and later *The Sid Caesar Show.* But when tape was introduced, it changed the dynamics. "By 1957 it didn't matter what you were doing," Caesar explained. "Everything was on tape because they [network executives] could control tape. But when you put a show on tape you lose the spontaneity. When you do it live, you know you can only do it once. Your whole body comes up with adrenaline because this is the performance,

Ernie Kovacs, one of television's most innovative comedians, proved that you can't always believe what you see on TV.

Courtesy of Stephen Cox Collection

this is it. Want to take it again? We did four takes; let's do five. And after the fourth or fifth take you lose it. You don't know what in hell you started. What they wanted was to control it. And they could sell it here, sell it there, take it around. But that was the end. And by 1957 I was exhausted."

Along with Sid Caesar, Ernie Kovacs was probably the most innovative comedian in TV history. Known for his big bushy mustache, a cigar, and a smile, Ernie Kovacs' evening show on WPTZ in Philadelphia was opposite my show. We knew each other, but since both of us were doing well, there was no rivalry between us. My show was a precursor of the news-service-entertainment *Today Show* or all the *Good Morning (Name a city)* shows. Ernie Kovacs' show wasn't like anything that had ever been done on TV before. When I sat on a tree limb and sawed it off, I fell out of the picture; if Kovacs had sawed off the limb he was sitting on, the tree would have toppled with him hanging there suspended in midair. When he did a cooking show, *Deadline for Dinner*, he beat up a head of lettuce for being too smart.

There's a theater term, *the fourth wall,* which refers to the invisible barrier between the audience and the performers. When a performer interacts directly with the audience, that's called breaking the fourth wall. Jerry Lewis did it, but no performer ever broke down the fourth wall like Ernie Kovacs. He went much further than anyone else in creating television comedy that was off-the-wall.

The strange thing is that unlike Milton Berle or Sid Caesar or Ed Wynn or so many other comedians, Kovacs never had a really successful show. He had his evening show, a cooking show, a quiz show, even briefly *The Tonight Show*, but unlike Berle, who was identified with Tuesday nights, or Caesar, who was identified with Sunday nights, none of Kovacs' shows were associated with a time slot. His shows were all over the place. From the beginning of his TV career in 1950 in Philadelphia until he died in an automobile accident in 1962, Ernie Kovacs was the master of sight gags, sound effects, technical innovations, bad jokes, blackouts, camera tricks, outrageous bits, and unbelievably silly sketches. He started *3 to Get Ready*—it was on Channel 3 in Philadelphia—with a live shot of his running a vacuum cleaner upside down on the studio ceiling. Live and upside down! Figure that one out! When the news and weatherman Norman Brooks predicted rain, Kovacs would get up on a ladder and pour water on him. Because it was almost impossible to get a microphone outside the studio in those days, he would do bits on Walnut Street outside the studio with the actors holding up cue cards with their lines written on them—so that viewers could read the lines themselves.

It was Kovacs who had a fire hydrant that squirted at a dog, water that poured out of a painting of the ocean, and a three-inch-tall woman who walked up his arm. All done live. As a woman undressed, her body parts disappeared. Office furniture and cooked turkeys danced in response to classical music. Once he drove by a construction site in a horse-drawn trash cart and remarked that the hole was so big he could "see all the way to China," at which point a man wearing a Chinese coolie costume climbed out of the hole, yelled something in pseudo-Chinese, and ran down the street. In one show Kovacs wore a wristwatch that marked the hour by chiming louder than Big Ben, and on another show when he played a newscaster in ancient Rome, he wore a miniature hourglass on his wrist. In a semitouching scene, a clown holding a circus poster on which he is featured, watches a beautiful woman of the streets—and the poster starts crying.

Among the many characters Kovacs created on his various shows were El Stupido, Rod Lovely, Superclod, Luigi the Barber, Al the Dog, a midget named Little Johnny Merkin, and probably his most famous, the effete poet Percy Dovetonsils. Kovacs recorded an album of the immaculately dressed—with cravat—Percy's poems entitled *Perthy Dovetonthilth Thpeakth*, which included the magnificent "O Sometimes I Wish I Were A Dog":

> O sometimes I wish I were a dog
> A Boxer or a Cocker Spaniel
> Or perhaps a German Spitz,
> Or maybe a Chihuahua named Manuel.
> I met a girl named Doberman
> And without a doubt it's a cinch, her
> Figure's the greatest I've ever seen
> Now I wish I were a Doberman Pinch-her!

Kovacs had a small group of actors with whom he worked, but foremost was his beautiful wife, Edie Adams, who played all the sexy roles—in addition to playing a gorilla musician in his Nairobi Trio. He also had a regular character on his morning show that no one ever saw. Years before Dave Garroway had J. Fred Muggs, Kovacs had Howard, the World's Strongest Ant. While the audience couldn't actually see Howard—apparently there were some technical difficulties—it did embrace him. Viewers believed in Howard enough to send in more than thirty thousand ant-sized gifts, most of them homemade, including false teeth, a mink-lined swimming pool, and several kegs of beer.

For Kovacs, every piece of equipment, every crew member, and everything that was needed to produce a television show was a prop to be used on that show. He was probably the first performer to talk to his camera crew and the boom operator and to go into the control room and start pushing buttons during the show. He played with the credits, introducing his summer replacement show *Ernie in Kovacsland* with the announcement, "Ernie in Kovacsland! A short program—it just seems long!" And he spoke directly to the viewing audience, telling them, "I'd like to thank you for inviting me into your living room this evening. It's just a shame you didn't straighten up a little."

Having fun with the cast and crew and the studio audience and viewers at home was one thing, but he also made fun of the commercials. His longtime sponsor was Dutch Masters cigars, and his commercials would often be skits. In one commercial he and his favorite straight man, Joe Mikolas, stood ten feet apart in a classic western showdown stance. Both men were smoking cigars. They drew their guns, and fired—and Ernie plugged Joe ten or twelve times. But instead of dying, Joe casually took a puff on his cigar—and smoke billowed out of all the holes.

That was Ernie Kovacs. So how did he vacuum the ceiling on live television? He helped invent the technology. His engineer cut off both ends of a Campbell's soup can and inserted two mirrors at forty-five-degree angles. The soup can was attached to a camera lens. When the cameraman turned the soup can, the mirrors would rotate the image, making it appear he was upside down vacuuming the ceiling. If you would like to see the kind of response this bit got, turn the dust jacket of this book upside down. Then the next time you're reading in public, sneak a look at the reaction you get.

These comedy-variety shows—*Variety* named them *vaudeo* because so many of them were hosted by former vaudevillians—were all at least an hour long, and there was a great variety of variety shows. Comic pianist Victor Borge had a show; dancer Donald O'Connor had a show; bandleader Spike Jones had several shows. Singers Dinah Shore and Perry Como had variety shows. Nat King Cole became the first African American to host his own variety show. A couple of years later, Red Skelton had a very successful comedy show. The problem was that these shows were expensive to produce and could be run only once. Unlike sitcoms and dramatic series, there was little interest in them in the syndication market. Variety shows lasted on air much longer than the great dramatic shows, but by the mid 1970s they had pretty much disappeared, part of the high cost of the success of the networks.

Everybody in radio was scrambling to find a
framework that would work on television. We all knew
what wouldn't work—standing in front of a microphone
and reading from a script. Unfortunately, that's what
we were best at . . . My major contribution to the
format was to suggest that I be able to step out of the
plot and speak directly to the audience, and then be
able to go right back into the action. That was an
original idea of mine; I know it was because I
originally stole it from Thornton Wilder's *Our Town*.

—GEORGE BURNS

O N THE OTHER SIDE OF THE FUNNY STREET WERE SIT-
coms (situation comedies), which were half-hour filmed
comedies with continuing characters. On radio the funny family
shows had been called soap operas or comedy serials; generally they
were only fifteen minutes long, but they were very popular. The word
sitcom wasn't even coined until 1951. Sitcoms were twenty-two minutes long, which left eight minutes for commercials. Most importantly, they were on film and could be shown over and over. They

could be syndicated and sold in every TV market in America. Over and over. And eventually in other countries as well.

What made sitcoms particularly appealing to the actors was an unusual deal made by Taft Schreiber, an agent with Lew Wasserman's MCA, the most powerful talent agency in the business at that time. Jerry Zeitman, who was a young agent there, tells the story: "We represented many of the most popular comedy shows on radio, Burns and Allen, Jack Benny, *Amos 'n' Andy*. I was told that Taft Schreiber went to see Bill Paley, who at that time was the owner and president of CBS. Taft said to Paley that he was going to move Benny and Burns and *Amos 'n' Andy* from NBC radio into television. The key line he spoke changed everything for an artist in television. Taft said, 'You're going to have exclusivity, but the artists are going to own their own negatives.' Who ever heard of an actor owning his own product? It was unheard-of. That one line was worth untold millions of dollars to actors. It made all the difference."

Later on, producer David Susskind explained Schreiber's idea to Eli Wallach. Wallach and his wife, Anne Jackson, had starred in a comedy named "Lullaby" on *The Play of the Week*. "The ratings were great," Wallach said, "and Susskind thought it could be developed into a series. Neither Anne nor I even knew what a series was. Susskind told us, 'I'll own a third, you'll own a third, and the network will own a third. And if it's successful, your children will never have to work again.'

"On the taxi ride home, we discussed it. There were a lot of good things about it. But then Anne turned to me and asked, 'Why shouldn't the children work?' That was it. We turned him down."

The formula for a TV sitcom was pretty straightforward. There were several regular characters, and each episode of a sitcom had one . . . situation. The story line usually centered around some kind of mistake, accident, snafu, or dubious scheme.

This format began on radio in 1926. The first comic serial was *Sam 'n' Henry*, the adventures of two African Americans—as written and performed by two white radio actors. On radio, white could be black. The show, broadcast on Chicago's clear channel WGN, was very popular throughout the Midwest, but when Freeman Gosden and Charles Correll, the show's creators and actors, asked permission to distribute the show to stations in other cities, the station management turned them down. When their contract with WGN expired, they moved to another station and created the first national radio program, *Amos 'n' Andy*. Amos and Andrew J. Brown remained among the most popular radio characters for more than two decades, at times attracting more than forty million listeners! One-third of the population of the United States was listening to the same show! It was so popular that in order to entice people to come to the movie theaters when the show was being broadcast, theater owners would wheel a radio onstage and let the audience listen to *Amos 'n' Andy*.

Television's first sitcom, which went on the air in New York in 1947, was *Mary Kay and Johnny*, a fifteen-minute show about a newly married couple living in New York's Greenwich Village. It starred recently married actors Mary Kay and Johnny Stearns, who were living in an apartment in Greenwich Village. It was done live, and it lasted three seasons on three successive networks, DuMont, NBC, and CBS. "Television was just one of those things you did to help pay the rent while you were looking for a real job in the theater," Mary Kay said.

Decades later people would describe *Seinfeld* as revolutionary because it was based on the small realities of life, but as Johnny Stearns remembers, "The show hit close to home. If Mary Kay got stuck in an elevator, it would give me an inspiration about us getting stuck in an elevator."

Beginning in 1948 *Mary Kay and Johnny* episodes were recorded on kinescope for national distribution. Unfortunately, these kinescopes survived only until the 1970s when ABC dumped all the old DuMont programs into the New York Bay and CBS trashed its own old kinescopes.

Several years before Lucille Ball and Desi Arnaz gave birth to Little Ricky, Mary Kay and Johnny had a baby—in real life as well as on the show. But unlike Lucy and Ricky Ricardo, Mary Kay and Johnny's small apartment had only one bed—meaning they must have slept together! However, there were several conventions that were carefully followed on all sitcoms after *Mary Kay and Johnny*: the husband and wife slept in separate beds and always in pajamas, nobody ever had to go to the bathroom (which was a good thing because there were no bathrooms), every TV family had two parents—

Courtesy of Stephen Cox Collection

although later several wives disappeared without explanation, leaving bachelor husbands trying to raise kids—and one had a job while the other stayed home. There often was a strange neighbor who walked in and out of the house without knocking or ringing the bell.

It was more than a decade after *Mary Kay and Johnny* that another married couple slept together on TV—and that couple was Fred and Wilma Flintstone.

During TV's early years there were a number of ethnic sitcoms, many of which had been successful on radio. The very first to make the transition to

Many of the early sitcoms were ethnic based and got their humor in part from ethnic stereotypes, something that might be very difficult to get on the air today. Gertrude Berg created the role of loveable Jewish Bronx housewife Molly Goldberg.

television successfully was *The Goldbergs*, the adventures of a middle-class Jewish couple, Jake and Molly Goldberg, who lived in a middle-class Jewish-dominated building in the Bronx. The great Yiddish actress Gertrude Berg played Molly. In a typical episode Molly Goldberg had to deal with a problem then facing many middle-class Jews: the Goldbergs' kids wanted a Christmas tree like their friends had. *Oy vey!* Such a problem! The warm and wise Molly Goldberg came up with an answer that has survived half a century: the first Chanukah bush. Another thing that most of these ethnic series had in common was an easily remembered catchphrase, something viewers could remember and imitate. *The Goldbergs* had a neighbor who would lean out the window to call to her friend in a singsong, "Yoo-hoo, Mrs. Goldberg?"

In 1949, the same year the Goldbergs were living in the Bronx, Irish-American Chester A. Riley was living *The Life of Riley* with his wife and two teenagers, a boy and a girl, in a neat suburban house in Los Angeles. Riley was the epitome of the lovable bumbler, a blue-collar worker at Cunningham Aircraft who could mistakenly believe that a coworker he overheard talking about killing a plant was plotting a killing *at* the aircraft plant! William Bendix played Riley on the radio and in a feature movie, but the first season on TV, Riley was played by Jackie Gleason. Bendix eventually took over and made Riley's favorite complaint, "What a revoltin' development *this* is," a nationally repeated catchphrase.

The Italian American Mama Rosa and her family owned a Hollywood boarding house favored by young actors in a short-lived 1950 show named, appropriately, *Mama Rosa*. Beverly Garland, who played Mama Rosa's daughter, has kept the first check she received for her work on that show—$9.23. Norwegian Americans were represented by the sugary-sweet humor of *Mama*, the story of the Hansen family living in San Francisco in 1910. And a few years later, the travails of resident aliens were portrayed in *My Favorite Martian*.

But the best known—and the most controversial—ethnic sitcom was *Amos 'n' Andy*. On radio, the Caucasian Gosden and Correll had played all the male characters, but obviously on TV the characters had to be African American. It took four years to put together the right cast and rehearse the stars to use the speech pattern of the radio characters. Amos was a philosophical cab driver who narrated most of the episodes. The main characters were actually George Stevens, the continually conniving head "Kingfish" of Harlem's Mystic Knights of the Sea Lodge, and Andrew H. Brown, the target of so many of the Kingfish's schemes. It was the Kingfish, for example, who sold Andy

Courtesy of Stephen Cox Collection

The ethnic sitcom *Amos 'n' Andy* had been a huge hit on radio, where the characters were played by white actors. Making the transition to TV required producers to find African American actors. The show was controversial, and after only two seasons pressure from the NAACP caused CBS to take it off the air.

the front of a house from a movie set, which Andy accurately described as "the thinnest house" he had ever seen. "The way I looks at it," Kingfish explained to Andy, "I examined the property. The house is stucco, and you is the stuckee." But their relationship was perfectly summed up when Kingfish was on trial and the prosecutor asked Andy, "Mr. Brown, would you tell the court how you became acquainted with George Stevens?"

"Yes, sir," Andy answered. "I was at the race track, and when I reached back for my wallet, I shook hands with Mr. Stevens."

And it was the Kingfish who famously replied, quite indignantly, when accused of yet another scam, "I rejects the allegation, and I resents the alligator!" The catchphrases from this show—"Holy mackerel!" and "Woe is me, woe is me, what is I gonna do?"—were almost weekly Kingfish complaints. Among the other characters were a shady lawyer, Algonquin J. Calhoun; the evvvvvvveeerrrr-soooo-sloowwwwww-moving janitor, Lightnin'; the Kingfish's wife, Sapphire; and her belligerent mother, Mama. "Lemme tell you something, Andy boy. If all the womens in Texas is as ugly as Sapphire's mother, then the Lone Ranger's gonna be alone for a long, long time."

When it began broadcasting in June 1951, *Amos 'n' Andy* was an immediate success—in the white community. In the African American community the reaction was mixed at best. Some black newspapers and magazines defended the show, pointing out that the characters included black men and women professionals, doctors, lawyers, judges, and businessmen, people of style and success. But the show went on near the beginning of the civil rights movement and many organizations, led by the NAACP, came out strongly against it. The NAACP said that "every character is either a clown or a crook," that "Negro doctors are shown as quacks," and "Negro lawyers are shown as crooks."

Amos 'n' Andy ran only two seasons, seventy-eight episodes, until

CBS reluctantly took it off the air. Television was the most important communications medium in America. With the civil rights movement heating up, advertisers were nervous about offending Southerners and wary about having their products connected too closely to African Americans. It was just easier for CBS to cancel the show.

Almost immediately *Amos 'n' Andy* became one of the most successful shows in syndication. But in 1964, bowing to continued protests, CBS yanked it out of syndication and prevented the old episodes from being broadcast.

The first African American sitcom was actually *Beulah,* which was adapted from the radio. Played by Ethel Waters, Beulah was a maid, a "queen of the kitchen," and in each episode she used her homespun wisdom to solve problems that her white bosses had created. *Beulah* was attacked by a lot of people, including the NAACP, for reinforcing stereotypes of black characters.

Amos 'n' Andy and *Beulah* were exceptions in the early 1950s for putting African Americans on television. In fact, after *Amos 'n' Andy* was cancelled, it took nearly twenty years before another all-African-American cast appeared on a television series. According to *Variety*, one major advertising executive had made it clear, "No Negro performers allowed." The legendary black singer Pearl Bailey was a guest on Milton Berle's first show, but after that, even he had difficulty booking African American performers. He explained, "I remember clashing with the sponsor and the advertising agency over my signing the Four Step Brothers to appear on my show, but I couldn't even find out who was objecting. 'We just don't like them,' I was told, but who the hell was 'we'? Because I was riding high in 1950, I sent out the word that if they don't go on, I don't go on. Ten minutes before showtime I got permission for the Four Step Brothers to appear. But years later I had no trouble booking Bill Robinson or Lena Horne."

Courtesy of Stephen Cox Collection

Many historians agree that *I Love Lucy*, starring Vivian Vance and Bill Frawley as Fred and Ethel Mertz (left), and Desi Arnaz and Lucille Ball as Ricky and Lucy Ricardo (right), was the greatest sitcom in TV history.

Most people don't consider Lucille Ball's *I Love Lucy* to be an ethnic sitcom, and maybe they are right, but I do have one word in response: "Babaloo!" Or as Lucy's husband, Desi Arnaz, who played her TV husband, Ricky Ricardo, might say about that, "Ed, you got some 'splainin' to do!"

Lucy and Desi played the first married interracial couple on TV, Lucy being white and Ricky being a Cuban bandleader. Apparently the bandleader part was OK; it was the Hispanic part that caused some problems. When the show went on the air in October 1951, CBS received a lot of nasty letters complaining about their mixed marriage not being appropriate for TV.

Although Lucy and Ricky's mixed marriage was unusual, their

being married formed the setting for the most common of sitcom situations—a married couple, usually with kids, gets involved in all kinds of mishaps. What can possibly be funnier than marriage? In addition to *I Love Lucy*, the family sitcoms of this era included *The Honeymooners*, which technically wasn't a sitcom but rather a skit on Jackie Gleason's comedy show for most of its run; *Father Knows Best* with Robert Young and Jane Wyatt; George Burns and Gracie Allen successfully playing George Burns and Gracie Allen in *The George Burns and Gracie Allen Show*; Chester Riley living with his family in *The Life of Riley*; bandleader Ozzie Nelson and his singer wife Harriet playing fictional versions of themselves in *The Adventures of Ozzie and Harriet*; *Leave It to Beaver*, featuring the adventures of the Cleaver family's youngest son, the Beaver; and nightclub performer Danny Thomas playing nightclub performer Danny Williams who lived with his wife and kids—until his wife died and he became a bachelor father in *Make Room for Daddy*. Which, of course, should not be confused with the real *Bachelor Father*, in which wealthy bachelor John Forsythe had to raise his niece, or Fred MacMurray's *My Three Sons*, or all the other shows in which a bumbling male is raising children, including *Family Affair, The Courtship of Eddie's Father, Nanny and the Professor,* and even *Flipper*!

But none of those shows—in fact no show in television history—was more popular than *I Love Lucy*. When Lucy gave birth to Little Ricky in a 1953 episode, 72 percent of the people sitting in front of their television sets were watching. Two years earlier nobody imagined this show would be that popular. Or popular at all.

"I remember that first year," said Dann Cahn, who edited the show from the very beginning. "One day on the lot, I ran into an old friend, Bud Molin, who was working as an assistant editor on three-minute music films that would play on jukeboxes. These were the earliest music videos. When I offered him a job with us, the man he

Courtesy of Stephen Cox Collection

While most sitcom couples were middle class and lived comfortably in houses or large apartments, bus driver Ralph Kramden and his wife, Alice, played by Jackie Gleason and Audrey Meadows, lived in a tiny Brooklyn apartment and struggled with the familiar problems of living from paycheck to paycheck.

was working for warned him, 'Bud, you're going to be looking for a job in three months. CBS will never pick up the option on *I Love Lucy* beyond the thirteen-week commitment.'

"Bud ended up staying at Desilu Studios for ten years."

Eventually Lucy would be nominated for nine Emmys and win two. Vivian Vance, who played the Ricardos' neighbor, Ethel Mertz, was nominated four times and won once. Bill Frawley, Ethel's husband Fred, was nominated three times. And Desi? Desi was never nominated. And all he did was . . .

"You know, Ed, as I got older people would ask me how old did I feel?
So I told them, I feel like a twenty-year-old, but there's never one
around."

Milton, enough. I'm talking about Desi Arnaz and . . .

"Desi Arnaz? I loved him. Loved him. I ever tell you about the guy who walked into a monastery smoking a Cuban cigar? Well, one . . ."

No. No, and that's enough! Enough!

When CBS wanted Lucy to bring her popular radio show, *My Favorite Husband,* to television, she insisted that her husband, Desi, play her husband, Desi. To convince the executives, who were concerned that there would be a negative public reaction, Lucy and Desi put together a vaudeville act and toured the country. The success of that act convinced CBS that Desi, a bandleader, could play a bandleader on the show.

Desi Arnaz changed television. The show's sponsor, Phillip Morris, wanted Lucy and Desi to do the show live in New York and then distribute kinescopes throughout the rest of the country, like every other show. But Lucy was a movie star and wanted to stay in Hollywood and do the show in front of a live audience because, as Jerry Zeitman explained, "Lucy wanted to hear the laughs. Gracie Allen wouldn't work in front of a live audience because she had all those wild crazy lines that had to be read exactly as they were written. Sometimes it would require several takes to get them right." Desi wanted to do the show on 35mm film and then edit it like it was a movie, believing that it might have lasting value and might someday be worth something. Desi wanted to preserve the show. However, network executives didn't believe anybody would want to watch a comedy twice, so there was no reason to spend considerably more money putting it on film. Desi convinced Phillip Morris to agree to it. CBS also reluctantly agreed, but with a condition.

I believe that this condition falls into the Worst-Negotiation-of-the-Century category.

Those tough network negotiators asked Desilu, Lucy and Desi's company, to pay part of the production cost and work for a smaller fee. And in return—now listen to how those clever college-educated bottom-line accountants outsmarted the simple bandleader from Cuba—in return Desilu received total ownership of the series. Lucy and Desi owned the show—a show that is still running somewhere every day (although they sold out their interest long ago), making Lucy and Desi the first TV stars to earn millions of dollars from their show.

I can just imagine the expression on the face of a CBS vice president the day he opened the newspaper to see that *I Love Lucy* was the most popular program on television. And then he discovers that the network had given away all the rights!

I Love Lucy was the first sitcom filmed live in front of an audience and marked a fundamental change in TV production. As CBS vice president Harry Ackerman explained at the time, "We are primarily in the live TV business. We definitely wanted to shoot *I Love Lucy* live. But the sponsor made us go to film. You can say that we went into the film business at the whim of the sponsor."

And because the audience was there, the show was done in sequence, as a story that made sense, rather than the usual way of shooting scenes out of order. Even though film allowed them to reshoot scenes, they didn't do very much of it, and a lot of dialogue mistakes were left in to make the show seem live.

Desi was also credited with inventing the three-camera technique, which became the standard way of shooting sitcoms. Actually, several shows already had been broadcast using three cameras, beginning with *Public Prosecutor* in 1947. But before Desi, most filmed shows were done with a single camera on a closed set. But as Dann Cahn explained, "We shot the first show with four cameras. We filmed every actor. We had a specially constructed Moviola editing machine, which allowed the director and me to see simultaneously the images from the cameras and hear the dialogue. After shooting the first show, we got rid of the fourth camera."

After the show was filmed, TV stations throughout the country and Canada received 16 mm prints, which eventually were sent back to Desilu. Desi gave complete, original sets of the prints—on 16 mm reels—to members of the cast and crew.

Eventually they did 180 half-hour episodes over six seasons, and then several additional one-hour specials. There was one basic plot: what kind of mess would Lucy get into this week? Ricky was a bandleader at the Tropicana nightclub, and many of the plots involved Lucy's trying to join him in show business or prove herself in the business world. Fred and Ethel Mertz were their drop-in-anytime-to-get-involved-in-the-plot neighbors, helping to define that role for subsequent sitcoms, leading directly to *Seinfeld*'s Kramer.

Although the show was set in New York—the Ricardos' apartment was supposedly on East Sixty-eighth Street—it was filmed on a movie sound stage in Hollywood that included bleachers for the audience. "The things we did on that set were amazing," Cahn said. One of the classic Lucy episodes, "Lucy in the Chocolate Factory," required Lucy to box chocolates on an assembly line. Chaos ensued when Lucy tried to keep pace as the assembly line of chocolate bonbons moved increasingly faster. "We built that whole chocolate factory on the set. People think it was a chocolate factory in Beverly Hills. Our prop department saw how the assembly line worked and made a mock-up of it. All on the set. In front of an audience.

"It got really complicated when Lucy and Ricky went to Europe and took a helicopter. I actually went to New York and flew with a double down the East River to a deck on the harbor. We took that film and projected it for the audience on the set, and built a full-sized model of the helicopter and landed it with Lucy inside on a replica of the deck right in our studio."

The most-watched episode in TV history to that time was Little Ricky's birth, which was managed without once using that provocative word *pregnant*. Lucy was "with child" or "giving birth," but she was never pregnant. She just got more and more "with child." But personally, my favorite episode was "Lucy Does a TV Commercial." I've done one sitcom in my career. In Tom Arnold's *Tom* sitcom, I played the longtime host of a morning talk show in Minneapolis, but I never did a TV commercial. Think about that; me, on television without doing a commercial. That's how viewers knew I was acting.

In this episode Lucy is hired to be the Vitameatavegamin girl. That's pronounced, vita-meata-vega-min, and it was a health drink containing vitamins, meat, vegetables, minerals, and . . . oh yes . . . alcohol, a lot of alcohol. Each time she rehearses the commercial, Lucy takes a sip or two, or three, of Vitameatavegamin. She gets more and more tipsy until it is time to go on the air. What happens is the usual disaster and public humiliation that happens on sitcoms: "Do you pop out at parties?" she asks. "Are you unpoopular? Well, the answer to all your troubles is this bittle lottle!"

I Love Lucy made Lucy and Desi wealthy, although apparently as time passed, Desi loved Lucy less and less. Maybe the episode that best summed up the relationship between them was the one with Superman's guest appearance. To please Little Ricky, Lucy tried to convince George Reeves, who played Superman on the TV show, to come to Little Ricky's birthday party. When Reeves turned her down, Lucy dressed up as Superwoman. Reeves changed his mind, and both Superman and Superwoman end up at the party. The exasperated Superman complains to Ricky, who replies that he has been married to Lucy for fifteen years. Reeves paused to consider that, and then said with admiration, "And they call *me* Superman!"

Most sitcom families were middle class. An exception was *The Honeymooners*, Ralph and Alice Kramden, who lived in a tiny

Bensonhurst, Brooklyn, apartment, a two-room walk-up barely large enough for the kitchen table, a sink and a couple of cabinets, and an antique ice box. The Kramdens struggled to survive on Ralph's paycheck from his job as a bus driver. *The Honeymooners* started as a six-minute sketch on Jackie Gleason's comedy variety hour, but became immediately popular. People could relate to a blue-collar couple looking for a nicer life. Eventually it ran one season, thirty-nine episodes, as a stand-alone show. There was one basic plot: Ralph has a scheme to make a lot of money and somehow manages to mess it up. Ed Norton— played by Art Carney—Ralph's upstairs friend who works in the New York sewers, helps Ralph with his scheme. The thing that made the Kramdens so popular was they were like a real married couple—they had their share of arguments, many of which ended with Alice commenting on Ralph's weight. When Ralph tried to browbeat Alice, for example, she would cut him up to size: "You're a big man, Ralph," she said, looking at his stomach. "And getting bigger every day."

Gleason had most of America using Ralph's catchphrases: "One of these days, Alice, one of these days. *Pow!* Right in the kisser," and "Straight to the moon, Alice." And no matter how badly Ralph messed up, somehow Alice still loved him, and each episode ended with him telling her, "Baby, you're the greatest."

In a Reuters poll taken in December 2006, that phrase, "Baby, you're the greatest," ranked as the fourth most memorable phrase in television history. (The greatest? Would you bring out the Mummers, please and have them blare the trumpets? The most memorable phrase in TV history is "Heeeeerre's Johnny!" spoken by your humble announcer. Thank you. Thank you very much.)

Maybe the only sitcom that featured more get-rich-quick schemes than *The Honeymooners* was *You'll Never Get Rich* (later renamed *The Phil Silvers Show*) in which vaudevillian Phil Silvers played U.S. Army Master Sergeant Ernest Bilko, the ultimate bumbling con man, a hustler with a heart of gold, which, by the way, if he could have figured out how to survive without it, he would have sold. It was Bilko's commanding officer, Colonel Ford, who best summed up the character: "Ernest Bilko was the only American soldier during the entire conflict of World War II to capture a Japanese prisoner—and hold him for ransom!"

There are a lot of people who believe George Schlatter's *Laugh-In,* which was first broadcast on January 22, 1968, was the most influential comedy in TV history because it broke the formula by being an endless series of unconnected bits, blackouts, one-liners, very short skits. Unconnected comedy. But Schlatter remembers when he had first used the approach more than four years earlier, in November 1963, the week President John Kennedy was assassinated. "I did Jonathan Winters' first TV special. Jonathan Winters had a bizarre comic mind. He was one of the greatest ad-libbers I've ever seen. He was very hard to write for because he was so inventive. His guest on that show was Art Carney. The week Kennedy was assassinated nobody felt like being funny. Everybody was really bummed. We didn't rehearse at all. It was supposed to air four days later. We weren't going to do it, but that would have left the network with a big hole in the schedule.

"So I got the NBC prop department to collect all the props in the building, and I put them on two

Courtesy of Stephen Cox Collection

Phil Silvers created the role of aptly named con man extraordinaire, Master Sergeant Ernest Bilko, who fought a never-ending battle, mostly against Army regulations.

tables in front of Winters and Carney. I told them, 'You just fool around while we're figuring this thing out.' I told our director, Dwight Hemming, 'Just shoot it. Whatever they do, just shoot it.'

"Dwight asked me, 'What are we going to do here?'

"I told him the truth, 'I don't have the foggiest notion. Just shoot it.' He shot it. We had maybe forty-five minutes of pure ad-lib. In those days you couldn't edit videotape the way you can now. You had to physically splice every cut you wanted to make. So what we had on tape was very funny, but there was no way to put that into any kind of form that made sense. The next morning I told the editors to cut it together. 'Cut joke to joke.'

"They pointed out that it just didn't make any sense because in those days you had to have an introduction to everything you did. I had an answer for them, 'Do you know what time it is? I've got to deliver this sucker real quick. Just cut the jokes together.' They did.

"I turned it in to CBS, and they screened it and liked it and asked me when I was going to finish it. I said, 'It *is* finished.' They said, 'It's not finished. It doesn't make sense.'

"I said, 'It's the newest thing in Europe. It's called *Comedie Verite,* and it's sweeping the continent. That's what everybody is doing there.' Whoa! They were surprised. They hadn't heard anything about it. 'Really?' they asked. 'Trust me,' I said. 'It's going to be big here very soon.'

"That's the show that we aired. It worked. Nobody understood what we were doing, but it worked. People laughed. And that was the editing technique we later used on *Laugh-In.*"

6

By 1954 there were still ten million Americans who had no access to television. The problem was that they couldn't get the signals. There was a system set up called the Community Television Antenna System. A receiving tower is constructed on the highest available point to pick up signals from remote network stations . . . by means of coaxial cable strung along telephone land power lines the signals were distributed. In one Appalachian Mountain community, the day the antenna system was installed every family but two stampeded to the local TV store to buy sets. One of the two taxpayers was in the county hospital. The other was a retired university professor who wasn't interested. The rest of the town made a show of it: they bought every set on display and flooded its proprietor for orders of more. They staged an informal parade, they made speeches in front of the Civil War monuments, and the mayor installed a set on the mall at City Hall. The justice of the peace handed out speeding fines while watching Garry Moore in a screen hidden under his bench and the boys in the general store were silent as they watched the antics of Red Buttons.

—*TV GUIDE*, SEPTEMBER 1954

B Y THE EARLY 1950s TV WAS COMING TO TOWN! EVERY town. Movie theaters were closing, and radio stations were figuring out how to survive. The networks were adding affiliated stations as rapidly as possible. Suddenly gold was worth its weight in broadcasting licenses.

"In order to have a network, you had to make deals throughout the country," broadcasting pioneer Stanley Hubbard explained. "Networks were allowed to own only five stations, I believe, at that time. You couldn't build a network with five stations, so you had to go out and get local TV stations to be part of your network. The networks paid the local stations to carry their programming with the commercials in them, which enabled the networks to charge advertisers considerably more. When the network started in Minneapolis, we got our network programming on kinescope, basically a movie of a TV program. We went to the airport every day to pick up the kinescopes. When the weather got bad in the winter, we would have some problems . . . Whatever time was left to fill—and there was a lot of it, obviously—that we did locally."

The Federal Communications Commission decided how many TV stations would be in each city and who would own those stations. When more than one person applied for a license, the FCC held a competitive hearing and made the award. It was like giving away money, and naturally there was a lot of politics involved. In Minneapolis, Stanley Hubbard's father had gone to a local bank to arrange financing for the only license being awarded to St. Paul. Apparently the bankers were impressed with his proposal because they turned down his loan request and applied for the broadcasting license themselves. The bank wanted to own the station! Hubbard contacted President Truman, whom he knew. "My dad told the president the story of how the bankers were trying to get the TV station, and Truman told him he would call the chairman of the FCC. The chairman told the president that they would have a competitive hearing, but that they were backed up for more than a year. Truman said, 'Have a night hearing.' They had the only night hearing in the FCC history. That's how my dad got his TV license."

In Austin, Texas, it was a lot easier. Lyndon Johnson was the Senate Majority Leader, and "the Johnson family fortune was made as a result of owning the only VHF license in Austin," explained former network executive Ed Bleier. "The station was actually in Lady Bird Johnson's name, but the FCC had no interest in putting competing channels into Austin."

Johnson wanted his station on the air in time to carry the Thanksgiving Day football game between the University of Texas and Texas A&M. It was a network telecast, and Johnson's station picked up the local feed and broadcast it from temporary facilities at the base of the transmitter. By the time the game started that night, most of the staff had gone home, leaving only an announcer who was scheduled to read a news update from a small glass-enclosed booth, and an engineer to make sure things ran smoothly.

At 10:00 p.m. the engineer moved the camera directly in front of the announcer, locked it into place, and went to the bathroom. Since there were only two people there, the engineer didn't bother to close the door. He turned on the light and began urinating—having absolutely no idea that the light behind him cast a perfect silhouette onto the glass booth of a man urinating.

In one sense the engineer's peeing had all the elements of a perfect local television program: it attracted a lot of attention, people talked about it, and it cost absolutely nothing.

At first the networks supplied only a few hours of programming each day. Local stations filled the hours before and after the network shows with quiz shows, man-in-the-street segments, amateur talent shows, a lot of charades, news and weather forecasts, and very old films. In Baltimore, Johns Hopkins University put "telecameras" into surgery rooms and televised operations. Cleveland featured a disc jockey who mouthed the words to the records he was playing. In Houston, singer Texas Ruby sang popular hymns. Milwaukee had several dance shows featuring schottisches and polkas, including professional, amateur, and just-who-do-you-think-you're-kidding dancers. In New York, the NBC affiliate, WNBT, ran a show on Sunday mornings called *Pet Time*, in which a camera focused on a dozen caged parakeets sitting on the trapeze, climbing parakeet ladders and staring blankly into mirrors. This was reality TV at its most real. The host explained, "It gives birds at home a psychologically happy reaction."

But it was talk shows that dominated local television. It did not take station owners long to discover that talk is cheap—and so were most of them, making it a perfect match. For the first couple of decades, at least one-third of all daytime programming was talk shows, either talk-variety shows or talk-interview shows. I did both. On some of my shows I would introduce my guests and speak to them briefly before they sang, or danced, or balanced twelve spinning plates simultaneously on the ends of long sticks, or did whatever it was they did. On other shows I simply interviewed guests and said my piece.

It became obvious almost immediately that the TV talk show was the best marketing tool since a girl on a calendar. Mike Wallace and his wife hosted one of the earliest talk shows in Chicago, *Mike and Buff*. CBS brought them to New York in June 1951. "If you had something to sell," he explained, "a book or a movie or whatever, television was the best exposure you could get. There has always been an exchange of currency between people who want a guest to fill airtime and the guest who wants the airtime so he can peddle his idea or his product or his candidacy."

The first great television talk show host, years before the term *talk show* was even used, was Arthur Godfrey. "The Old Redhead" was one of the biggest radio and TV stars of the time, but the real secret to Godfrey's success has remained a secret, sort of like the purpose of Stonehenge. "The thing that makes Arthur Godfrey remarkable as a hit entertainer," wrote *Time* magazine, "is his relative lack of a definable talent. He can neither sing, dance, act, nor perform with skill on a musical instrument. Yet today [1949] he is the top moneymaker and the outstanding personality on the air . . . He is seen and heard—and apparently loved— by forty million people." *Time* forgot one thing. Godfrey could not tell a joke either. He could, however, play the

I patterned my career after Arthur Godfrey, whose amiable style made him one of the most popular personalities on TV. *Time* magazine said, "He can neither sing, dance, act, nor perform with skill on a musical instrument. Yet today he is the top moneymaker and the outstanding personality on the air."

ukulele and almost single-handedly made it as popular as it is today. Godfrey had his own explanation for his success, "It's because people believe in me. How the hell else can you explain it?" Whatever it was that Arthur Godfrey did, he did it better than anyone who had come before him. And he did it seven days a week on radio and television. I admired him for it, and I wanted to do whatever it was that he did as well as he did it.

Starting in 1948, Arthur Godfrey was one of the early radio stars to make the transition to TV. His radio show, *Arthur Godfrey Time*, his television show, *Arthur Godfrey and His Friends*, and his show that was broadcast simultaneously on both radio and TV, *Arthur Godfrey's Talent Scouts*, all were in the top five in the Hooper ratings. He was amiable, folksy, and he was endlessly fascinated by one subject: himself. He believed people were interested in him, so he spent much of his time telling his listeners everything about his life, from what he had for dinner to how much he weighed to what he planned to have for breakfast. And he enjoyed having fun with his sponsors. When he was selling a shampoo made of eggs and milk, for example, he pointed out, "And if your hair is clean, it makes a fine omelet."

One other thing about Godfrey that seemed to appeal to people was that he expressed his emotions on the air. Live. Whatever he was feeling, that's what he did and said. He cried on radio when broadcasting the funeral of President Franklin Roosevelt, which was understandable. But apparently he also cried on television while listening to an all-girl quartet perform a soulful rendition of "Down by the Old Mill Stream." Crying? "Down By the Old Mill Stream" is not even a sad song.

Before Jack Paar walked off *The Tonight Show* because the censors wouldn't let him tell his W.C. joke, Godfrey was at the center of the biggest controversy in TV history. It was in 1953 . . .

*"Censors? I never had a problem with the censors. I told the truth,
I was out in Vegas and I visited the Hoover Darn.
Flew there in a heckacopter. I went and . . ."*

Milton! Go back to your chapter right now.
You understand? Right now.

One of Godfrey's talents was discovering young talent, and he brought of lot of those people together for television's *Arthur Godfrey and His Friends*. Among them were the McGuire Sisters, Tony Marvin, the Hawaiian Haleloke, bandleader Archie Bleyer, Pat Boone, and a tremendously popular, handsome young Italian singer named Julius La Rosa. Godfrey had discovered La Rosa while he was serving in the navy and hired him on the spot. For two years he performed on Godfrey's morning radio show and on his television show as well as making personal appearances. La Rosa was so popular that he received more fan mail than Godfrey did. People thought of them almost as a father and son until the evening in 1953 when Godfrey announced after La Rosa had finished singing "Manhattan," on *Arthur Godfrey and His Friends,* "This was Julie's swan song with us."

Do you think Donald Trump was the first boss to fire someone on the air? Godfrey did it when Trump was building sand castles. He fired La Rosa right there, right on the air. La Rosa was stunned. The audience was stunned. America was stunned. Nothing like that had ever happened before. In a press conference the next day, Godfrey explained that La Rosa had "lost his humility" and had refused to attend a ballet class Godfrey insisted all his *Friends* attend. He also claimed that La Rosa had asked for a release from the show, "and I will never stand in the way of anyone trying to improve themselves. We wish him Godspeed."

It turned out that the real reason La Rosa was fired was because he had hired an agent-manager rather than relying on Godfrey's staff to run his career, an act Godfrey saw as a betrayal. There were also some rumors concerning La Rosa's relationship with Godfrey's favorite McGuire Sister, Dorothy, but this didn't really come out; after all, this was 1953 when people had egos, not libidos. There was a huge uproar—most of it in support of "that nice young singer." Someone released a critical song entitled "Dear Mr. Godfrey." The phrase "no humility" became a punch line for comedians.

The week after he was fired, Julius La Rosa received 130 offers. He appeared on Ed Sullivan's variety show, *Toast of the Town,* which started a feud between Godfrey and Sullivan. Sullivan said he would continue to hire anyone Godfrey fired—and if Godfrey himself was fired, he could be on the show too!

La Rosa went on to have a moderately successfully career, but the controversy was devastating to Godfrey. It revealed to his fans that he wasn't really such a laid-back, aw-shucks kind of guy. Instead, he was a tough businessman, practically a dictator. He remained on television until 1959 when he had a battle with lung cancer.

It was a thrill for me when he hosted *The Tonight Show* for a week when Johnny was on vacation. I loved watching him do whatever it was he did. Both Godfrey and I were pilots, and during that week he took me for a flight over New York. And as we were flying up the East River, high above that magnificent city, I did have one thought: don't ask him about La Rosa until we're on the ground.

One setting that seemed like a natural for a talk-variety show was a nightclub, because people went to real nightclubs to talk and to watch performers. Carl Reiner made his first TV appearance on Maggi McNellis' *Crystal Room* in 1948. "The room was set up like a nightclub," he said. "There were people sitting at a table, and she would come over and talk to you. It was half an interview show, and then you would get up and do something. There was no nightclub like that in the world. They paid you $125, which seems like a lot for five minutes' work, but it really wasn't because a lot of people were seeing it, and you were ruining your act for other club dates." Maybe the most realistic nightclub of all was Sherman Billingsley's The Stork Club, a name synonymous with fame, class, and money, in no particular order. For almost five years, starting in 1950, *The Stork Club* was broadcast from The Stork Club. It was almost like being there, as Billingsley interviewed celebrity guests and introduced performers. The key word here is *almost*. Billingsley proved that a great nightclub host makes a great nightclub host—but not necessarily a great TV star. He wasn't very good at it, and the show never really caught on.

The TV world in those early days was mostly a man's world —as pretty much was the rest of the world. With the exception of Lucy, Molly Goldberg, Mama, and a few others, women played mostly supporting roles. There were almost no female network executives. Advertising was all male. A majority of the commercials featured men. Women were stay-at-home wives on sitcoms, supporting stars on dramas, and they never read the news or hosted quiz shows. They were a necessary device on soap operas. The exception was that women did host talk shows. Talk shows allowed women to show what they had.

From the Author's Collection

And if you couldn't sing, tell jokes, dance, or balance plates—but you were beautiful—you could become a female TV personality like Faye Emerson, who was known for her beauty, intelligence, pleasant personality, and low-cut blouses. She was also one of television's biggest stars in the late 1940s and early 1950s.

Arthur Godfrey would have been proud of me for that line.

One of the biggest stars of television in the late 1940s and early 1950s was a minor movie actress named Faye Emerson, who was known for her beauty, intelligence, pleasant personality, and low-cut blouses. Male viewers, in particular, knew her for the low-cut blouses. She was known as the First Lady of television, Mrs. TV, and "the woman who put the *V* in TV." *The Faye Emerson Show* went on the air in 1949, and famed columnist John Crosby wrote, "Miss Emerson fills a ten-inch screen very adequately, very adequately. I assume [her show] is aimed primarily at women, but I know men,

141

including this one, who are helplessly fascinated by it for reasons which never occurred to CBS."

The controversy about whether or not her clothes were too sexy became so important she actually conducted a vote on her show. I don't think anyone was surprised that 95 percent of voters wanted her to keep her clothing exactly as it was. She said, innocently, "I wear on TV just what I'd ordinarily wear at that hour of the night. I don't think children can be adversely affected. They're probably not up at that hour, and, anyway, have you ever seen the clothes worn by women in comic books?"

We must have been reading different comic books. Betty and Veronica never dressed that way.

Faye Emerson—who was married to President Franklin Roosevelt's son Elliott before she was married to Skitch Henderson, who Johnny Carson hired to lead *The Tonight Show* band when he took over—probably got more "exposure" on TV than any other woman until then. By 1950 she was hosting talk shows on both CBS and NBC—something that had never been done before. Faye Emerson wasn't just a pretty woman. She was also known as "the girl with the high IQ in a low-cut gown." Edward R. Murrow picked her to be his substitute when he was unable to host his interview program, *Person to Person*. The secret of her success as a talk show host, she once explained, was that she liked to "chitchat," and she was smart enough and well-informed enough to talk about everything from women's earrings to congressional hearings with her guests. "I'll touch on anything—as long as it's not too heavy. The only thing I don't touch are people's personal lives. And I never rap people or anything, because I don't think I'm in a position to do so."

In addition to hosting her own programs and appearing as a guest panelist on several quiz shows, Faye Emerson had a five-minute segment called "The Woman's Touch" on *Night Beat*, which was hosted by Mike Wallace. Her feminist point of view and pretty liberal politics were acceptable as long as her clothes fit snugly.

Faye Emerson wasn't the first woman to have her own talk show. As early as 1948 Frances Buss directed a "woman's magazine" show entitled *Vanity Fair,* hosted by Dorothy Doan. "One guest I remember," said Frances, "was Maria von Trapp, the character Julie Andrews played [in *The Sound of Music*]. She was in New York trying to get support for her children. We had Maidenform as a sponsor. People said how in the world is Dorothy going to do Maidenform commercials?

Her Sunday night job as a regular panelist on *What's My Line?* made Arlene Francis one of television's most popular and highest paid women. But she also hosted Pat Weaver's Midday Show, *Home Show*, and her own *Arlene Francis Show*—seen here in 1957. Hugh Downs is on the left.

You did not show a woman in a brassiere in those days. She held up one of those brassieres in front of her and showed it as though it were the finest Irish lace."

Among the many other women who hosted talk shows were actress Arlene Francis with her early afternoon *Home Show*; Eloise McElhone, who was praised by critics for her ability "to talk endlessly about nothing"; Mary Margaret McBride, who drew as many as six million mostly female listeners to her top-rated radio talk show, but became the first TV talk show failure when the 1948 *Mary Margaret McBride* show lasted less than three months; Sloan Simpson, former model and the socialite ex-wife of New York's flamboyant mayor Bill O'Dwyer; and former model Jinx Falkenberg, who cohosted a show with her husband, Tex McCrary. Maggi McNellis' *Leave It to the Girls*, a *View*-like show based on the premise that a panel of four women in low bodices were better than just one Faye, would dissect a male guest or discuss pressing relationship issues like "Can a romance that is dead be revived"; and Eva Gabor undercut all her talk show rivals by often having her very attractive sisters, Magda and Zsa Zsa, and even her mother, Jolie, on her talk show. Perhaps the most unusual show was hosted by beautiful actress Lili Palmer, then married to

The first TV personality to challenge Milton Berle in the ratings was Bishop Fulton Sheen. But that was not unexpected because, as he said when accepting an Emmy award, he had what was certainly the greatest writing staff in TV history: Matthew, Mark, Luke, and John.

Rex Harrison, who wore high-necked dresses and discussed cultural topics, at times reciting Greek poetry, reading George Bernard Shaw's eulogy, and critiquing British theater—with background music of German lieder played on guitar.

As the networks expanded, so did competition. Only a few years after viewers had been thrilled by a test pattern, they had choices. The toughest hour on TV was Tuesday nights at 8:00 p.m. when Milton Berle competed against Frank Sinatra. The trade papers referred to it as "the obituary spot"—when it came to competing against them, nobody had a prayer.

Which made it the perfect spot for the man who brought his own prayers.

In 1952, DuMont gave the time period to New York's archbishop, the Most Reverend Fulton J. Sheen, who previously had conducted the first religious service broadcast on national television. Bishop Sheen had been a professor at Catholic University when I was a student there, and we used to sneak into his class to hear him speak. Basically his show was simply his lectures—just himself and a blackboard. The network received no income from the show, but it didn't pay Bishop Sheen anything either. *Life Is Worth Living* was a tremendous success, drawing as many as thirty million viewers. For a half hour Bishop Sheen stood in front of the camera and spoke without a script on subjects like communism, morality, and love. Milton Berle's popularity dropped ten points in the Trendex rating.

Milton? If you've got something to say, now's the time . . .

"Well, he was using old material too."

Thank you, Milton.

The Archdiocese of New York was thrilled by Bishop Sheen's success. A spokesman said, "We turn down requests for tickets that

Edward R. Murrow (right) and Charles Collingwood helped establish CBS News as journalism's most prestigious television network through programs like *See It Now* and a series of socially-oriented documentaries. When Murrow left *Person to Person* in 1959, Collingwood hosted the program for three years.

sound as if they come from girls' schools. We don't want any squealing. First thing you know, he would turn into a clerical Sinatra . . . He's telegenic. If he came out in a barrel and read the telephone book, they would love him."

The show ran for almost four years. In 1952 Bishop Sheen won the Emmy as television's Most Outstanding Personality. In accepting the award he made sure to pay tribute to what was certainly the greatest writing staff in TV history, "my writers, Matthew, Mark, Luke, and John." After his show went off the air, the very popular Bishop Sheen continued to make guest appearances, showing up as the mystery guest on *What's My Line?* and even appearing on *Dean Martin's Celebrity Roast* of Joe Namath.

The ultimate celebrity interview show was Edward R. Murrow's *Person to Person,* which broadcast on CBS beginning in 1953. It was a simple format: Murrow sat in an easy chair in New York, smoking a cigarette, and interviewed two guests each week in their own homes, offices, or special environment somewhere in America as they showed Murrow and viewers around the place. Locations ranged from Sophia Loren's apartment overlooking Hollywood to the warden's home on Alcatraz. Murrow's intention, he said, was to show "extraordinary people doing ordinary things," and "revive the art of conversation." That sounds pretty simple, but the technology needed to get it done was incredibly complex. Murrow once described television as "the five-ton pencil," meaning it took five tons of equipment to get a show on the air. For *Person to Person* they had to move that equipment into the celebrity's house or apartment. Usually technicians put up temporary towers to relay the signal, but at least once they had to slice off the top of a mountain to establish a line of sight from the location to the transmission tower. *Person to Person* was more a triumph of technology than a simple interview show.

I have fond memories of *Person to Person* because it was responsible for much of my career. When I lived in Philadelphia, *Person to Person* came to our little development to interview my next-door neighbor, Dick Clark, who was then hosting *American Bandstand*, the MTV of the 1950s. It was like an electronic army moved in. Truckloads of equipment were unloaded; long cables were stretched across the streets; all kinds of lights were set up. It was all very exciting. After the show, the owner of the complex, Dan Kelly, threw a party for CBS executives and technicians and asked me to host it. One of the guests at that party was Chuck Reeves, whose office in New York was down the hall from that of Art Stark, the producer of the game show *Who Do You Trust?* Not too long after the party, Reeves overheard Stark telling the host of the game show, a young comedian named Johnny Carson, that their announcer was leaving and they had to find another announcer as quickly as possible. Reeves suggested the guy who had hosted the *Person to Person* party in Philadelphia. Which is how *Person to Person* was responsible for my career.

Although Edward R. Murrow was considered America's greatest journalist, *Person to Person* had very little investigative reporting. About as deep as it got was Murrow asking legendary conductor Leopold Stokowski if the piano he was showing viewers was in tune.

Murrow visited many of the most celebrated people in America. Senator John Kennedy and his wife, Jackie, showed him their home, especially the model of Kennedy's PT-109. Italian diva Maria Callas explained seriously that she particularly liked the quality of American lingerie. Marlon Brando played the bongos. Harpo Marx did the entire interview without saying a single word. Sammy Davis Jr. proudly introduced Murrow to his grandmother. *Person to Person* visited John Steinbeck, Margaret Mead, Bogie and Bacall, Orson Welles, former President Truman, and, of course, Milton Berle, who promoted a serious novel he had just written. Murrow talked to two guests a week, every week, for almost nine years. The most controversial was probably Cuban dictator Fidel Castro, who appeared on the program—wearing pajamas—less than a month after overthrowing Batista, causing Murrow to say, "You must have had a very busy week. How do you feel?" Fidel Jr. was there, too, holding a puppy. "Is it yours?" Murrow wondered. It wasn't.

The show wasn't rehearsed in any traditional sense, but it was extremely well planned. Every move a guest made had to be thought through so that wherever the guest went, there would always be a camera in place. At times an interview required as many as six cameras. With videotape or on film this would have been simple, but it was all live. They even used a split screen occasionally, showing both Murrow and the guest (the first time many viewers saw that technique), and a unique-high-frequency wireless microphone. CBS executive Charles Cappleman worked as the production executive on the West Coast for several years. "On Monday morning I would go with a technical person to the home of a guest and decide what we needed to do to keep from destroying it while we were there. I'd make notes like, 'get a drop cloth to put on the carpet here' and 'get a scrim to go over that window to get rid of the sunlight.' Meanwhile the telephone company would figure out where to park its truck to put up the microwave tower. There were cables all over the place. I remember as we were leaving Vincent Price's home I came outside and saw a technician wrapping up his garden hose. 'That's not a camera cable,' I told him. 'Let's put it back.'"

Some guests brought special problems to the broadcast. Actress Tallulah Bankhead was one of the most outrageous, flamboyant, outspoken, charismatic, and beautiful women of her time. She described herself as "pure as the driven slush," and once told a potential boyfriend, "I'll come and make love to you at five o'clock. If I'm late, start without me." Imagine a combination of Lindsay Lohan and Paris Hilton with great intelligence and a sense of humor. Imagine all that on TV. Imagine the censors the day before. And imagine the preparation for the broadcast. Unfortunately, Tallulah Bankhead had recently had a breast enlargement operation and was very proud of it. She spent considerable time making crew members sit on her lap to look at her brand-new breasts. The people who were there that day remember hearing the extraordinary voice of Murrow—the booming voice that had reported events of World War II with the famous opening line, "This . . . is London"—basically pleading through a loudspeaker that carried his voice throughout the entire house, "Get her to cover her tits!"

Murrow left the show in 1959 and was replaced by Charles Collingwood, who hosted it for three additional years.

Murrow's *Person to Person* interviews were mostly fluff. Mike Wallace, however, conducted television's first really hard-hitting interviews on DuMont's local New York station, WABD. This was the same Mike Wallace who had been picking up elephant droppings a few years earlier. *Night Beat,* which earned Wallace the reputation that eventually got him to *60 Minutes,* went on the air in 1956. As Wallace remembers, "My pal, my partner, my producer Ted Yates suggested we do a late-night interview show following the newscast. At that point all television interview programs were pabulum. Easy questions and easy answers. And he said, 'There are all kinds of questions we could ask that have never been asked. Let's really go after some of these people in an interesting way. Make them think; make them react.'"

Night Beat was the perfect talk show. The entire set consisted of two stools and a black backdrop. Wallace sat on one of the stools, smoking a cigarette, while his guests sat opposite him, cigarette smoke curling into their faces and a spotlight in their eyes. The show was on four nights a week and had two guests each night. The budget for the whole thing might have been five bucks. But what made *Night Beat* so different was that Wallace and his crew did extensive research, and he asked the type of questions that had never been asked on television. "We became occasionally abrasive, frequently irreverent, sometimes confrontational," remembers Wallace. "It was new and different." For example, he asked famed restaurateur Toots Shor, "Why do people call you a slob?"

"Me?" Shor answered. "Jiminy Crickets, they musta been talking about Jackie Gleason."

When he asked celebrated gangster Mickey Cohen how many men he had killed, Cohen told him, "I have killed no men that, in the first place, didn't deserve killing."

He asked Planned Parenthood founder Margaret Sanger if birth control should be available for unmarried women, and even asked society party giver Elsa Maxwell her age!

You have to understand, asking a woman her age in front of a million people was a huge deal. "We prided ourselves that we were permitted to ask and get answered any question imaginable. We were asking the questions the audience would have liked to ask. This was something new in television. We were making people squirm a little." Nobody on TV had ever been so blunt, so confrontational. When much of the country still refused to believe homosexuals existed, Wallace asked top dress designers, "Why is there such an extraordinary number of male homosexuals in the fashion industry?" He interviewed members of the Ku Klux Klan and people who were addicted to drugs and controversial figures like Hugh Hefner, Salvador Dali, Norman Mailer, civil rights attorney Thurgood Marshall, and stripper Lili St. Cyr. Labor leader Mike Quill responded angrily to a question about his religious values by warning Wallace, "I'm ready anytime you want to repeat the stupid question," and then walked off the show.

Supplied by Globe Photos

Mike Wallace rose from shoveling elephant droppings on a children's show and hosting beauty pageants on a wrestling show in Chicago to become one of the nation's most respected—and controversial—journalists, practically creating the confrontational interviewing technique he later displayed for decades on *60 Minutes*.

Once, when he was doing a piece on Johnny Carson, I agreed to be interviewed. He had a really interesting technique. He sat as close to me as possible, closer than any other interviewer I had ever spoken with. In fact, our knees were touching. What that did was make me uncomfortable so that I could not fall back into giving my usual answers.

Wallace became known as "Mike Malice" or "The Terrible Torquemada." The audience wasn't used to anything like this. Sid Caesar even parodied Wallace's hard-hitting style on *Your Show of Shows*, playing a guest being questioned by Wallace who started sweating under the pressure. I mean, really sweating—sweating buckets of water, rivers of water, an ocean of water just poured off Caesar as "Wallace" grilled him.

Night Beat was so successful on DuMont's local New York station that ABC bought the show, changed its name to *The Mike Wallace Interview*, and broadcast it once a week. ABC president Leonard Goldenson bravely told Wallace, "You will not succeed in this job unless you make the building shake every two weeks."

Several weeks later newspaper columnist Drew Pearson told Wallace on the air that Senator John Kennedy's Pulitzer Prize–winning book, *Profiles in Courage,* had been ghostwritten. This was big news. Kennedy was getting ready to run for president, and something like this could cost him the nomination. Wallace pressed him on that statement. "And he, Kennedy, accepted a Pulitzer Prize for it?"

"He did," Pearson insisted.

The next day Kennedy's father, Joseph Kennedy, ordered his lawyer to "sue the bastards for fifty million dollars." The Kennedys wanted ABC to fire Wallace. The network wanted Wallace to withdraw the claim, but he refused. On the next *The Mike Wallace Interview* show, an ABC executive stood in front of the camera and retracted the story. That wasn't the only legal threat Wallace earned. It turned out that Goldenson wanted the building only to shiver rather than shake, so the show was cancelled after a single season. But Wallace had done his job. He had changed the nature of talk TV.

Murrow's *Person to Person* represented the friendly, personal interview programs, a format that was eventually mastered by people like Larry King, Charlie Rose, and Barbara Walters. *Night Beat* was the first of the hard-hitting programs that led to *60 Minutes, 20/20, The Phil Donahue Show*, and many local interview programs. And Joe Pyne? Joe Pyne created the attack interview, forging the rocky path for people like Morton Downey Jr., Jerry Springer, Los Angeles' Wally George, and a whole studio full of cable characters.

Joe Pyne's confrontational interviews were to talk television what pro wrestling is to televised sports. *The Joe Pyne Show* was a pioneer of tabloid TV. You could call him "the first angry man." His show was sort of a daily train wreck. Pyne started as a radio talk show host and made his TV debut in 1954 on a local television station in Delaware, eventually being syndicated to about 240 stations. Pyne tried to book the most provocative guests for his shows, from the high priest of the Church of Satan to a man who had been married seventeen times. His subjects ranged from UFOs to the war in Vietnam to UFOs *in* Vietnam. He interviewed American Nazis, every kind of eccentric, and hippies. "The subject must be visceral," he said. "We want emotion, not mental involvement."

On the air, he sat behind a desk and, just like Murrow and Wallace, always had a lit cigarette in his hand. But unlike those two men, he began by baiting his guests—and then attacked, ridiculed, and insulted them, leading his audience in frenzied Jerry Springer-like jeers. If he didn't invent this kind of show, he certainly perfected it, once admitting "I have no respect for anyone who would come on my show," failing to comprehend the irony in the fact that he was there every day.

Or maybe not. Both Pyne and his audience took great delight in his snarled insults. He loved to tell guests, "Go gargle with razor blades." Or "Why don't you take your teeth out, put 'em in backwards, and bite your throat!" He liked to tell people, "I could make a monkey out of you, but why should I take the credit?" The line he perfected on radio, used on TV telephone callers, and which is still used on radio today was, "Get off the line, you creep!" Pyne had lost a leg during World War II and had a wooden leg. When long-haired rocker Frank Zappa was on the show, Pyne hissed, "So I guess your long hair makes you a woman," to which Zappa immediately responded, "So I guess your wooden leg makes you a table."

Pyne claimed he kept a gun in his desk and was suspended for a week once for showing it to an African American guest after the Watts riots. Pyne threw guests off his show, ordering them to "take a hike," and occasionally the show did get violent. People got pushed; objects got thrown. Once the entire set got knocked over. People watched the show with fascination, knowing anything could happen.

Unfortunately, Pyne had at least one thing in common with Murrow. Both men died of lung cancer from smoking.

CBS had tried several people as host of *The Morning Show*, which was an attempt to compete with *The Today Show*. There was no audience and no budget. They would book anyone who wrote a book—obscure books that couldn't get on *Today*. Since nobody cared, we did silly things. There was a girl who could eat underwater. So we decided to use her. We got a glass tank, filled it with water and put her in it. There was a weather map on the glass. (Host) Dick Van Dyke would say, "There's a cold front over Colorado," and she would circle it— underwater and with her cheeks puffed out. Another time we had an archer come in. She stood at the end of the studio. There would be a cold front over Colorado and she'd shoot an arrow across the studio and into the map at Colorado. We found a lumberjack who could throw an ax. There was a cold front over Colorado and this big double-bladed ax whizzed half the length of the studio and landed in Colorado.

—PRODUCER CHARLIE ANDREWS
TODAY SHOW BY ROBERT METZ (PLAYBOY PRESS, 1977)

B ECAUSE TALK SHOWS REMAINED THE MOST INEXPEN-
sive type of programming, TV and advertising executives continually looked for new ways to package them. The legendary NBC

executive Pat Weaver understood the value of talk more than anyone else, probably because of his advertising background. Before joining NBC, Weaver had been the vice president in charge of radio and television at the huge advertising agency Young & Rubicam. The time slot in which the networks didn't even try to compete in the early 1950s was the early morning. That was considered the perfect radio time. It was accepted as fact that most people were too busy in the morning getting ready to go to work or school to stop and watch television. The industry called the morning time period "Siberia." But people would listen to the radio as they moved around their house and catch up on the latest news, weather, and other information they needed. It was estimated that 75 percent of homes had the radio turned on between 7:00 and 9:00 a.m. A lot of the local TV stations didn't even bother going on the air in the morning, and those that were on the air generally aimed their programming at very young children, figuring mothers would put the kids in front of the set while they got their husbands ready for work and older children off to school.

Where other people saw a test pattern, Pat Weaver saw a potentially huge audience, and so he created a talk-interview-news-service-entertainment early morning show he called *Rise and Shine*, a name he eventually changed to *Today*. Other people called it "Weaver's Folly." Weaver's concept was simple, as he wrote in a long memo: "We cannot and should not try to build a show that will make people sit down in front of their sets and divert their attention to the screen. We want America to shave, to eat, to dress, to get to work on time."

Weaver had tremendous plans. Instead of a host, he wanted a "communicator" to sit at a desk in New York City and report news from around the world. The studio would be huge with glass windows and a balcony from which viewers could watch the show below them. The studio would contain the most sophisticated communications equipment, and throughout the show phones would ring, teletype machines would clack, pictures would be printed from the tele-photo machine, and reports from around the world would inform and entertain viewers.

But he didn't have the studio or the communicator. At first the show was supposed to share space with the children's show *Howdy Doody*, although Weaver was able to convince his bosses to empty a television-set show-room in Radio City, the RCA Exhibition Hall, and broadcast from there. Instead of a bal-cony, people would watch the show through the storefront windows.

I vaguely remember that there was a lot of doubt that

Courtesy of Stephen Cox Collection

NBC president Pat Weaver revolutionized TV programming by creating both the *Today* and *Tonight* shows, in addition to the midday *Home Show* and radio's long-lived *Monitor*, of which I was one of the hosts for several years. He also helped to create participation advertising, in which several companies bought spots on a program rather than sponsoring the entire show.

NBC's new morning show would work. Even Pat Weaver knew that people weren't going to *watch* his show. He wrote, "I urge you to destroy any mental image you have of just another morning program. We are building a program that will change the listening habits of this nation . . ." *Listening* habits? People *watched* television and *listened* to radio. That's the way the world worked.

Weaver had an answer for that too. "The listener will become a viewer whenever his interest in the audio reaches the point where it interrupts his preparation for work or school and replaces it in impor-tance to him." Because the audience would constantly be changing, Weaver intended to repeat material several times during each telecast.

This was an ambitious undertaking. *Today* has become the second-longest continuously broadcast show in television history, and the concept still doesn't seem as if it would work! Weaver was going to broadcast from a showroom, but he still needed a communicator. Supposedly he was looking for a comedian to host the show and was considering Fred Allen, Bob Hope, and . . . and here it comes . . . yes, Milton Berle.

"They told me I'd have to get up at four o'clock to do the show. I said what's the big deal, that's what I do right now. Then they said 4:00 a.m. in the morning. In the morning? I said I thought I was supposed to be telling the jokes. Thank you, thank you very much.

    OK, I'll be going back to my chapter now.

Eventually they picked Dave Garroway, an eccentric, laid-back, creative host of a Chicago talk-variety show, *Garroway at Large*. It was the same kind of show I was doing in Philly—a little of this and a little of that, as long as it didn't cost anything. I used to close my late show, *McMahon & Company*, by having a lovely girl blow out a candle, and the station would go dark. Garroway had a tag gag, something funny he did at the end of every show. For example, he would say, "This show came to you from Chicago, the friendliest city in the world." He would then turn around and walk away, and there would be a knife in his back.

Garroway's conversational, informal style was different from the typical serious, formal manner. He said that he was successful because he didn't try to talk to an audience, but rather he looked into the camera and spoke to one person. I never forgot that, and I have tried to do the same thing.

Outside of Chicago, Garroway was unknown, so very few viewers were going to turn on *Today* to see him. Weaver planned *Today* to be the longest show the networks had ever done: three hours long every

Courtesy of Stephen Cox Collection

Weaver believed TV should educate as well as entertain and insisted his shows include cultural and current event segments such as this appearance by Richard Nixon, with David Garroway, on *Today*.

day, but only two hours would be broadcast into each time zone. A lot of material from the first hour would be repeated for new viewers in the third hour.

The whole thing seemed impossible. Nobody thought the show would work—except Pat Weaver. And Pat Weaver believed *Today* would change the world. The show went on the air on January 14, 1952. *Today* "begins a new kind of television," Garroway told viewers. The first show was pretty much a disaster. Garroway asked a reporter in Frankfurt, Germany, to "tell me the news in your part of the world."

"The big news is the weather," was the reply. "We're really chilly."

The show did a remote interview with the Chief of Naval Operations, who was arriving for work at the Pentagon. When asked how the Navy was doing, Admiral Fechteler replied, "I guess it's all right. It was there last night all right, when I left it."

Gradually, the show got better, but critics still disliked it, suggesting that "NBC go back to sleep in the morning." Sponsors weren't interested. But from the very first morning, viewers did watch it. The first two weeks the show was on the air, NBC received sixty-five thousand letters commenting on Garroway, on the set, making suggestions, and even a few complaints. That was amazing! The show struggled along for a year. And finally, after millions of dollars had been invested, after the most modern communications equipment in existence had been used, after NBC's news bureaus around the world had done their part, *Today*—the show that would become a television institution—the entire staff in New York—all of it—was saved by a monkey.

J. Fred Muggs is easily the most important chimpanzee in television history. He would sit on Garroway's lap making monkey faces, doing monkey business, starring in little skits, and almost always dressed in one of the 450 costumes made for him. The show even introduced a female companion for him, Phoebe B. Beebee. Young kids loved him and encouraged their parents to watch the show in the morning. With that rapidly growing audience came sponsors. Dow was introducing Saran Wrap and felt the morning was the perfect time to advertise—just as women all over America were taking leftovers out of their refrigerators. The success of the clear plastic wrap convinced dubious advertisers that the show could sell products. And *Today* became a success.

It was like a movie plot. The monkey saves the show and becomes an international celebrity. Muggs dedicated supermarkets, commissioned Navy ships—I'm not kidding, that really happened—and toured the world. The only American star more popular than him in Japan was Marilyn Monroe, and when he was there, he was cared for by fifteen geisha girls. Muggs was one smart monkey, eventually learning five hundred words as well as the value of his fame. He costarred with Garroway for almost four years and by the time he was taken off, the *Today* format was firmly established. Both CBS and ABC eventually created their own morning shows, but they have never been able to catch *Today*.

Garroway ended each show by looking into the camera, raising the palm of his right hand, and wishing viewers "Peace." He hosted the show until 1961. Muggs got his own show on a local New York channel, but it failed very quickly. After that he appeared occasionally on other shows and as of 2004 was living in retirement in Florida.

The advantage radio had over television was you could listen to it while you were doing something else. You could drive your car, work in the store, eat dinner, and the radio would be playing in the back-

Courtesy of Stephen Cox Collection

Broadway Open House—with (from left) announcer Wayne Howell; Jerry Lester, who hosted the show on Tuesdays, Thursdays, and Fridays; musical director Milton Delugg; and the beautiful Dagmar—was Weaver's first attempt to create a late night show.

ground. Generally it was only at night, after the chores of the day were done, that people would sit down by the radio set and really listen to it. The executives who created TV knew that TV didn't work in the background, and they assumed people would watch TV only for those few hours after dinner and before going to bed. The networks filled those evening hours with their programming, leaving the rest of the day to local stations. Pat Weaver was one of the few people who believed television had the power to change the way we lived. He looked at those time periods the networks ignored as opportunities. For the early morning he created *Today*. And for late-night he created *The Tonight Show*.

Weaver's first experiment in late-night programming was a talk-variety show called *Broadway Open House* that went on the air in May 1950. Originally he picked a Steve Martin–like comedian named Don "Creesh" Hornsby to host the show. But two weeks before the show went on the air, Hornsby died of polio, and Weaver hired two complete casts to replace him. Comedians Morey Amsterdam and Jerry Lester each hosted the show two nights a week. Within months Lester proved he had something special: a beautiful, ditzy blonde known as Dagmar. Dagmar's apparent talent was sitting on a stool and breathing. The more deeply she breathed, the more she displayed her talent, but it was enough to make her a major female TV star.

Weaver knew what he was doing. *Broadway Open House* was jokes and dames, and the more of each, the better. One member of the crew, known as the "cleavage stuffer," had the job of inspecting the women who appeared on the show just before they went onstage and, if they were revealing too much cleavage, handing them tissues to cover their assets.

It was arguably the greatest single job in TV history.

Dagmar later recorded a song with Frank Sinatra, appeared on Bob Hope's very first TV show, and guest-starred on the first telethon in

TV history, a twenty-four-hour-long fund-raiser for the Damon Runyon Cancer Fund. Supposedly Jerry Lester got jealous of the attention Dagmar was getting and quit after a year. But his *Broadway Open House* had proved that some viewers would watch late-night TV.

Meanwhile, in 1950 CBS brought to New York a young comedian named Steve Allen who had created an ad-lib, anything-goes show on local TV in Los Angeles. At CBS he was sort of a utility comedian, appearing

More than any performer, Steve Allen, a brilliant comedian CBS had brought to New York, created the nighttime talk show format for NBC as the first host of *Tonight*.

on quiz shows, variety shows, substituting for Arthur Godfrey, even hosting *Songs for Sale*, an *American Idol*-type show for young songwriters. In 1954 Pat Weaver hired him to host *Tonight*, his new late-night show for NBC. More than any performer, Steve Allen pioneered the nighttime talk show format. Allen said, "I did what I had already done on radio—reading question cards, interviewing people up in the aisles, having people yell out songs to see if I could play them or the band could play them, making funny phone calls, reading angry letters to the editor, the things we think of as late-night entertainment."

And he did it all, at least at first, without writers. It was all ad-libbed.

"At the production meeting they were planning the show, and they said, 'Do you want any writers?' And I said, 'To write what?' because I had always ad-libbed the show. They said, 'OK, forget that.' I started out with no writers at all."

The show went on the air in September 1954, not too long after coaxial cable finally connected the two coasts, making it possible for the whole country to watch the same show live. Louis Nye, a regular performer on a local show, was sitting with Steve Allen's wife, Jayne Meadows, the night of the first broadcast. She remembered him saying, "This will never go. America will never understand this crazy show."

"You're wrong," she told him. "It will be the biggest smash hit, and it will run forever."

Allen began the first ninety-minute *Tonight* show broadcast by warning viewers, "In case you're just joining us, this is *Tonight,* and I can't think of too much to tell you about it except I want to give you the bad news first. This program is going to go on forever. If you think you're tired now, wait until you see one o'clock roll around . . . We especially selected this theater for this very late show because this theater sleeps around eight hundred people."

Many of the aspects of the late-night format we accept as natural and obvious started with twenty-nine-year-old Steve Allen. He sat behind a desk and his guests sat to his side. He had a live orchestra, he used articles from newspapers, he made crank phone calls, and he had musical performers. He did regular skits like "The Question Man," who figured out the question after you gave him the answer. His guests covered the whole range from comedians to politicians. A lot of talented young performers appeared on his show, future stars like Jonathan Winters, Tim Conway, the Smothers Brothers, Jim Nabors, Lou Rawls, and Jackie Mason. Steve Allen said he discovered Steve Lawrence and Eydie Gormé "in the backseat of a car." The list even includes Andy Williams and the Muppets. He was creative and spontaneous and often opened his show sitting at a piano, just playing with the keys, doing a monologue.

Steve Allen dived into a swimming pool filled with gelatin; he held elephant races out in the street; he attached a hundred tea bags to his body and jumped into hot water to become the world's largest tea bag. One night he ran outside the studio dressed in a police uniform and hailed a cab; when the cab stopped, he quickly threw a giant salami into the backseat and ordered the driver to rush that sausage to Grand Central Station as fast as possible. I used to watch his show every night, as someone who wanted to do a similar show more than as a viewer, but I loved it. I thought he was one of the most inventive performers I'd ever seen.

Years later Steve often appeared with Johnny Carson. He would carry a small tape recorder, and during breaks he would take out his tape recorder and record an idea. It was his notepad. Nobody had more ideas than he did. Johnny used to introduce him by saying something like, "Steve Allen was supposed to come out five minutes ago, but he needed to finish a symphony and then write a book."

Steve Allen proved that Pat Weaver's belief that a late-night talk-comedy variety show would find an audience was absolutely correct. Late-night became a destination. Rather than fitting television into their lives, viewers began changing their lives to watch television.

But NBC still didn't understand how valuable late-night television was and decided that since Steve Allen was so successful Monday through Friday between 11:15 p.m. and 1:00 a.m., it should move him to Sunday nights opposite CBS's hugely successful *The Ed Sullivan Show*. For several months Allen continued doing *Tonight* three nights a week—Ernie Kovacs was substitute host the other two nights—while also starring in *The Steve Allen Show* on Sundays and making a movie, *The Benny Goodman Story*.

"After a few weeks of that," he recalled, "I realized I couldn't do justice to the important show, the one in prime time. *The Tonight Show* I could do in my sleep. So I eventually did walk away from it." As his replacement, he suggested that either Ernie Kovacs or a low-key raconteur named Jack Paar should take over the show. Instead,

NBC created a nighttime version of *Today* entitled *Tonight! America After Dark*, and even hired a regular member of the *Today* cast, Jack Lescoulie, to host it. The show had a magazine format and used respected reporters like Bob Considine, Irv Kupcinet, and even columnist Earl Wilson to do pieces on everyone from the Marx Brothers to starlet Jayne Mansfield. This was long before *Nightline*, but apparently the audience was a lot more interested in being entertained than being educated. Within six months *Tonight! America After Dark* was cancelled, and in 1957 Jack Paar began hosting *Tonight Starring Jack Paar*.

Several years later Jack Paar and I would both be living in Bronxville, New York, and from time to time I would see him at the hardware store or the post office. Surprisingly, he was a very shy man. He would sort of nod to me, which I always took to mean, "You're doing OK, kid." But truthfully, it could also have meant, "You look familiar."

Every announcer loved Jack Paar. As he once said, "It's almost impossible to dislike me because I do nothing." As Regis Philbin described it so accurately, Paar represented all of us. "When I saw Jack Paar come out and not deliver a streak of jokes, but sit on the edge of his desk and . . . talk about what he had seen . . . I thought, well, maybe—I wasn't a comedian, I wasn't a singer, I wasn't even a disc jockey—but I thought that just maybe I might be able to do what he was doing."

Like Steve Allen, Jack Paar shaped the *Tonight* show to fit his personality. He didn't do many skits or sketches, and even those people appearing regularly on the show were conversationalists rather than performers. Rather than opening the show with a joke-filled monologue, he would sit on a stool and tell humorous stories. In a very low-key manner, Paar talked about his life and his family, his wife and daughter, and even his pet dachshund. However wild his story, he would assure his audience, "That's absolutely true. I kid you not."

Paar opened up his life to viewers like no one before him. He never hesitated to reveal his emotions to the world, admitting, "I cry when they put new Coke bottles on the shelf in the supermarket," and an agent claimed, "You can pierce him with a Kleenex."

Among his regularly appearing guests was Cliff Arquette, playing his character Charlie Weaver, an old hillbilly type who liked to bring everybody up-to-date about the goings-on back home in Mt. Idy. He would read a letter from Mama, who would tell him, "We had a fire in the bathroom. Lucky it didn't spread to the house," and "I was going to send you that five dollars I owe you, but I see I already sealed the envelope."

Sitting next to him might be the handsome immigrant from Italy, golf pro Guido Panzini, who admitted to Paar that American women confused him: "There'sa lotsa hanky, but no panky!" When immigration authorities could find no record of Mr. Panzini, he admitted that he was actually Irish-American actor Pat Harrington Jr.

And sitting next to Panzini might be the lovely French gamine Genevive, whose accent got progressively worse and funnier the longer she was in America, or the professional hypochondriac and piano player Oscar Levant. Levant had held his own at the famed Algonquin Round Table, and on Paar's show he admitted to viewers, "Roses are red, violets are blue,

Courtesy of NBCU Photo Bank

NBC replaced Steve Allen as host of *Tonight* with Jack Paar, who created a show that was an extraordinary nightly display of wit and intelligence and made *Tonight* just about the hottest show on television. Paar appears here with his announcer, Hugh Downs, on the last *Tonight* show he hosted.

I'm a schizophrenic, and so am I," and when asked how he liked a particularly syrupy singing act, Levant replied, "I can't watch them. I'm a diabetic."

Paar crowded his guest couch with literate, funny, unusual people, people who loved the English language. Betty White was a regular; Peter Ustinov, Nipsey Russell, and Jonathan Winters appeared often; ditsy comedian Dody Goodman appeared frequently; society journalist Elsa Maxwell, America's "hostess with the mostest," was a regular; Joey Bishop became famous sitting on Paar's couch. Jack Paar's *Tonight* show was an extraordinary nightly display of wit and intelligence.

But Paar also brought serious guests to late-night TV, including Fidel Castro and Eleanor Roosevelt, as well as both 1960 presidential candidates, John F. Kennedy and Richard Nixon. After both men had appeared on the show, *New York Times* reporter Scotty Reston wrote, "Now there are two litmus tests for candidates: who can stand up to Nikita Khrushchev and who can sit down with Jack Paar."

Paar also introduced great young talent like Phyllis Diller, Bill Cosby, Carol Burnett, and Bob Newhart. And every single night, he kept a seat in his audience for his most faithful fan, the elderly Mrs. Miller. Sometimes he would single her out, asking sweetly after a joke failed, "But you liked it, didn't you, Mrs. Miller?"

Paar made *Tonight* just about the hottest show on television in any time slot. It was the original must-see TV because the next morning people were going to be talking about it. As TV critic Jack Gould wrote, "Mr. Paar almost alone has managed to preserve the possibility of surprise." When he took over the show, only forty-six affiliates carried the show; within a year almost every one of NBC's 170 stations broadcast it nightly. Viewers never knew what Paar was going to say or do. In addition to walking off the show when his water-closet joke was censored, he picked fights with Ed Sullivan (who had complained that he had to pay his guests considerable sums while Paar paid them only the mini-

I hosted the very late night show *McMahon & Company* at 1 a.m. in Philadelphia, often after commuting to New York to work with Johnny Carson on *Who Do You Trust?* and to audition for commercials.

From the Author's Collection

mum $320 fee) and with the aging columnist Walter Winchell. He started a campaign against Cuban dictator Fulgencio Batista and tried to arrange a trade of tractors in exchange for the release of prisoners captured at the Bay of Pigs. When the East Germans built the Berlin Wall, Paar broadcast *Tonight* from Berlin for a week—creating a national controversy when senators complained that American troops were being used to help produce a television show. As he admitted, "When trouble isn't following me, I'm leading it."

Steve Allen and Jack Paar had created and defined late-night television. They had turned dead air into extraordinarily valuable property. And they did it so well that it seemed almost impossible anyone else could equal their popularity or change the format. In 1962, just when it seemed as if he had run out of surprises, Jack Paar revealed his biggest surprise. At the height of his popularity, he was leaving the show. For real. No backsies. He just felt like he had done it long enough. He was going to host a weekly show in prime time.

Have you ever see a grown network cry?

In addition to commuting to New York to be the announcer on Johnny Carson's quiz show *Who Do You Trust?* in 1962, I was hosting a late-night talk-variety show in Philadelphia, *McMahon & Company,* on one of the five NBC-owned and operated local stations. *McMahon & Company* was a variety show that went on the air at 1:00 a.m., after *Tonight.* We were more of a very-early morning show than a very-late night show. The network had similar shows on each of its "O-and-Os"—stations it owned and operated. It was completely up to the host to determine what kind of show he wanted. I had a piano player, a few musicians, and guests. A lot of stage plays opened in Philly on the way to Broadway, and by the time my show went on the air, those performances were done for the night, and a lot of major stars would come on the show to sell tickets.

I'm sure the network looked at me as a possible replacement when

From the Author's Collection

Johnny Carson set the tone of *The Tonight Show* by opening the very first program with a monologue. It was terrific and he went on to perfect the art in more than 4,000 monologues over the next thirty years.

Paar decided to leave, but I never heard a word about it. Many different people were suggested, although Paar said that Johnny Carson was "the one man who could or should replace me."

Just between you and me, what did Johnny Carson really have to offer besides boyish good looks, a brilliant comic mind, impeccable timing, infectious enthusiasm, undeniable charisma, and a warm personality? If I had known that that was all they were looking for . . .

There could not have been a more perfect choice. Johnny was able to take the format that

The Great Carnac the Magnificent, who knew the answers to questions sealed in an envelope, was one of the favorite roles played by Johnny.

Allen and Paar had established and make it his own. He did the sketches and bits like Allen and introduced an amazing variety of people to America as Paar did.

Johnny still had six months left on his *Who Do You Trust?* contract when NBC announced he would be Paar's replacement, so a series of temporary hosts filled that time, including Merv Griffin, Art Linkletter, Robert Cummings, and Joey Bishop. Johnny and I had gotten to be friends working together, but I didn't know if I was going with him to *Tonight*. I had heard that NBC wanted Paar's announcer, Hugh Downs, to continue on the show to establish a sense of continuity. But one night after we had done *Trust*, Johnny and I were sitting at the bar at Sardi's, the famous Broadway restaurant, when he said, "So when we take over the show . . ."

"Wait a second," I interrupted. "Did you say, when *we* take over the show?"

"Oh yeah," he said. "I'm taking you. You know that. Don't be dumb."

I don't know for certain, but I have heard that Carson made a deal with the network. He would accept a producer under contract to NBC, and in return I would become the announcer. That gave the network some control of the show, and it got me the job. It also worked out well for Hugh Downs because he became host of *The Today Show*.

Hugh Downs turned out to be very helpful to me. He let me do the commercials in rehearsal for several weeks before we began. That gave me a feel for the studio. I got to know where to stand, where to look, and I met the people I would be working with. So when we went on the air, I felt comfortable doing the commercials. It was everything else I wasn't sure about.

Several weeks before our first show the entire production staff went down to Ft. Lauderdale, Florida, and planned the show. That's where sketch characters were born, and where a basic structure was laid out. But very little was said about my role.

Hours before we were going on the air for the first time, as Johnny and I were walking downstairs to the stage for a rehearsal, I said, "John, I want to discuss something with you. How do you see my role down there tonight?"

I've never forgotten his answer. It described perfectly the next thirty years. If I close my eyes, I can hear him right now: "Ed, I don't even know how I see my own role. Let's just go down and entertain the hell out of them."

Johnny did a very different *Tonight Show* than Steve Allen or Jack Paar. His personal life was much less public than either man—except for all those divorces and contract battles with the network—but he was always the center of the show. He built a great monument on their foundation, establishing forever the parameters of nighttime talk shows.

People often ask me about my most memorable moment on the show. I tell them the truth: every moment. It's impossible to pick out any particular moment, any night, any guest that was the most memorable. But there was that one night when I was absolutely terrified. Our guest was Joan Embry from the San Diego Zoo. She brought a lion with her, a show lion, well trained, but still a lion. He came out, he rubbed against me, he did his act, the audience applauded, and then he left. The lion was a trooper.

But then Joan brought out a Bengal tiger—a live 400-pound Bengal tiger. Until that moment I had never realized how large a Bengal tiger could be. "Isn't he beautiful?" she asked. Here's a good piece of advice: never insult a Bengal tiger. "Nice boy," I said. Unfortunately, he took a liking to me. We were head to head, and his head was bigger than mine. He was just staring at me. Now, I didn't know what was on his

Courtesy of Stephen Cox Collection

The Tonight Show A-team (from left): Doc Severinsen, director Bobby Quinn, Johnny, producer Freddie deCordova, and yours very truly.

mind; maybe he had a toothache, maybe he had a cold or didn't feel good, or maybe he had had a fight with his mistress. And then he smelled the lion.

I was frightened, I mean truly frightened. I didn't know what to do. He locked into that lion scent. I knew I had an option; I could end my career by walking off the show, or I could end my career by being eaten on live TV by a Bengal tiger. Fortunately, Joan picked up on it and led him away.

It's not possible to even begin to sum up the years we spent together. I could write a book about it—in fact, I already have. But when I think back on the thousands of nights we spent together, when I look at what we accomplished, it is clear that no one understood the real objective of a talk show better than Johnny Carson. "Entertain the hell out of them."

There was a big battle going on between NBC and CBS
over which color system the FCC was going to approve,
a decision that was going to be worth untold millions
of dollars. I was working in a special unit in Chicago,
experimenting with color. Green tended to titillate or
waffle. Red would not come out totally red sometimes.
Some colors against black and white would become
gray and disappear. Orange was good for TV; blue was
very good. And we learned one other thing; if you were
wearing a certain shade of blue and you were standing
in front of a blue screen, that blue you were wearing
would key out; it would disappear. When the shows
weren't on the air, we had a beautiful, voluptuous,
redheaded "color girl" sitting in front of the camera so
the engineers could work on the color shading.
Redheads only; brunettes wouldn't work. These girls
had to have certain skin shades and wear specific
makeup. This picture was broadcast only to the lab,
and sometimes to the program manager's office and
the general manager's office. Well, one day the
engineers convinced the color girl that she had to wear
a blue sweater. She did, and that part of her body
dropped out. Then the engineers got a nude picture of
a woman from a magazine and keyed it in, creating a

very special effect.That ended the day this picture
accidentally got fed into the station manager's office.

—WOODY FRASER, PRODUCER

TELEVISION NEWS BEGAN ON JULY 1, 1941, WHEN WCBW,
the CBS station in New York, broadcast the first news telecast
by a licensed commercial station. On December 7 and 8, 1941, CBS
newsman John Daly did hour-long reports about the attack on Pearl
Harbor—but the only picture shown was an American flag being
blown by a fan off camera. That same visual was used on December 8,
when CBS televised President Roosevelt's speech to Congress declar-
ing war on Japan and Germany.

World War II was covered on a daily basis by radio and weekly by
newsreels. Television just didn't have the technology to compete.
During the war some TV news shows used wall maps and globes to
show where the actions were taking place. In 1945 DuMont successfully linked New York and Washington into the first officially
licensed network to announce that a second atomic bomb had been
dropped on Japan, and when Japan surrendered a few days later,
DuMont showed a blackboard on which had been written in chalk
"Japan Offers to Surrender."

In February 1948 NBC began broadcasting a ten-minute daily
news program, *The Camel Newsreel Theatre*. John Cameron Swayze,
who was rarely seen on the air, read stories directly from the AP and
UPI newswires while newsreel-type footage was shown. Within a
year the show had become the *Camel News Caravan,* and Swayze
added occasional in-studio interviews and commentary to the program. CBS began telecasting a fifteen-minute news show hosted by
Douglas Edwards in late 1948. That show had a much more original

format—Edwards sat at a desk, holding news copy in his hand, and read it! CBS also used film. Edwards told an interviewer, "Once we showed film received five minutes *after* we went on the air! It was something hot, and our assistant rushed down Park Avenue on a motorcycle, skirts flying to get the damn thing here. But we got it on the air."

As with any live show, there were mistakes. "One evening," Edwards said, "we ran a clip of Ted Williams hitting a home run upside down and backwards. I looked at the camera, and there was only one thing I

John Cameron Swayze hosted NBC's first television newscast, *The Camel Newsreel Theatre.* He was a popular newscaster who is best remembered for his opening and closing phrases, "Let's go hop scotching around the world for headlines" and "That's the story folks—glad we could get together."

could say, 'Now you know what Ted Williams hitting a home run looks like upside down and backward.' Another night I was running over the list of keynote speakers at the Republican convention, and I came to the name Dwight Green, the governor of Illinois. As I announced that Green's picture would be on the screen in a few seconds, a sinister-looking devil flashed on. The devil was for a commercial for chewing tobacco."

Although the news was probably the format that could most easily be adapted from radio to television, the challenge for the new medium of television was how to bring its new capabilities to the same old stories that people were reading in the newspapers, hearing on radio, and seeing as weekly newsreels in the movie theaters. Whether on radio or television, the news essentially consisted of a newscaster reading the news. On radio, newscasters and reporters had become stars, men whose somber voices were instantly recognizable and trusted. Newscasters didn't become known as the anchormen until 1952, when Don Hewitt used that phrase to describe Walter Cronkite's role at both the Democratic and Republican presidential conventions. It was a phrase taken from sports, Hewitt explained, when the anchor ran the last and most important leg of a relay race.

There were people who thought creating a newscast on TV was an expensive waste of time. Nobody was going to sit in front of the TV set and *watch* news. It was generally assumed that television was going to focus on entertainment, a thing to watch for relaxation, rather than providing information.

The legendary sportscaster Jack Whitaker started at WCAU in Philadelphia in 1950 as a newscaster and the news writer. "The news was pretty simple," he remembers. "One man would sit behind a desk. We didn't have teleprompters or cue cards. If you didn't want to sit at a desk with your head buried in the script, you memorized the show. I used notes, but there was a lot of memorization and ad-libbing. We knew the story, and we explained it to our viewers. We didn't show any film at all. It was too expensive, and we didn't have the time or the facilities to produce it. The only thing we could show were photographs. We used Associated Press photos and put them on easels. The Korean War was going on, and we would get a picture of a B-17 bombing from the AP, and as I was reading the story, the camera would pan side to side or up and down. That's the way we got motion. If we were talking about President Truman and the White House, we would show a picture of Truman, then the Oval Office, and then maybe General MacArthur."

I also remember doing that at WCAU to illustrate local stories. A staff photographer would take a series of pictures representing the story, and we would put them on an easel. For example, we would take pictures of a police car approaching a crime scene, and as we reported the story on air, a stagehand would flip the pictures so it looked like the car was moving closer. Nobody objected. Truthfully, I don't think anybody cared. The news was just something you watched until the next real program came on the air. Serious news came from the radio.

At first, news broadcasts were only fifteen minutes long, which was plenty long enough according to Walter Cronkite, "because that's all the news

Courtesy of Library of Congress, New York World-Telegram and the Sun Newspaper Photography Collection

Walter Cronkite was recruited to join CBS in 1950 by Edward R. Murrow. Cronkite was the anchor for CBS's coverage of the Democratic and Republican national conventions in 1952. By the 1970s he was cited as the most trusted man in America. He is pictured here on the set of *The Morning Show*, which he co-hosted briefly in the 1960s.

there was." There were not many feature stories, human interest stories, or investigative journalism—just the news. The network news, usually starting at 6:00 p.m., was fifteen minutes followed by fifteen minutes of local news. When WCAU started an eleven o'clock newscast, Jack Whitaker thought, "Nobody is going to watch the news at eleven o'clock. But then they hired the most famous radio newscaster in Philadelphia, John Facenda, and the eleven o'clock news became a big hit."

Technical changes came gradually. Don Hewitt, who directed *The CBS-TV News* long before becoming the producer of *60 Minutes*, projected slides on a screen behind Douglas Edwards so that viewers could see both him and the picture. The teleprompter, which was invented by a Broadway actor named Fred Barton in 1953, revolutionized news broadcasts. It was an electrically controlled box directly beneath the camera lens on which the script was written in large letters so you could appear to be looking directly into the camera while reading your lines. It was great. It allowed newscasters to get out from behind their desks. The invention of the videotape recorder in 1956 made it possible to tape studio interviews ahead of time. Those first Ampex recorders were much too big to use outside the studios, but within a couple of years smaller recorders made it possible to tape stories on location. That's when a fifteen-minute news show became not nearly long enough, and in the early 1960s both network news and local news went to a half hour.

In those early days newscasters also did the commercials. On the *Camel News Caravan,* for example, John Cameron Swayze reported the news while smoking a cigarette, and there was always a spiral of smoke rising from a cigarette in an ashtray on his desk. Camel prohibited any story that involved cigars from being broadcast on the news—the only exception being British prime minister Winston Churchill, who was allowed to be shown holding his famous stogie.

Mike Wallace remembered that when he hosted the local news in New York, "I would do the commercials for Bond Clothes and suggest to our viewers that when they went to the Bond Clothing store, they should say, 'Mike sent me.'" John Cameron Swayze's tagline for Timex watch commercials, "Takes a lickin' but keeps on tickin'" became far better known than the line he used to end his news broadcasts, "Glad we could get together."

Early newscasters also hosted quiz shows. John Charles Daly hosted ABC's nightly news, and on Sundays he was the moderator of the CBS quiz show *What's My Line?* Swayze was a panelist on several quiz shows, including one he created, *Who Said That?* And in 1958 he hosted a dating show called *Chance of a Lifetime*, in which a panel tried to match eligible singles in the audience. Mike Wallace also emceed several quiz shows, including *The Big Surprise* and *Guess Again*, a game show that lasted only two weeks. Even Walter Cronkite briefly hosted the 1954 game show *It's News To Me*, which had first been hosted by John Daly, in which a celebrity panel decided whether news stories were real or fabricated. Newscasters on local stations sometimes even had to host children's shows. By the mid-1950s the networks had learned that the news could be a serious—and profitable—business, and anchors were limited to news-oriented programming.

To replace John Cameron Swayze, NBC introduced in 1956 the concept of coanchors, Chet Huntley reporting nightly from New York and David Brinkley from Washington, D.C. While previous anchors had been radio personalities, Huntley and Brinkley were products of TV journalism. Their on-camera rapport made the show popular, and their closing phrases, "Good night, Chet" and "Good night, David, and good night from NBC news," became some of TV's most parodied catchphrases. Because of their popularity, the broadcast, which was originally fifteen minutes long, was expanded to a half hour in 1963.

In response to NBC's Huntley and Brinkley, CBS gave its anchor chair to Walter Cronkite. But Cronkite became more than

Courtesy of Library of Congress, New York World-Telegram and the Sun Newspaper Photography Collection

In 1956 NBC replaced John Cameron Swayze with nightly news reported by coanchors Chet Huntley (left) in New York and David Brinkley (right) in Washington. The show developed a strong following and was popular until Chet Huntley's retirement in 1970.

just a news anchor. He was also the voice of the news for CBS, the go-to guy when any serious event was transpiring. Cronkite hosted the long and often tedious rocket launches at the beginning of the space program, and brought a kind of humanity to that complicated technology. As astronaut John Glenn's rocket climbed slowly from the launchpad, Cronkite could be heard over the tremendous roar of the engines urging, "Oh, go, baby, go!"

And on November 22, 1963, it was Cronkite who slowly took off his glasses, rubbed his eyes, and announced, "From Dallas, Texas, this news flash, apparently official: President Kennedy died at 1:00 p.m. Central Standard Time—2:00 Eastern Standard Time—some thirty-eight minutes ago."

Then he put his glasses back on. As he later remembered, "I choked up; I really had a little trouble; my eyes got a little wet. [The Kennedy era] was just lost to all of us. I grabbed hold before I was actually [crying]."

The power of the network news, and of Cronkite and Huntley and Brinkley in particular, grew so strong that President Lyndon Johnson, when told that Cronkite had come out publicly against the Vietnam War, said sadly, "If I've lost Walter Cronkite, I've lost the country."

FOR MANY VIEWERS THE MOST IMPORTANT PART OF LOCAL news broadcasts was the weather. Maybe there was nothing they could do about the fighting in Korea, but at least they could find out if they had to wear a raincoat in the morning or what the temperature was going to be when the kids left for school. And television made the weather profitable. People would watch the weather report, which enabled stations to sell advertising.

The first American TV weather forecast was probably that done in 1940 by Jim Fidler on an experimental station in Cincinnati. New

York City's first regular weather report began in October 1941 by WNBT. In that case March really did go out like a lamb—Botany clothing sponsored a cartoon character named Woolly Lamb who sang the weather: "It's hot, it's cold. It's rain, it's fair. It's all mixed up together—but I, as Botany's Woolly Lamb, predict tomorrow's weather." There is no record of Woolly Lamb's accuracy.

In fact, the accuracy of television forecasts generally was not held in high esteem. Some TV weathermen were prohibited from giving warnings about bad weather to prevent scaring viewers.

Anybody could be wrong. The key to success as a weatherperson was being wrong entertainingly. In agricultural areas, where knowing the next day's weather really mattered, a professional meteorologist, usually someone who had learned the craft in the army, would give a lecture on meteorology. But in other areas, where there was competition for ratings, entertainment value was more important. Almost immediately the weather forecast became the segment for gimmicks, cartoonists, clowns, and eventually very pretty girls—or "weather bunnies."

When the CBS network bought WCAU, it made Jack Whitaker the weatherman, even though he did not want to be one. He said, "I didn't want to do weather, but I wanted to be unemployed even less. So I became a weatherman."

That's how I became a weatherman too. I did the weather every Sunday night on WCAU. "Don't forget to take your umbrella to work with you," I would say. "It looks as if we might get some rain." Or, conversely, "No rain tomorrow." That was all that people wanted to know—was it going to be raining in the morning? Since it rained less than one day a week, I had a great shot at being right. My qualification was that I was under contract. The only thing I knew about the weather was what I had learned in the Marine Corps. I had my map and a weather report that I assumed was taken from the National Weather Service.

There was little to set one weatherman apart from another, so weathermen looked for something to make themselves distinctive. They would wear raincoats or carry umbrellas, squirt shaving cream on a map to indicate a snowstorm, use puppets or dolls, stick magnetic suns or angry dark clouds on metal maps, and scrawl all over maps with markers. One weatherman sat at a piano and sang his forecasts. One of the most popular weathermen was cartoonist Tex Antoine, who would draw the appropriate clothing, a heavy coat or a bathing suit, on a character named Uncle Weatherbee. Antoine would stand in front of an artist's easel and illustrate the nation's weather. He would finish by writing the temperature in big numbers and then turn those numbers into a weather-related illustration. It was a very popular gimmick.

And then there was weather bunny Tedi Thurman who was best known for her own weather front. She became a bit of celebrity, appearing with Jack Paar on the *Tonight* show, with a suggestive reading of the weather. Once she peeked out from behind a shower curtain to report, "The temperature in New York is 48. And me, I'm 36-26-36."

THE THIRD SEGMENT OF EVERY LOCAL NEWS BROADCAST has always been the sports—scores and highlights. Sports and television have fit together better than beer and football. A lot of historians believe sports was the primary reason that TV was initially successful; and just as many historians believe that television enabled most sports to prosper.

The first bit of information viewers wanted when sports reporting started was the horse-racing results. And the station that could get the results first usually attracted the most viewers. Believe me, I learned about the importance of horse racing when I was hosting *Five Minutes More*. A man named Dan Kelly had become a close

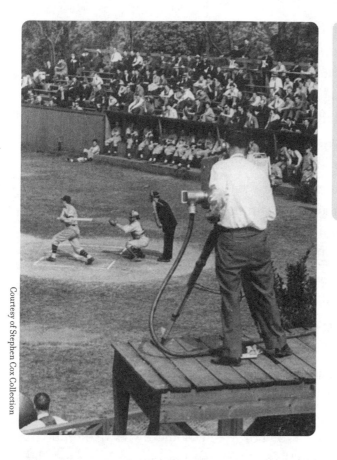

In 1939 Columbia University played Princeton in the first baseball game to be televised to New York's 480 5-inch by 7-inch sets. Only one camera was used, causing announcer Bill Stern to admit, "We prayed every batter would strike out because that was the only thing the camera could record."

Courtesy of Stephen Cox Collection

friend—as well as my landlord. Dan owned thoroughbreds and raced them at Garden State Park in Cherry Hill. One day he whispered to me that he had a horse going off at long odds that I should bet on. "This is a good one, Ed," he said. "Put a lot of money on it." Well, that was big news, and I just couldn't wait to share it with all my viewers. That night I shared my big tip with them on the air—and the next day they all started betting on Dan Kelly's horse . . . *all* my viewers. That horse went from being a long shot to the odds-on favorite in a few hours. Dan Kelly was not happy about that!

What set sports apart from other programming was that sporting events required almost no preparation. A particular game or match was going to take place whether or not it was televised. That meant no scripts, no rehearsals, no temperamental directors, no censorship problems, nobody forgetting his lines. It meant just setting up the cameras and turning on the power.

NBC broadcast the first sporting event in the United States on May 15, 1939, televising a 2,388-mile, six-day bicycle race, with Joe DiMaggio firing the starter's gun. What is generally recognized as the first sports event televised in America was a college baseball game between Columbia and Princeton, played two days after the bicycle race had started, but before it finished. And the first major-league baseball game was broadcast in August that year, a doubleheader between the Brooklyn Dodgers and Cincinnati Reds from Ebbets Field. The reviews of the broadcast were mixed: it was possible to see the players in the field but impossible to follow the ball.

By the following season the Dodgers were televising a game a week. They weren't too worried about people staying home to watch the game because very few people had TV sets in their homes. In 1946 the New York Yankees sold the broadcast rights to their home games to DuMont for $75,000! While some owners continued to worry that TV would hurt attendance, the Washington Senators' Clark Griffith had a pretty good answer, explaining, "Television doesn't show you enough. You can't follow the play. If it ever becomes good, I'll throw it out."

As with just about every other format, sports broadcasting had to be invented. Legendary baseball director Harry Coyle remembered, "We didn't know anything about televising baseball. In fact, we didn't know anything about television. We used two portable cameras to cover a game at Yankee Stadium, and they were located in cages hanging behind first and third base. In those days 'portable' meant anything with two handles. It might have weighed four hundred pounds, but if it had handles, it was portable.

"There was no such thing as technique. The most common suggestion we got from people was why didn't we just show the whole field with one camera and leave it there. But each year we would try something new until we finally decided to experiment with a camera in right field. What we were waiting for was a home run to right field. We figured we would see the ball coming toward the camera, and it would be a great shot. Sure enough, somebody hit a long shot to right field, directly at the camera. I got excited; this was going to be great, but when I looked at the monitor, all I saw was the grass. Grass? I didn't understand it.

"I found out after the game that our cameraman was a big baseball fan. He had brought his glove to the game, and when the ball was hit, he got so excited he forgot all about the camera. He picked up his glove and tried to catch the ball; the weight of the lens pulled the camera straight down."

CBS actually issued a press release in 1946 to announce it had hired commentators and "camera directors with some knowledge of the game," pointing out that a TV announcer has the hard job of "interpreting for the ignorant without annoying the informed."

Initially, there were two sports that sold TV sets: baseball and boxing. The very first network broadcast of a sports event—and I use the word *network* pretty loosely, meaning more than one city—was the 1944 featherweight championship fight between Willie Pep and Chalky White, which was also the first presentation of *The Gillette Cavalcade of Sports*.

The June 1946 heavyweight championship fight between Joe Louis and Billy Conn at Yankee Stadium attracted an estimated 141,000 viewers. Louis's December bout against Jersey Joe Walcott had an estimated one million viewers, but more importantly, on the Monday and Tuesday after the fight, RCA sold 2,400 television sets. The 1947 World Series between the Yankees and the Dodgers was carried by all

Television's first sports superstar was Gorgeous George, the original showman of professional wrestling. He was a competent but ordinary wrestler until he developed his flamboyant persona. His credo was "Win if you can, lose if you must, but always cheat."

three New York networks as well as other stations on the East Coast, and an estimated 3.9 million people saw at least some of the series, making it television's first mass audience. So many people watched the fights or baseball games in bars that Fred Allen said, "There are millions of people in New York who don't know what television is because they're not old enough to go into the saloons yet."

Boxing was the perfect sport for television. Two fighters were inside a ring small enough to be covered by a single camera that didn't have to move. By 1948 *The Gillette Friday Night Fights* had become one of the most popular shows on TV. Viewers just couldn't get enough boxing. New York State even had to change the traditional colors of boxing trunks, from purple and black or red and white to black-on-white and white-on-black for the black-and-white cameras.

Even amateur events like the Golden Gloves were popular. Frances Buss, who directed some of the earliest bouts, recalled, "We had put up a boxing ring in the studio, and on Saturday nights we showed the Golden Gloves. The boxers would dress one floor below the control room. I never went down there, never. One Saturday night a bout ended, and we waited for the next fighters to come up—and we waited. After waiting a long time, we found out that the fighter who had been defeated wasn't feeling very well and was being examined by the doctor. Unfortunately, a fighter in the next fight was supposed to wear the injured fighter's trunks. These two fighters were sharing one pair of trunks, so the second boxer couldn't come upstairs until he got those trunks. We waited a long time that night."

Television's first sports superstar was a little guy named George Wagner. Wagner had been a relatively unsuccessful professional wrestler until he bleached his straight black hair to a curly pale blond, put on an elegant robe, hired a formally dressed valet to lead him into the ring and spray the ring with perfume—and changed his name to Gorgeous George.

The one, the only, the original Gorgeous George, a master showman who originated the concept of entrance music, became the villain America loved to hate. The man practically invented cheating—if it's possible to cheat in professional wrestling—using the sharpened bobby pins he wore in his hair as a weapon, poking them into his opponent's thigh. He was so popular that when he was wrestling, bars put out signs in front reading, "Gorgeous George. Television. Tonight!" His matches regularly sold out because he put on a great act. Fans laughed at him and cursed at him, and on occasion came close to rioting. When he was jeered by a female fan, he was known to respond, "I told you not to come down tonight, Mother."

Gorgeous was credited with selling more TV sets than anyone else before Milton Berle, and helped establish TV as an entertainment medium that could attract many *thousands* of viewers. Professional wrestling was a great show, with the obvious good guys versus the unbelievably evil bad guys—always refereed by an incompetent man whose toughest job was turning his back just in time to miss the good guy being hit over the head by the villain. At Madison Square Garden, wrestling shows usually outdrew boxing matches, causing famed promoter Ned Irish to note, "At least 40 percent of the customers were women, and there's nothing you can attribute that to but television."

While wrestling promoters insisted the sport was legitimate, the fact that a wrestler who was hit over the head with a folding chair, then tossed out of the ring onto the cement apron, then pounced on and pummeled by two bruisers could appear unscathed and ready to fight the next night, did raise a few questions.

Stanley Hubbard helped put on the weekly wrestling show for his father's TV station in Minneapolis and remembered, "When I was a senior in high school on Friday afternoons, I used to help set up the ring for wrestling. Then during the match I would lay under the ring and when I got a cue that it was time for a commercial, I would bang on the bottom. One guy would pin the other one, and then we would go to a commercial. And the wrestlers *still* insisted it was real. I would tell them, 'You guys are faking it,' and they would tell me, 'No it isn't; when we heard you banging, we got the energy.'"

Roller Derby was also perfect for television and attracted a lot of viewers. Teams of five men and five women skated around a banked track and basically tried to throw other skaters over the railing. It was mayhem on wheels—and the women were tougher than the men. Their tattoos were bigger, and they had nicknames like Toughie. Roller Derby went on the air in 1949, and by the end of the first season, the five-match Roller Derby World Series sold out Madison Square Garden for five consecutive days.

Two years after the end of World War II, almost one quarter of television broadcast time was sports, but television's focus on sports was reduced as the networks started paying more for original programming, drawing producers from other media to create shows for TV. There was also the problem of overexposure. There were only so many good boxers, for example, and the fourth time you've seen a wrestler get hit over the head with a chair it begins to get boring.

Television was changing American culture, and there were going to be clear winners and losers. Boxing was just devastated. The great editor of *Ring*, Nat Fleischer, said, "In 1949, receipts from fights around the country dropped 50 percent. Attractive matches still do well at the box office, but TV is hurting the small clubs, which can't get leading fighters." Roller Derby was off TV by 1953 and became, basically, a traveling sideshow.

Pro wrestling lost some of its popularity, but sort of hung around on local stations until Vince McMahon—no relation to me, but still a fine name—promoted the World Wrestling Foundation as a soap opera with weapons and made it a very popular TV show and arena event.

While major-league baseball attendance dropped slightly, the minor leagues were destroyed. Before TV was widely available, a local minor-league team was the best baseball a fan could see. But when the big-league teams started telecasting their games into smaller cities, people stayed home to watch them. Why pay to see a minor-league team when you could see a major-league team for free in your own home? The International League's Newark Bears, whose teams were sometimes as good as major-league squads, went out of business. Teams from coast to coast, even entire leagues, folded.

College football, which had proved to be very popular on TV, decided to do something to stop dropping attendance. At the 1950 meeting of the NCAA, at which the impact of television on sports—as well as the news that TV would be broadcasting an atomic bomb test—was discussed, Asa Bushnell, commissioner of the powerful Eastern Athletic Conference, suggested, "Television and the atom bomb have been hooked up a lot at this conference. Let's wait until the bomb destroys our stadiums and not let television do it first." As a result, the NCAA proposed a game-of-the-week format, in which one game would be shown in each region. In response, the University of Pennsylvania sold the rights to televise its eight home games to ABC for $250,000, but it was forced to reject the deal when the other Ivy League schools announced they probably wouldn't play on TV. Trying to calm the situation, NBC president Joe McConnell pointed out that "back in 1932 there was the same fear of radio, and for a while, colleges barred football broadcasts."

An ABC vice president looked into the future and saw the time when sports would be owned by the networks, "at a fabulous price, of course." Then he added, "We'll have silent football. It will be played indoors under perfect conditions. The weather will always be just right, the grass the proper height, the ball will never be slippery. In this test-tube world the players won't be bothered by the roar of the crowd because the crowds will all be watching at home! And they'll be comfortable. There will be no one at the game except the sponsor, and he will be behind a glass cage."

And I will bet you one thing: when people heard this said in 1950, they laughed.

None of this really affected professional football because in those days nobody cared very much about pro football. W2XBS, NBC's experimental station, broadcast the first pro football game, the Philadelphia Eagles against the Brooklyn (football) Dodgers, in October 1939. The eight-person broadcast crew used two cameras, and football's first play-by-play announcer and first color commentator, Skip Walz, also directed the camera shots by pointing to whatever he was talking about. "It was a cloudy day," he said, "and when the sun crept behind the stadium, there wasn't enough light for the cameras. The picture got darker and darker, and eventually it went completely black and we had to revert to a radio broadcast."

In those early years the NFL could barely give away the TV rights to its games. In 1953 a loosely structured network of eighty-seven Westinghouse and DuMont stations agreed to telecast the NFL's eleven-game schedule. Five years later, several million viewers watched the New York Giants and the Baltimore Colts play for the NFL championship. It was one of the greatest football games ever played, but it couldn't be seen in the largest TV market in America because it was blacked out of New York City to make sure the Giants sold out Yankee Stadium.

Football proved to be the perfect game for television, and television proved to be the cash register for football. CBS created the pregame show in 1961 with *Pro Football Kickoff*, hosted by Johnny Lujack, which was fifteen minutes long and originated from a different stadium each week. CBS also introduced the instant replay during the 1963 Army–Navy game.

Like football, college basketball was initially much more popular than pro basketball. In 1953 the sixty-one-station DuMont network signed a deal with the National Basketball Association to show games on fourteen consecutive Saturday afternoons—as many as possible featuring the Boston Celtics' Bob Cousy, who would dribble or pass the basketball *behind his back*, an amazing feat a lot of people tuned in to see for themselves. For whatever reasons, pro basketball has never really enjoyed tremendous success on TV.

There is absolutely no good reason, however, for golf to be successful on TV. It's a slow game. Even when golfers are playing, there's very little action, and that action is one person swinging a club. And then when he does connect, it's just about impossible to follow the golf ball in the air. A round of golf takes longer than a pro football game, and a match consists of several rounds taking several days. Golf is expensive to televise because a course is eighteen different holes, and there are numerous players shooting at the same time. Most people don't bet on golf, so they don't watch it for that reason. But there is something about the game that captures hearts—and tempers.

Golf also got very lucky. In 1953 the Tam O'Shanter World Championship was the first golf tournament to be nationally televised when the owner of the club at which it was being played *paid* ABC to put it on the air! Let me repeat that. The owner of the tournament paid the network to broadcast his golf tournament. As pro golfer Lew Worsham approached the par-4 eighteenth hole, he trailed the leader by one stroke. His tee shot left him about 115 yards from the hole. He used a wedge to drive his second shot forty-five feet from the hole, and, as viewers watched, it rolled right in for a tournament winning eagle. The first golf tournament to be televised nationally was won by one of the greatest shots in the entire history of golf. Worsham's miracle attracted tremendous attention and helped turn golf into a popular TV event.

In the 1950s CBS and NBC were the dominant networks, and ABC and DuMont were struggling. ABC was more of an afterthought than a viable network. That changed in the early 1960s when ABC invested in sports programming, hoping to attract a younger audience that might hang around for its other shows. Among the first people hired was producer Roone Arledge, who had previously produced the Shari Lewis puppet show, *Hi Mom!* Jim McKay remembered, "I had been at CBS for eleven years. I had one show scheduled in the spring, the Master's Golf Tournament . . . While I was down there I heard some guy named Roone Arledge was trying to reach me from New York. I returned the call, and Arledge said, 'We're going to put on a show as a summer replacement. It's just for the summer. That's all there is. We're checking a number of people to see if they're available. Would you be interested?'

"I tried to sound as casual as I could when I said, 'Yeah, I'd be interested in that.' I did not tell him that this was my last show for CBS, and after that I didn't know what I was going to do.

"I think he did mention during that call that the show would involve a certain amount of travel. A few days later he called back and said, 'Well, Jim, how much money do you want?' Just like that.

"I said, 'I don't know. We'll talk about it when I get back to New York.'

"He told me he had to know right away, and when I asked him why, he said, 'We're having a press conference in a half hour to announce who the host of the show is going to be, and it's going to be you, but we have to have a deal.'

"I hadn't talked to my wife, Margaret, about this. My wife was terrific at this kind of stuff. So I thought of the biggest number I could imagine and said, 'A thousand dollars a show.' He said OK, and that's how I was hired to do *Wide World of Sports*. And for thirty-seven years it was pretty steady work." McKay was the right choice to host what became one of the most popular and enduring shows in TV history.

Wide World of Sports was put together mostly because ABC had lost the rights to broadcast baseball, and so it had a time slot to fill on Saturday afternoons. Arledge decided to feature low-budget sports, sports that few people had seen—in fact, people didn't even know a lot of them existed. Arledge took advantage of the newly available videotape to prerecord these unique sports events all over the world.

The show featured eclectic sports like logger and firemen competitions, curling and hurling, jai alai, surfing, demolition derby, thrill seekers like Evel Knievel, as well as more familiar sports like figure skating and track-and-field events. "The rule of thumb from the start was that we would not do what later became known as 'junk sports,' made-for-TV sports," said Jim McKay. "These had to be things that existed before we came along . . . because the emotions of the people had to be real." No matter how unusual the sport was, it really meant something to the participants, and the show treated each sport with respect.

"[We did] the World Barrel Jumping Championships from Grossinger's Hotel in Catskill, New York," said McKay. "When a guy

. . . broke the seventeen-barrel barrier, which was like the four-minute mile to people in barrel jumping, his wife cried. The other guys picked him up and carried him around the rink in triumph. You realize that to these people this was big.

"There came to be a thing called the World Championship of Demolition Derbys . . . The same guy won it two years in a row. So I went down with my tongue deeply embedded in my cheek to interview this guy. All I remember is he was from Manassas, Virginia . . . I said, 'Here you go, Mr. World Champion, two years in a row. How long do you count on doing this?' He looked at me and shrugged. 'Well, I work real hard on my cars and I go to church a lot.' And I realized he was serious. This was the biggest thing in his life." Taking each sport completely seriously set the tone for the show and probably enabled it to become a foundation of sports on television.

When *Wide World of Sports* was first broadcast, McKay recalled, "Roone said, 'I think the opening stinks.' I agreed, and so we put some words together, not knowing they would still be heard thirty-eight years later: 'Spanning the globe to bring you the constant variety of sport, the thrill of victory, and the agony of defeat, the human drama of athletic competition.'" Those words became part of our language.

And those words came to represent the objective of all sports broadcasting in America, which is to bring to viewers that emotional high that keeps them coming back to the next game and the game after that. And the viewers bring with them the sponsors whose money enables the networks to support the leagues, so that viewers can continue to see the thrill of victory and the agony of defeat.

9

If we were to do the Second Coming of Christ in color for a full hour, there would be a considerable number of stations that would decline to carry it on the grounds that a Western or a quiz show would be more profitable.

—EDWARD R. MURROW

A S LONG AS TELEVISION ONLY REPORTED NEWS STORIES with some pictures, it really had no great advantage over radio. But the Kefauver Committee hearings, which began in May 1950, demonstrated the unique ability of television to present a story. Tennessee senator Estes Kefauver's investigation into the existence of organized crime lasted fifteen months, and his committee called more than eight hundred witnesses. It was televised from New York City, and for the first time Americans got a good look into the structure and power of the Mafia. The most famous and vicious mobsters in America all appeared on the same TV show, competing against programs like

In 1950 the U.S. Senate investigated organized crime in interstate commerce. The broadcast of the Kefauver Committee hearings made Frank Costello, a powerful Mafia boss, the most famous gangster in America since Al Capone. An estimated 30 million viewers watched his hands as he testified because the condition for his testimony was that his face not be shown on TV.

Kukla, Fran and Ollie. Life magazine described the effect of the hearings: "The week of March 12, 1951, will occupy a special place in history . . . people had suddenly gone indoors into living rooms, taverns and clubrooms, auditoriums, and back offices. There . . . looking at millions of small frosty screens, people sat as if charmed. Never before had the attention of the nation been riveted so completely on a single matter."

Among the people who testified were the famous gangster moll Virginia Hill, "prime minister of the underworld" Frank Costello, and enforcer Willie Moretti. Costello agreed to testify only if his face wasn't shown on TV, so the cameras remained focused on his constantly moving hands. An estimated thirty million viewers spent dozens of hours watching Costello's hands, sometimes clasped, sometimes waving, but always in motion. When the committee asked Costello about his finances, he responded with the phrase that was to become one of the most famous ever spoken on television, "I refuse to answer on the grounds it may tend to incriminate me."

Costello did answer lots of other questions though. For example, when asked how the government could reduce gambling in America, he answered in what had by then become his familiar Italian accent, "If you want to cut out gambling, there's just two things you need to do. Burn the stables and shoot the horses."

Willie Moretti became a TV star by providing comic relief. When asked how he managed to afford two large houses and two new luxury cars, he told the committee, "I gambled." In 1948, he explained, "I didn't win too much on horses, but I had a sure thing going for me. I had President Truman [in the election]. I win ten thousand dollars on that Dewey don't carry New York City by 640,000. Even money." Asked who introduced him to Al Capone, he said, "Listen, well-charactered people, you don't need introductions; you just meet automatically." Moretti's two hours of testimony made him a celebrity. He held press conferences and allowed reporters to stick with him—all the way until he was killed.

While the Kefauver hearings proved the power of television to capture the public's attention as never before, Edward R. Murrow proved that television could be the most powerful communications medium in history.

Murrow was probably radio's most famous reporter. His reports from England, opening with the phrase, "This . . . is London," brought World War II home to America. As Nazi bombs devastated the city, Murrow lay in a gutter and held up his microphone so listeners could hear the bombs falling.

After collaborating with producer Fred Friendly on *Hear It Now*, a series of very successful record albums that weaved together historical events, speeches, and Murrow's commentary, Murrow and Friendly turned the concept into a successful radio show. Supposedly Murrow did not like that newfangled TV, but he adapted to it very quickly. John Frankenheimer remembers working as an assistant director on an election coverage. "Cronkite was there, Eric Sevareid was there, all of the CBS correspondents, and Murrow. Each of them had a desk, and Walter Cronkite would say, 'Here is Winston Burdett,' and the red light would go on, and Burdett would start speaking. I was down on the floor with Murrow, and he said, 'John, get me a telephone.' I said, 'Mr. Murrow, there's no place I can plug it in.'

"He said, 'I don't care. Just get me a phone.' I went to an office and literally ripped the phone off the wall and came back with it in my hand. He took the dangling cord and put it in his desk drawer. He said, 'Let me know when they're coming to me.'

"I could hear the director screaming, and I said, 'They're coming to you now.' Murrow put the phone to his ear, the red light went on, and he said, 'Very good, I'll call you right back.' Then he hung up the telephone and said into the camera, 'This is Edward R. Murrow.'"

The TV version of *Hear It Now*, called *See It Now*, went on the air in November 1951, with the first simultaneous live transmission from both the East and West Coasts with Murrow speaking to reporters in both New York Harbor and San Francisco Bay. *See It Now* was the first newsmagazine on television. William Paley, who ran CBS, invested a lot in Murrow and let *See It Now* operate as an independent unit. Mili Bonsignori, one of television's first female film editors, was with the show from the beginning. "We were separate and apart from the CBS organization. We had no bosses over us; nobody told us what to do or when to do it. Fred Friendly was the only one in the cutting room who could tell me what to do. Murrow would say a word, and I would do it . . . No executives came into that cutting room to see what we were doing. We never screened the shows for them, not once. Even Paley saw it first on the air."

See It Now demonstrated that people would watch controversial programs. One early show simulated coverage of a bomb attack on New York. In December 1952 the show went to Korea to show American troops at war far away from home. And in 1953 Murrow used the power of television to make a political stand that changed America.

During the Cold War, many Americans believed Communists were infiltrating all aspects of our culture in order to shape our thinking and eventually take over America. The television networks, like the motion-picture industry, refused to hire people and also fired people who were on a blacklist—a list of people who supposedly had Communist leanings or who attended Communist-related meetings. It was just an awful time, made more so because of the fact that there really was no actual blacklist that people could look at. Americans turned against Americans. And if you were identified as being on the list, there was very little you could do about it.

Producer Stan Rubin remembered, "There came a time when I couldn't hire a writer without checking with someone in the front office who had to check with someone else to see if that person was approved."

"There was a number you had to call," John Frankenheimer remembers, "and you would read your list of actors. You never knew who was on the other end of the telephone. And they would call you back the next day, and you would hear a voice say, 'This one is OK. This one, no, not OK.'"

Blacklisted writers used "fronts," people who allowed the blacklisted writers to put their names on a script. It was silly. It was an open secret, but everybody went along with it. Longtime network executive Dick Shepherd remembers when an executive wanted to meet a front to discuss script changes. Legendary agent Swifty Lazar "called the executive and said, 'I talked with Mr. Smith, and unfortunately he's in New York. His mother is critically ill and probably isn't going to live another week, so he can't come back to California to discuss this script. But his closest friend on earth [the blacklisted writer] will do him a favor and meet with you to discuss the changes you want made in the script . . . .'"

The blacklist cost a lot of people their careers. Actress Pert Kelton was replaced as Ed Norton's wife, Trixie, on *The Honeymooners*. Actor Phillip Loeb was forced to quit *The Goldbergs*, and three years later he committed suicide. Even Lucille Ball, the biggest female star in television, had a problem when the House Committee on Un-American Activities revealed that in 1936 she had registered to vote as a Communist and signed two Communist party petitions. But the committee did add that it had found no evidence that she had been a member of the Communist party or been active in any movements. This was Lucy! America's sweetheart! She explained that she registered to please her grandmother. Desi Arnaz told the audience at a taping, "Lucille is 100 percent American. . . . I want you to meet my favorite redhead; in fact, that's the only thing red about her, and even that's not legitimate."

Edward R. Murrow despised the blacklist. After famed radio personality John Henry Faulk was blacklisted, he couldn't get a job and was about to lose his house. Murrow gave him two thousand dollars to cover the mortgage. Faulk thanked him, but pointed out, "I don't know when I can pay you back."

Murrow replied, "This isn't a loan. It's an investment in America."

Although he signed a loyalty oath when CBS required its employees to do so, Murrow attacked the blacklist, which he believed was a witch hunt, on *See It Now* with "The Case of Milo Radulovich." Radulovich had been a lieutenant in the Air Force Reserve with a spotless record, but he had been dismissed because his immigrant father had subscribed to subversive Serbian newspapers that printed Communist ideas. Mili Bonsignori remembers working on that program. "Murrow and Friendly felt it was such an important show that I think they put their own money in it. At the time they told us, I was really floored. I thought it was the bravest thing they ever did. And the show worked because Radulovich was reinstated in the Reserve, and it opened the door for people to be a little braver. You know,

See It Now allowed disgraced U.S. Senator Joseph McCarthy the opportunity to respond—unedited—to Edward R. Murrow's legendary attack on his credibility.

Courtesy of Stephen Cox Collection

everyone was capitulating to McCarthyism. It was a horrible time to live through. Even if you weren't guilty, you felt guilty."

With the success of the Radulovich story, Murrow and Friendly decided to go directly after Senator Joseph McCarthy, certainly one of the most powerful men in America at that time. With no evidence of any kind, McCarthy could destroy a person's career—and life. During one speech he held an envelope high in the air and proclaimed, "I have here in my hand a list of 205 people that were known to the Secretary of State as being members of the Communist party, and who, nevertheless, are still working and shaping the policy of the State Department." It was an amazing accusation. McCarthy never named those people, explained where the list came from, or gave any evidence that it was true.

Murrow and Friendly decided to expose McCarthy, and the weapon they used was television. The March 9, 1954, broadcast of *See It Now* may be the most important show in television history because it established forever the power of television. Mili Bonsignori remembers Murrow saying, "'We are going to convict him out of his own mouth,' and that's what we did." The show consisted of clips of McCarthy and then Murrow's providing evidence that the senator was using half-truths, hearsay, and fabrications to destroy the reputations of innocent people and support his own political opinions. It was devastating.

At the end of the show, Murrow said, "We must not confuse dissent with disloyalty . . . We will not walk in fear, one of another. We will not be driven by fear into an age of unreason, if we dig deep in our history and our doctrine, and if we remember that we are not descended from fearful men—not from men who feared to write, to speak, to associate and to defend causes that were, for the moment, unpopular. This is no time for men who oppose Senator McCarthy's methods to keep silent . . .

"The actions of the junior Senator from Wisconsin have caused alarm and dismay amongst our allies abroad, and given considerable comfort to our enemies. And whose fault is that? Not really his. He didn't create this situation of fear; he merely exploited it—and rather successfully. Cassius was right: 'The fault, dear Brutus, is not in our stars, but in ourselves.'

"Good night, and good luck."

The country shook in an earthquake of opinion. Murrow had used television as it had never been used before and gave it a backbone. Television journalism was never the same.

About a month later, McCarthy provided a filmed response in which he described Murrow as "the leader and cleverest of the jackal pack." But it was too late; Murrow had destroyed McCarthy's credibility.

Murrow and Friendly get all the credit for this program, and they deserve it. But Alcoa Aluminum also deserves credit for sponsoring "A Report on Senator Joseph R. McCarthy." Murrow and Friendly put their careers on the line. Alcoa risked its business.

Television also provided the knockout punch to McCarthy about one month later. The U.S. Army had accused him of using his power to force the army to give preferential treatment to a friend of his. The Senate's Army-McCarthy hearings were televised for thirty-six days and seen by more than twenty million viewers. Toward the conclusion of the hearings, the army's prosecutor, a courtly man with a flair for dramatics named Joseph Welch, challenged McCarthy's key aide, Roy Cohn, to provide a list of the 130 Communists McCarthy had claimed worked in defense plants. In response, McCarthy attacked a young lawyer in Welch's Boston law office who had once been a member of the National Lawyers Guild, an organization with an association to the Communist party.

Perhaps speaking for many Americans, Welch said, "Until this moment, Senator, I think I never gauged your cruelty or your recklessness . . ." McCarthy tried to interrupt, again attacking the lawyer, but Welch continued. "Let us not assassinate this lad further, Senator. You've done enough. Have you no sense of decency, sir? At long last, have you left no sense of decency?" As the television cameras focused on Joseph Welch and as millions of viewers watched, he gathered his papers, stood up, and left the room. The spectators followed. McCarthy was left sitting at his table, ranting, his own credibility destroyed. Finished forever.

See It Now continued to cover controversial subjects, including an interview with J. Robert Oppenheimer, who was involved in the creation of the atomic bomb and was later removed from his position after being accused of being a Russian agent; a story about the effects of the Supreme Court's decision to integrate public schools; and, ironically, Murrow even did a story about the link between smoking cigarettes and lung cancer.

The same year that "A Report on Senator Joseph R. McCarthy" was broadcast, 1954, CBS News was officially created by combining into a single unit the news and public affairs departments of CBS radio and television. Within two years *See It Now* had been replaced by the far more profitable game shows. It survived until 1958 as a series of specials.

In 1953 CBS created *You Are There*, a docudrama that re-created epic events in world history as they might have been covered by CBS television correspondents, with historical figures responding to reporters' questions and explaining their actions. The host was Walter Cronkite. The show began with the words, "Walter Cronkite reporting," and then set up the moment in time. "April 18, 1861. Seven Southern states have seceded from the Union. Others may follow. Civil war may be the consequence, and Ft. Sumter and Charleston Harbor . . ." The show always concluded with Cronkite telling viewers, "It was a day like all days . . . and you were there."

You Are There was used to attack the blacklist and the political hysteria surrounding Joseph McCarthy. In the first two seasons, almost every script was written by a blacklisted writer working under a front. Many of the subjects dealt with the meaning of liberty and patriotism—"The Signing of the Magna Carta," "The Defense of the Alamo," "The Treason of Benedict Arnold," for example. "Ironically," as Cronkite remembers, "the further back in history we went, the more contemporary the parallels became . . ." "The Death of Socrates" (399 BC), starred John Cassavetes, Robert Culp, and Paul Newman as Plato. Socrates was, according to Cronkite, "the perfect hero for the 1950s because he would not back down. None of us had any doubt about what that program was about." "The Crisis of Galileo" (1633), which told the story of Galileo being tried by the Inquisition for his belief that the earth rotated around the sun, "was not only a tragic one, but also was a story that specifically confronted the rituals of congressional inquisitions more directly than any other program that we did."

The networks not only re-created history with *You Are There*, but they used historical footage to create programming and documentaries that were both educational and entertaining. "Victory At Sea" added a symphonic score by Richard Rogers to naval footage from World War II. "The Big Picture" used military public relations and training films to tell its stories. In 1954 Walter Cronkite began hosting *The Twentieth Century*, which told historical stories using historical footage.

Documentaries were usually hour-long shows that told a story or investigated a situation. Most people thought of documentaries as those really boring films they made you sit through in school—but at least the lights were turned out so that you could get some sleep. But the networks loved them because they didn't cost much to produce and they satisfied the FCC's requirements that the networks broadcast some educational programming. Now, truthfully, a lot of those documentaries weren't very interesting. CBS, for example, had a strict rule that music could not be used in a documentary. The networks wanted to make sure that no one confused serious documentaries with anything entertaining.

That began to change one afternoon in 1957 on Sixth Avenue in New York. David Wolper, a young producer, bumped into the American representative of a Russian production company from whom he had previously bought cartoons and short films. The man told him he had just gotten several hours of footage from the Russian space program that he intended to sell to the networks. The Russians had just put the first satellite, Sputnik, into orbit—and people were excited, interested, and even a little scared. Until then Wolper had been selling programming to local stations, mostly old travelogues like *Let's Visit the Orkney Islands*, D movies like *Hitler—Dead or Alive*, cartoon series like *The Funny Bunnies,* and old movie serials like *Flash Gordon* and *Don Winslow of the Navy.* His résumé was hardly that of a guy who was going to challenge the networks.

Wolper instantly bought the footage for ten thousand dollars. "But I didn't intend to make a tedious documentary," he said. "The battle for supremacy in outer space was a great story, and I knew if I could tell it in an exciting way, I could find an interested audience . . . I knew very little about the history of documentaries . . . I didn't know the 'rules,'

David Wolper, sitting behind a Movieola, created educational entertainment—a new form of television. His tremendous output resulted in more than seven hundred films and winning fifty Emmys.

so I couldn't follow them." In addition to the Russian footage, Wolper got film from the U.S. Department of Defense, captured German film from the Library of Congress, and even some home movies from the widow of space pioneer Robert Goddard. "I didn't know my film was not supposed to be entertaining in addition to being informative," Wolper remembered. "To make it more exciting as well as appealing to the networks, I signed the famous film composer Elmer Bernstein to write the music and hired a controversial young reporter named Mike Wallace to narrate the show."

Then he began trying to sell the finished documentary, *The Race for Space*, to the major networks. "From somewhere I obtained a model rocket about ten feet long that I intended to use in my sales pitch. Jack Haley [who worked on the show] and I took our rocket to New York. When we changed trains in Chicago, Haley hoisted the front of the rocket on his shoulder, and I picked up the tail, and we casually walked through the station. People stared at us as if they had never seen two guys in business suits carrying a big rocket before."

In 1957 sponsors still purchased blocks of time from the networks, so David Wolper found a willing sponsor, the Shulton Company, which made Old Spice toiletry products, and then tried to make a deal with a network. CBS turned him down, explaining it would not broadcast public affairs programming that it had not produced. And, by the way, what was with that music in a documentary?

Both NBC and ABC claimed they had similar policies. If someone were going to do boring programming, it would be them! DuMont was fading as the fourth network and really didn't have enough affiliates to make it worthwhile. "I was desperate," Wolper said. "All my experience in television had been as a syndicator, selling programs to individual stations . . . It occurred to me that I could set up my own network consisting of one station in each market . . . I discovered that in most cities network affiliates were willing (and legally able) to preempt regularly scheduled network programming to show *The Race for Space* . . . In some cities we actually placed the program on three stations for the same night. In New York, for example, we placed the program on three independent stations to run at 9:00, 10:00, and 11:00 p.m. The show was a huge ratings success."

Several years later, during a Congressional hearing into the networks' use of their economic power, a CBS vice president explained that one reason it had turned down Wolper's show was to prevent sponsors from interfering in the development of news and public-affairs programming. Referring to Mike Wallace, who years earlier had done cigarette commercials, he said, "We think it's quite inappropriate to have a newsman in a program that measures the missile gap be one who is identified with the measurement of the quarter inch by which Parliament cigarette filters are recessed. I think that alone justifies the wisdom of our policy if television journalism is to fulfill its role as a responsible journalistic source." A few years later CBS hired Mike Wallace as one of the hosts of its new investigative program, *60 Minutes*.

Beginning with *The Race for Space*, David Wolper introduced a new format to television: the entertaining documentary. Informational television had been limited to a few syndicated shows like Art Baker's *You Asked for It*, in which viewers would mail postcards requesting stories like a live reenactment of William Tell shooting an apple off his son's head, and *Ripley's Believe It or Not*, originally hosted by Robert Ripley.

Rather than focusing on educational or intellectual subjects, David Wolper made documentaries about subjects people really liked, using fascinating footage they wanted to see. He made a series of TV documentaries about the movies—*Hollywood: The Golden Years, Hollywood: The Great Stars, Hollywood: The Fabulous Era*, and even *The Legend of Marilyn Monroe*—and then he turned the footage into a thirty-one-program half-hour series, *Hollywood and the Stars*. He made several films about World War II, including *D-Day, The Sixth of June,* and *December 7th—Day of Infamy*. Wolper adapted the technique used in nonfiction filmmaking to TV, shooting original film in addition to using footage compiled while working on documentaries, when he created series like *Biography* and *The Story of . . .* , which profiled men in fascinating professions like test pilots and matadors. Wolper's cameras brought TV viewers to places they had never been, in particular *The Undersea World of Jacques Cousteau*. He eventually made more than seven hundred films and won fifty Emmys.

While David Wolper was making educational entertainment, the networks continued to develop and improve their ability to do serious investigative reporting. *See It Now* was eventually replaced by *CBS Reports,* which looked into nonentertaining subjects like "Murder and the Right to Bear Arms," "Eisenhower on the Presidency," and "Storm over the Supreme Court," a three-part series. But probably the most controversial of the *CBS Reports,* and a show that demonstrated TV's ability to influence public policy, was Edward R. Murrow's classic documentary about the lives of migrant workers in Florida, *Harvest of Shame*.

Fittingly broadcast the day after Thanksgiving 1960, *Harvest of Shame* was Murrow's last major program, and it shocked America by describing the terrible conditions under which fruit pickers were forced to live to earn as little as a dollar a day. The show was produced by David Lowe, who had started in TV producing the children's show *Captain Video*—and had done a quiz show with that kid Johnny Carson, *Who Do You Trust?* Lowe did all the investigative reporting and filmed the show, and Murrow narrated it. But Murrow also did something most documentaries didn't do—he editorialized, calling for federal legislation to regulate the agricultural industry.

Many people believe *Harvest of Shame* is the greatest documentary in TV history. It was so brutal that it was shown in the Soviet Union as an example of the way American workers were exploited. Ironically, Murrow left CBS to head the United States Information Agency, and in that position he had to request that the British Broadcasting Company not show *Harvest of Shame* in England. His request was turned down.

CBS also made the documentary *Hunger in America,* which focused on the reality that thousands of Americans did not have enough to eat. At the time it had a policy requiring documentary producers to provide a balanced report, making sure both sides of every issue had an opportunity to present their case. In this case, as Mili Bonsignori remembers, "Nobody denied that there was hunger, but the producer, Martin Carr, wanted to find somebody who said hunger was good for you, because that would provide balance. And so they found a commissioner of welfare or something in Texas who said, 'We've always had hungry people. They're just lazy.' So that's how we got the other side of that issue."

It was CBS News that in 1960 broadcast the first debate between John Kennedy and Richard Nixon, a broadcast that changed American politics forever. Before 1960, what was most important in politics was the way a candidate thought, rather than how he looked. As Howard K. Smith moderated the debate, viewers saw the young, handsome Kennedy sitting next to the rather grim-looking Vice President Nixon. Those images changed the dynamics of the election—and history—because it was the first time that makeup made the difference in a presidential election. Nixon was using the wrong make up, which made it look like he hadn't shaved, and his appearance became a campaign issue.

I'll tell you a story. In 1968 when Nixon was considering whether to run a second time for the presidency, he appeared on *The Tonight Show*. One of my neighbors happened to be working with him, and asked me to offer some advice about how to "look good" on television.

I met with Nixon in his office and said, "The most important thing to do when you're on TV is to include everybody. Make contact with the people who are watching at home as well as those people in the studio. Try to find common emotions, things that people watching at home can relate to. If Johnny asks you how you feel about something, tell him you feel the same way about it as every person in the audience has felt at one point in their lives."

When Nixon appeared on the show, the first question Johnny asked him was whether he was going to make a second run for the presidency. "Actually," Nixon replied, "I think you ought to run for president. Let me tell you a few things. I'm an expert on how to run for the president. Not on how to win, but on how to run. You come over on television like gangbusters. And I'm an expert on how important that is."

Johnny asked him, "You're not going to lend me your makeup man, are you?"

"No," Nixon said firmly, "I'm going to lend him to Lyndon Johnson!"

Nixon must have liked how he looked on TV that night because he hired *The Tonight Show*'s makeup man to work with him during his successful campaign. And when he won the election against Hubert Humphrey—whom I voted for, in case you're wondering—he asked me to produce the inaugural gala for him.

After the 1960 election, TV became the single most important campaign tool for every political candidate—and helped to raise the salaries of makeup people.

There are some things a son or daughter won't tell you . . . Do you expect him to blurt out the truth—that he's really ashamed to be with the gang because he doesn't see the television shows they see? How can a little girl describe the deep bruise inside? Can you deny television to your family any longer?

—AMERICAN TELEVISION DEALERS AND MANUFACTURERS ASSOCIATION ADVERTISEMENT (1950)

ONE OF THE BIGGEST PROGRAMMING MISTAKES MADE when television was being established was the popular belief that stations shouldn't waste money creating programs for kids because kids didn't have money of their own, they didn't smoke, and they didn't buy cars. It was thought that families would sit together watching television, so almost all of the original programming was aimed at adults. The few children's shows that were on the air were mostly done as a public service—and with the hope that it might help sell some TV sets.

Buffalo Bob Smith poses with the stars of his show, puppet Howdy Doody, who could speak, and Clarabell the Clown, who could not. *Howdy Doody* aired on NBC for 13 years— from 1947 to 1960. At that time, Buffalo Bob Smith and Howdy Doody had done more shows than anyone else in network history.

The theory was that if the kids yelled loud enough, the parents would buy one.

The show that proved children's programming could attract a large audience and sell advertising was *Howdy Doody,* hosted by Buffalo Bob Smith, which ran for thirteen years. *Howdy Doody* began as a children's radio quiz show, *The Triple B Ranch,* hosted by Bob Smith, who would greet his audience every day, "Ho ho ho, howdy doody!" In addition to hosting the show, Bob Smith, who came from Buffalo, provided the country-bumpkin voice for Howdy Doody. In 1947, NBC's programming director, Warren Wade, decided to try the show on television. As Buffalo Bob remembered it, "The name of the show at first was *Puppet Playhouse* because we had hired this puppeteer who had many puppets. We had sort of a serial with puppets, old-time movies, and little stunts with kids in the clubhouse.

"Warren Wade told us on December 23, 1947, that we were going to be on television the following Saturday. And he told us we had to have Howdy on. I said, 'We don't have a puppet,' but he insisted we had to have Howdy on. So for the first three weeks we pretended that Howdy Doody was in my desk drawer, and the camera had a shot of the desk drawer, and I would say, 'Are you in there, Howdy?'

"Then the camera would take the shot and he would say, 'Yeah,

I'm in here, but I'm too bashful to come out.' That third week I opened up the desk drawer, and that was the first time people saw Howdy.

"We had nobody to learn anything from. We were like pioneers. We had a great act with French poodles from Radio City Music Hall on the show. And the puppets. We didn't even have a sponsor for the first three months. We started just on Saturday afternoons from five o'clock to six. Then we added weekdays. One of the things that made *Howdy Doody* so popular was that we were the first show many stations put on the air. In many markets there was no daytime television, just a test pattern all day long. When TV set installers would go to a home, they would have to tune the set to something. Kids would come home from school, sit in front of the television, and listen to the recorded music and watch the test pattern until I got there at 5:30 and said, 'Say, kids, what time is it?' And the whole world blasted out, 'It's Howdy Doody time!' If they were watching television, they were watching *Howdy Doody*."

Now I want you to do yourself a favor. Sing the *Howdy Doody* theme song out loud. Don't just think it; sing it. You don't have to shout it; you can keep it low, but do it out loud. I guarantee, I absolutely guarantee, it will make you smile. The *Howdy Doody* theme song was sung to the tune of "Ta Rah Rah Boom De Ay." You know that tune. It was used because the musicians' union had not signed a contract yet, so the show couldn't use live music, and "Ta Rah Rah Boom De Ay" was in the public domain. Now sing along with Buffalo Bob Smith . . .

> It's Howdy Doody time,
> It's Howdy Doody time,
> Bob Smith and Howdy too,
> Say Howdy doo to you.

Let's give a rousing cheer,
'Cause Howdy Doody's here.
It's time to start the show,
So, kids, let's **GO!**"

Admit it, that felt good. That alone was worth the price of admission to this book. I admit it, it's not exactly an aria, but it is definitely a classic.

The Howdy Doody most children knew had red hair that appeared black on TV, big rosy cheeks, big ears, a broad smile that never changed (mainly because Howdy was made of wood), and forty eight freckles—one for each state. (Alaska and Hawaii had not yet become states.) But he was not the first Howdy. The first Howdy, as Bob Smith recalled, "was grotesque. 'Ugly Doody' we called him. The toy buyer from Macy's came to our show one day and asked if we had ever thought about licensing the puppet because they had gotten requests for Howdy Doody dolls. The man who made the puppet got wind of this and thought that he should figure in the royalties that would be coming from the licensing. Well, NBC had paid him five hundred dollars to make the puppet, which was a lot of money. The deal was closed. NBC said, 'No, you don't have any licensing rights. It's Buffalo Bob's name; it's Buffalo Bob's idea. We own the puppets and the name.'

"He said, 'If you think it's yours, I'll just take my puppet and go home.' And he did. He walked out of the studio and took the puppet. Howdy Doody was puppetnapped! We immediately called someone else, and I gave him the voice and said, 'This is what he sounds like. What do you think he should look like?' We got back beautiful sketches and said, 'Go make him.' It was two weeks before we had another puppet.

"In the interim we wanted Howdy on the show. Nineteen forty-eight was an election year, and we decided Howdy would run for president of all the kids in the United States. We had no ratings system at that time and had to get some way to show the salesman that people were watching." NBC offered free campaign buttons and received sixty thousand requests, which represented about one-third of all the TV sets in American homes. The kids were watching—and sponsors noticed. Within a few days all the advertising time had been sold to major companies who wanted to reach the children's market.

Ventriloquists like Edgar Bergen with his dummy, Charlie McCarthy, had been successful on radio, which was something I could never understand. What was so impressive about not seeing the ventriloquist move his lips on *radio*? Howdy was no dummy. He was a marionette with a person pulling his strings and speaking his lines. In addition to Howdy, the puppets included Doodyville's Mayor Phineas T. Bluster, the always-silly Dilly Dally who could wiggle his ears, and Flubadub. Princess Summerfall Winterspring began life on the show as a marionette, but was then magically transformed into a live Indian princess. Chief Thunderthud's catchphrase, "Kowabonga," which basically meant, "Wow!" became part of every kid's vocabulary. But next to trustworthy, reliable, sensible Buffalo Bob and Howdy, the most popular character on the show was Clarabell the Clown. Clarabell didn't speak. Instead Clarabell made his opinion known by honking a horn a certain number of times.

The original Clarabell was played by Bob Keeshan—the same Bob Keeshan who a few years later changed his name to Captain Kangaroo—and the character's creation was an accident. Keeshan was a page at NBC and had worked with Bob Smith on an early morning radio show. After *Howdy* went on the air, Smith hired him as one of TV's first cue card holders. As Smith explained, "One day a kid had won a prize, and I needed something, and I said, 'Bobby, get me that little prize, please.' So he walked on camera and handed it to me. He was wearing a T-shirt.

"After the show my boss, Warren Wade, said, 'I saw that guy walk on camera wearing a T-shirt. Is that good television?' I asked him what he meant. 'Well, if he's going to be on, let's dress him up as something. Don't let him walk on in a T-shirt.' The only thing we had in the wardrobe prop room was this zebra-striped clown suit. I asked Bob if he minded wearing it, and he said it was fine.

"One day I needed something, and he walked on camera dressed in his zebra-striped clown suit—he didn't have any makeup on—and handed it to me. I thanked him and he said, 'You're welcome, Bob.'

"After the show Warren Wade called me again. He said, 'Hey, that guy with the clown suit? He talked.' I agreed he had talked. 'Well,' Warren said, 'Don't let him talk.' I asked him why and he explained, 'Because if the union comes in and he talks, we're going to have to pay him actor scale.'

"So I told Bobby not to talk when he comes on camera. 'OK, fine,' he said. 'I didn't have anything to say anyway.' So he started not talking.

"A couple of months later, Ringling Brothers Barnum and Bailey Circus came to New York, and to promote the circus they would send over an act for us every day, and in return we gave them a plug. One day they would send a juggler, the next day something else. We got a great act for no money, and they got valuable plugs. One day they sent over two of the greatest clowns in history, Emmett Kelly and Felix Adler. They saw Keeshan sitting in his clown suit and said, 'What's he?' They then put face paint on Bob and gave him a big nose and the big painted smile, and we christened him Clarabell. And it was Clarabell for the next twenty-five hundred shows. He never talked because it was cheaper that way. We gave him two horns, a happy horn and a very dejected horn, a yes horn and a no horn. We copied that from Harpo Marx. And that's how Clarabell came into being."

Incidentally, Clarabell's makeup was done by Dick Smith—the eventual Oscar-winning Dick Smith who did the makeup for *The Exorcist* and *The Godfather* and many other great films. The same person who made up Clarabell also made up the girl with the spinning head. When I put on my clown outfit for *The Big Top*, I didn't look anything like Clarabell, but the truth is that to kids all clowns look alike—and they kept mistaking me for Clarabell.

Howdy Doody was one of the first shows to introduce what would become an American classic: children's show merchandising. Eventually there was a Howdy Doody comic book, a record, wind-up toys, a humming lariat, a beanie, T-shirts, and a Howdy Doody dummy.

By 1956 the networks had decided to fill the early evening time period with programming that would appeal to adults, and NBC moved *Howdy Doody* to Saturday mornings. The cost of creating the show was just too expensive for that time slot, and it went off the air in September 1960. At that time Howdy had done more shows than anyone else in network history. At the end of the last show, Clarabell, who by then had been played by several different actors, turned and looked at the audience and said, "Good-bye, kids." Those were the only words Clarabell ever spoke.

While *Howdy* was aimed specifically at children, the people-and-puppet show *Kukla, Fran and Ollie* was the first to appeal to both kids and their parents. In fact, about 60 percent of the audience was adults. Kukla and Oliver J. Dragon (Ollie) were puppets whose actions and voices were created by the never-seen Burr Tillstrom. Fran Allison would stand in front of their stage and talk to them. That was pretty much the structure of the show, Fran talking to two puppets and their friends—if you believe that puppets really can have friends.

What made the show popular was that the characters were very well developed, with families and histories and, much like the Muppets many years later, very human qualities that made them par-

Puppet clown Kukla (left) with creator Burr Tillstrom and co-stars Oliver J. Dragon and Fran Allison. *Kukla, Fran and Ollie* appealed to both children and their parents and was the first network program to be broadcast in color.

ticularly lovable. For example, Ollie, the one-toothed dragon, would roll on his back when he wanted affection or bang his chin on the stage when he was frustrated. The show was never scripted. It was just conversation based on the latest events in the puppets' lives. If you really stretched your imagination, it was possible to believe that after the show Kukla and Ollie, as well as Fletcher Rabbit, Madame Ooglepuss, and even Beulah Witch, took off their makeup and went home to their families to prepare for the next evening's show. To protect that image, Tillstrom refused to allow his characters to be marketed, because he didn't want kids to see them inert or just lying in a pile on a shelf.

The audience really embraced the concept; when Kukla blew his nose on a stage curtain, viewers sent in 250 handkerchiefs. When mailman Fletcher Rabbit sang the sad song, "There's Never Any Mail for the Mailman," he received thousands of letters. As executive Charles Cappleman explained, "These were loving people; they were open people; they had no script. They had an idea of where they were going, and it started and it went."

The show originated in Chicago and was broadcast nationally from 7:00 to 7:30 p.m. by NBC beginning in January 1949. By 1950 six million people were watching nightly, which made it competitive with shows like Milton Berle's *Texaco Star Theater*. Just think how Uncle Miltie must have felt when he discovered his biggest competition was a clown and a one-toothed dragon. When the network cut the show to fifteen minutes in 1951, its ratings actually improved. NBC was barraged with three thousand letters, and fans organized to create a public fund to sponsor the show.

Kukla, Fran and Ollie ran for a decade and was the first network program to be broadcast in color. But even with its great popularity, it had some difficulty finding sponsors. The show's audience ranged from four-year-olds to . . . much older. Companies like McDonald's didn't exist, and few products appealed to that wide an age range. In 1957 the show went off the air, although Tillstrom and his puppets did make appearances from time to time.

Incidentally—and I suspect you can win some bets with this little fact—the name *Kukla* was taken from the Greek word for *doll*.

As soon as stations realized there was an audience—and sponsors who would pay to reach that audience—children's programming exploded. At one point there were more than fourteen hundred children's programs on local TV stations. Producer Woody Fraser, who created *The Mike Douglas Show* and helped discover Regis, remembers, "Anyone working at a station that could be pressed into service to do children's programs did it. Sometimes it was the weatherman, sometimes it would be one of the news anchors. Those were the days when anchormen were playing clowns."

At least two programs did something very creative—they franchised their format to local stations. "The idea was to give children someone to identify with in their own city," Fraser explained. "As great as programs like *Howdy Doody* or *Captain Kangaroo* were, you weren't going to see them at the opening of your local supermarket, but you could run into Bozo the Clown, for example."

Kids could see Bozo the Clown at their local supermarket because there were lots of Bozos in the world—more Bozos than you can imagine. There were hundreds of Bozos. Bozo the Clown began life as a storyteller on a children's record in 1946. The popularity of the record convinced KTTV in Los Angeles to create *Bozo's Circus* three years later. Rather than selling the series around the country, they licensed the rights to the character and the format to local stations while advertising Bozo the Clown nationally. Each local market hired a Bozo of its own. In Washington, D.C., for example, Willard Scott, who later created the role of Ronald McDonald, was the local Bozo. The show itself was sort of a kids' variety show with cartoons, games and contests, scripted skits, and children's performers. Eventually there were Bozos on 240 stations in forty different countries.

Romper Room, a show for preschool kids that took place in a kindergarten classroom setting, allowed stations to choose between a syndicated version or creating a local telecast. The local telecast gave stations the advantage of having a local personality who could make personal appearances to promote the show. It was a well-run operation. Each local station would hire its own host, usually an elementary schoolteacher, and send her to Baltimore for a weeklong course in being a *Romper Room* host. If a local teacher was temporarily unable to host the show, a substitute host was flown in from Baltimore.

Parents enrolled their children in the local *Romper Room*, where the curriculum included subjects like finger painting and ring-around-the-rosy. Parents then filled out their own child's report card. If children were able to convince their own parents, who loved them deeply, to give them good marks, they were rewarded with a small prize given out only in special stores, which also happened to sell an entire line of *Romper Room* merchandise. Just think of the beauty of that deal. If you give your own child high marks, you get to take him to a store where you can spend a considerable sum of money on *Romper Room* products. If you give your child poor marks, he doesn't earn a prize, and you get his anger for the rest of your life. This was some TV show!

The show itself consisted of the usual collection of songs, games, and stories read by the hostess, Miss Whatever City. At one point there were more than 150 Miss Whatevers across America. The curriculum was scripted and carefully planned so that the hostesses in all cities taught the same material at the same time. And all the shows ended the same way. Miss Whatever looked through her magic mirror—a round frame on a handle—directly into the camera and spoke to specific children by their first names.

And, no, Willard Scott never played Miss Washington, D.C.

Within a few years every station was broadcasting several children's shows. The most basic show consisted simply of a host reading a picture book to a group of adoring children. On occasion a two-person cast would include an artist to illustrate scenes from the story as the host read the book. The more elaborate version was DuMont's *The Magic Cottage*. As the hostess, Pat Meikle, told a story, fairy-tale characters would emerge from her magic blackboard.

In addition to *Romper Room*, there were several television "schools." The most popular was NBC's *Miss Frances' Ding Dong*

Photo courtesy of AP images

Miss Frances' Ding Dong School was first broadcast in Chicago and quickly became so popular that it went National in November 1952. Although Frances Horwich began supervising all of NBC's children's programming in 1954, *Ding Dong School* was cancelled in 1956 and replaced by *The Price is Right.*

School, taught by Frances Rappapport Horwich and advertised as "The Nursery School of the Air." Miss Frances spoke directly to children and always had a project for them to do. She taught children how to grow a sweet potato or make animals from twisted pipe cleaners. She drew with kids and read to them, and 95 percent of all American preschoolers with access to TV sets were said to be attending *Ding Dong School* by 1953.

Children's programming also included puppet shows, circus shows, and fantasy shows. One of the most creative was *Mr. I. Magination,* in which host Paul Tripp played a train engineer who each week took his viewers to Inventorsville, Ambitionland, Seaport City, or I-Wish-I-Was-There Land, where they met everybody from test pilot Scott Crossfield, to other kids, to puppets who acted out the lives of historical characters. What set *Mr. I. Magination* apart was Tripp's inventive use of props. A washtub became the Atlantic Ocean, and a blue screen became the tunnel through which the train traveled to various fantasy lands. Tripp had a sizeable cast for a children's show, which included young actors Richard Boone and Walter Matthau, who dressed in costume to manipulate puppets and move props on the show. And some of the shows were directed by a young actor named Yul Brynner.

The Big Top, featuring Ed McMahon and His Merry Band of Clowns, was a popular children's show in Philadelphia—and a very good one, if I do say so myself. The show always started with me—it had to because I had the title printed on my bald clown's head—and ended with our strongman, Dan Lurie, Sealtest Dan the Muscle Man, who had the closing credits written on his muscles. In between we had acrobats and dog acts, jugglers and roller skaters, motorcycle racers and daredevils. It was a variety show for kids, who packed the Camden Convention Center every week. Our job was to keep them laughing for three minutes, several times each show. I created all of our bits, and most of them ended with my partner in mime, Chris

Keegan, getting hit or wet or knocked down or dumped on by a pile of sawdust or cornflakes or water. Whatever I did wrong, he suffered. If I picked up a ladder, he was going to get hit. If the bit involved water, he was going to get wet. If I picked up a heavy weight, he was going to get hit on the head. It was all very satisfying for me.

This is me on *The Big Top*, proving that those people who called me "a big clown" were absolutely correct. I starred on this children's show with my "Merry Band of Clowns."

I was on that show eight years before I hung up my nose for good. Compared to most children's shows, *The Big Top* was an elaborate production. We really did put on a circus every week.

Interestingly, although most elementary schoolteachers at that time were women, the two most enduring hosts of children's TV shows were men: Mr. Wizard and Captain Kangaroo. If you're wondering why the very popular Mr. Fred Rogers is not included, it's because he didn't move into his neighborhood until the late 1960s.

No children's program was more educational than *Watch Mr. Wizard*. Don Herbert, a former B-24 bomber pilot who flew fifty-six missions over Europe during World War II, came up with the concept of doing interesting science experiments on TV that could be done at home by kids.

(When I wrote that sentence, I couldn't help but remember when the great comedian Alan King told Johnny on *The Tonight Show* that he had recently bought a chemistry set for his teenage son, and it had been a terrible mistake. "Oh, really?" Johnny asked. "Why was it a mistake?"

"Because every time we have an argument," King explained, "the

Watch Mr. Wizard was very successful at making science exciting and understandable to children. Mr. Wizard was Don Herbert, and the show stayed on the air in original or repeated programming from 1951 until 2000.

kid picks up a full test tube, holds it over his head and screams, 'We'll all go together!'")

Watch Mr. Wizard began broadcasting on NBC's Chicago affiliate in 1951. It was considered public service, so none of the local stations carrying the show had to pay for what was, basically, a sixth-grade science class. Mr. Wizard and a young assistant performed experiments that were simple enough to do at home—such as showing how to get an egg inside a bottle without breaking it. He popped popcorn using infrared rays without breaking the cellophane covering. He showed how an airplane flies by tying a paper plane to a fan. Eventually there were more than fifty thousand Mr. Wizard science clubs across the country with a membership of more than half a million kids who tuned in to learn why a cake rises, what rain is, and how static electricity makes your hair stand up. Almost three hundred schools used the show as the basis of homework.

However, the do-it-at-home stuff sometimes got a bit sticky. Jeffrey from New Jersey wrote in 1955 to describe his effort to make an alcohol lamp using a milk bottle, just as Mr. Wizard had showed him. Unfortunately, rather than allowing the stick—the makeshift wick—sufficient time to become saturated in alcohol, his mother had lit it too soon. The resulting explosion blew out the kitchen window, Jeffrey complained, and bits of the bottle smashed into the front of the house across the street.

Johnny enjoyed having Don Herbert on *The Tonight Show*. He always brought an experiment with him that only a kid could do— and Johnny would become the kid. One night Mr. Wizard became the first person to electrocute a pickle on national television by running a current through the pickle. The pickle juice carried the current, and the whole pickle lit up.

Watch Mr. Wizard was cancelled by NBC in 1964, but between 1983 and 1991 Don Herbert hosted *Mr. Wizard's World* for Nickelodeon. *Mr. Wizard's World* ran in reruns until 2000, making it the longest-running show in Nick's history.

And now, boys and girls, it's time for the question and answer part of our book.
Knock knock.
(You) Who's there?
Alaska.
(You) Alaska who?
Alaska to duck, 'cause here they come.
(Then a whole load of Ping-Pong balls drops on poor Captain Kangaroo's head.)

OK, how about this poem?
Roses are red, violets are blue,
I like it most, when Ping-Pong balls fall on you!
(And then a whole load of Ping-Pong balls drops on poor Captain Kangaroo's head.)

OK, OK, I've just got one more.

Knock knock.

(You) Who's there?

Reddy.

(You) Reddy who?

Reddy or not, here they come!

Absolutely the most violence any kid was going to see on *Captain Kangaroo* was when a whole load of Ping-Pong balls dropped on the poor Captain's head. OK, one more, but this time let me give credit to the proper characters:

Mister Moose: Knock knock.

Captain Kangaroo: *Hmm*. Who's there?

Mister Moose: Jessie.

Captain Kangaroo: Jessie who?

Mister Moose: Jessie any Ping-Pong balls around here?

Bob Keeshan became the mop-haired, walrus-mustached, big-bellied, grandfatherly Captain Kangaroo several years after creating the character of Clarabell on *Howdy Doody*. He believed that there should be a show for kids that was less frantic, quieter, softer, slower paced, gentler, calmer, nicer, sweeter, and warmer than *Howdy*—and just about every other kids' show on the air at the time.

Captain Kangaroo—the name came from the fact that he wore a jacket with very large pockets—went on the air weekday mornings in October 1955 and lasted until 1984. Not very much happened on the show, and it didn't happen five mornings a week on CBS for thirty years, making *Captain Kangaroo* the longest-running children's series in network history.

There were people who criticized Johnny Carson for doing the same show every night—claiming that all he did was tell a few jokes and then speak to a few guests. That's sort of like complaining that Marilyn Monroe didn't have perfect teeth. And there were people who criticized the Captain for doing the same show every single day, day after day, week after week, year after year. Well, he did, and kids loved it. The show opened to the jingle of the keys to the Treasure House. And for the rest of the hour, Captain Kangaroo would walk through the Treasure House, stopping to talk with familiar characters

Bob Keeshan, who created the character of Clarabell on *Howdy Doody*, became the mop-haired, walrus-mustached, big-bellied, grandfatherly Captain Kangaroo for nearly thirty years—from 1955 until 1984.

like Mister Green Jeans, who would have with him an adorable domestic animal (anything from a midget pony to a kinkajou); Mister Moose, who inevitably was going to trick poor Captain Kangaroo into saying the terrible words "Ping-Pong balls"; the greedy Bunny Rabbit, who would manage to get carrots from the kindly Captain; Miss Worm; Mister Bainter the Painter; and Dancing Bear.

And then at some point Captain Kangaroo would need the answer to a question and suggest, "Let's go ask Grandfather," and wake up the grandfather clock, who would usually have a poem for the boys and girls at home.

And then the Captain would show a cartoon, most often starring Tom Terrific, who would change into a variety of shapes to save his adorable but very lazy dog, Mighty Manfred the Wonder

Dog, from the evil Crabby Appleton, a villain who was admittedly rotten to his core.

And then, the Captain would read out loud. From a book. Sometimes from the same book he had read several times before. Books like *Caps for Sale, Mike Mulligan and His Steam Shovel, The Little Red Lighthouse and the Great Gray Bridge,* and *Make Way for Ducklings.* Captain Kangaroo provided all the sound effects himself as he read.

And then he might even have a real person visit, like Bill Cosby, who showed up often at the Treasure House. And Captain Kangaroo always had good advice for all of us: "Remember the magic phrases 'please' and 'thank you.' Always have good manners, respect other people, and play fair. Be nice to animals."

And it worked. Kids loved him. More importantly, parents loved him. At one point when CBS threatened to cancel the show, more than ten thousand parents protested, causing CBS to cancel the cancellation because, as a network exec admitted, "We were terrified of the mothers." Maybe he remembered the advice that the Captain gave at the end of every show: "It's another Be-Good-to-Mother Day."

Kids? I love kids? Did I ever tell you the one about the three kids who walked into a bar mitzvah? One of them had a duck on his head and . . .

Milton, this is neither the time nor the space.

So I guess you don't want to know what the duck said to the rabbi?

Let's just ignore him.

At the other end of the children's show universe was *Lunch with Soupy Sales.* This was a wild, raucous, irreverent show filled with bad jokes and puns and slapstick, much of it improvised, and almost always ending with Soupy getting hit in the face with a pie.

Soupy had hosted the first teenage dance show in America in 1950. Interestingly, the owner of the Cincinnati station who fired him also fired at the same time a young writer named Rod Serling. He got rid of two of the most creative guys in early TV at once! Not a wise decision. Soupy followed that with *Club Nothing!*, a basic talk show that gave him his first sense of television freedom. In 1953 *Lunch with Soupy Sales,* a local Detroit show, made Soupy the most popular TV personality in that city. Eventually he moved to Los Angeles, and ABC broadcast the show nationally, the first and only Saturday morning show on the network *without* cartoons.

In many ways *Lunch with Soupy Sales* was a parody of children's shows. Other kids' shows had the usual characters—sweet puppets and costumed actors—but *Lunch with Soupy* had unusual characters. White Fang, the Meanest Dog in the USA, was so big that the only part of him that fit onto the screen was a giant white paw. Black Tooth, the Sweetest Dog in the World, was seen only as a giant black paw. Both Fang and Tooth spoke in grunts, which only Soupy Sales could under-stand and interpret. The other puppet characters included Hippie the Hippo and Pookie the Lion. Regulars included Soupy's girlfriend, Peaches, played by Soupy in drag; private detective Philo Kvetch, also played by Soupy; The Mask; and the infamous Onions Oregano, not played by Soupy.

During each show there

Courtesy of Stephen Cox Collection

The unpredictable Soupy Sales' real name was Milton Supman, which he changed to Milton Heinz in recognition of his sponsor. As a comedian who sold soup it was natural that he become Soupy Sales. His shows were wild and raucous and almost always ended with Soupy getting hit in the face with a pie.

would be a knock at the door in the rear of the set, and behind it would be a mystery guest. Often it would be a pretty famous celebrity—even Frank Sinatra, Sammy Davis Jr., and Tony Curtis made guest appearances—who got hit in the face with a pie. For a time, getting hit in the face with a pie on *Lunch with Soupy Sales* became a bit of a status symbol in Hollywood. Other times it would be a character, such as a visiting psychiatrist. "Tell me, Doc," Soupy would ask him. "Is it possible for a man to be in love with an elephant?"

"No," the psychiatrist would say flatly. "A man cannot be in love with an elephant."

"In that case," Soupy would reply, holding up a silver hoop that looked like a bicycle wheel, "do you know where I can get rid of this engagement ring?"

But no matter what happened, and to whom it happened, the end result would be . . . a pie in the face.

The show ran, with interruptions, through 1966. Eventually it was syndicated. Soupy Sales had a big hit record, "The Mouse," and a dance that went with it. He appeared in a movie comedy, *Birds Do It*.

But the event for which Soupy Sales will live forever in TV lore, an event that many people believe was the greatest ad-lib in television history, happened on New Year's Day in 1965. Apparently upset that he had to do the show on a holiday, and with about five minutes to fill at the end of the show, he suddenly whispered to his young viewers that they should sneak into their still-sleeping parents' bedroom, take their father's wallet out of his pants on the floor, and "take out those funny pieces of paper with pictures on them, and put them in an envelope and mail them to me at Channel 5 in New York. And you know what I'm going to send you? A postcard from Puerto Rico!"

He got a two-week suspension from the network and a little cash—from a twenty-seven-year-old who wrote that if Soupy Sales really did take the money and move to Puerto Rico, it would be the best money she ever spent.

While the ability of computers to react to feedback has made the word *interactive* common today, a truly creative and truly interactive children's show ran from 1953 to 1957: *Winky Dink and You*, hosted by Jack Barry. A kid would send off fifty cents and receive a "Magic Window"—a piece of transparent plastic to put on the TV screen—a few crayons, and a cloth. Jack Barry would tell the children where to draw on the Magic Window and then everyone would say the Magic Word, "Winko!" and the lines the kid had just drawn would become part of a bridge, for instance, that Winky Dink would use to walk across a river.

The problem was that some kids never bothered to send in their fifty cents and just used their own crayons—right on the TV screen. Columnist Ken Beck says that when his father discovered what he had done, he "got a spanking from Pop later that night. It took a lot of scrubbing to get those crayon marks off." Creativity has its cost.

The one thing that just about every kids' show had in common was that they showed cartoons. The cartoons weren't considered art, and they weren't considered clever, but kids loved them. At first, the TV cartoons were movie cartoons that were so old they were out of copyright.

Farmer Al Falfa, also known as Farmer Alfalfa, was created in 1916 and was a star of silent movies, who became successful on TV. He changed his name for a time (to Farmer Gray) and eventually even got his own show, *Farmer Alfalfa and His Terrytoon Pals*. The plots were all very similar. Farmer Alfalfa is tormented by sadistic mice. He tries to kill them in every possible way, but they won't die, and they come back, more than ever before—thousands of them—attacking him, climbing out of his sink and bathtub, crawling all over him even as he swats them into the wall, an endless number of them. The cartoons consisted of very simple black-and-white animation—mostly mice.

Eventually producers started making original cartoons. In New York, Herb Sheldon went on the air with *Kids Today* in 1946 and for more than a decade hosted several different cartoon shows—including Sandy Becker's three-hour-long weekend show, *Wonderama*. Ray Heatherton became *The Merry Mailman*, in which, dressed as a mailman and standing in front of a curtain, he introduced old movie cartoons. Later he added songs, stories, performers, some sketches, and even healthcare advice. Kids who wanted more of an authority figure than a mailman to introduce their cartoons could turn the dial and watch Officer Joe Bolton on *Clubhouse Gang*.

William Hanna and Joe Barbera created many of the memorable cartoon shows for early television, including *The Huckleberry Hound Show*, *Yogi Bear* (who was "smarter than the average bear"), *The Ruff and Reddy Show*, and *Jonny Quest* (and later *The Jetsons* and *The Smurfs Adventures*).

The best thing about cartoon characters for many network executives was that they never demanded to renegotiate their contracts, never complained about working on holidays, didn't eat much, never needed makeup, and never used drugs or alcohol. Even better, cartoons could be broadcast over and over with no loss of quality, unlike kinescopes. Among the many cartoon characters who appealed to kids—and truthfully, to a lot of adults also—were Quick Draw McGraw, Little Audrey, Magilla Gorilla, Underdog, and, of course, Jay Ward's Rocky and Bullwinkle. Bugs Bunny even got his own show, the *Bugs Bunny Theater*, as did the Looney Tunes family.

Andy's Gang, hosted by the raspy-voiced big galoot Andy Devine, was a Saturday morning children's variety show that included movie serials and other features to make it different from other early shows with just cartoons. Andy was a veteran movie character actor who had played Wild Bill Hickok's lovable sidekick, Jingles. When the show first went on the air in 1950 it was known as *Smilin' Ed's Gang*, hosted by Ed McConnell, but Devine took over five years later, and the name changed. One thing was constant—the sponsor was always Buster Brown shoes. Buster Brown's theme song opened the show and was probably the best-known kids' commercial. It began with Buster greeting the audience, "Hi. I'm Buster Brown, I live in a shoe. This is my dog, Tige. He lives there too!" And then he sang the song, "I got shoes, you got shoes . . ." C'mon everybody! "Everybody's got to have shoes, but there's only one kind of shoes for meeeeeee!" Shout it out! Let me hear you! "Good old Buster Brown!"

The show consisted of Andy introducing episodes of a serial— which usually featured an Indian boy named Gunga and his friend Rama, who had more problems each week with elephants than most people have in a lifetime—telling some stories, and eventually having a chat with puppet characters. These were very strange puppet characters. In fact, I suspect that one of the reasons kids liked *Andy's Gang* was because his TV gang wasn't really very nice. It was led by the really nasty Froggy the Gremlin, a tuxedo-wearing frog; Midnight the Cat, who wore a kind of sad dress and danced awkwardly; Grandie the talking piano; and a hamster named Squeeky the Mouse. And, no, I don't know why the hamster was called "the mouse" either.

Each week Froggy would appear out of thick air—a cloud of smoke—to the words "Plunk your magic twanger, Froggy," and create trouble by causing the guest to do something incredibly stupid. If an opera singer was on the show to explain how to paint a wall, she would say, "And now I'm going to take this can of paint and . . ."

Froggy would finish the sentence, "dump it over my head. Hee hee hee."

And then she would.

The guest would turn angrily to Froggy and take a swipe at him, but he would disappear in a puff of smoke, safe to reappear and be the foil for the next week's guest.

The ultimate children's variety show—the most memorable of them all, the show that all these years later will *still* make adults stand up and start singing proudly—was a club with a very special leader. "Who's the leader of the club that's made for you and me?" (Admit it, you can't even read it without singing it in your mind.)

M-I-C, K-E-Y, M-O-U-S-E

Hey there, hi there, ho there,
You're as welcome as can be!
M-I-C, K-E-Y, M-O-U-S-E

Mickey Mouse! Donald Duck!
Mickey Mouse! Donald Duck!
Forever let us hold our banners high.
High! High! High!

Come along and sing a song
And join the jamboree
M-I-C, K-E-Y, M-O-U-S-E

The *Mickey Mouse Club* was created by Walt Disney and was to kids what *American Bandstand* was to teenagers. It was the show kids had to watch every day. The club was a variety show with the requisite cartoons, a filmed adventure serial, music, comedy, dancing, and performances. The members of this club consisted of a group of kids just like you and me—except they were better looking and more talented and starred on TV—called the Mouseketeers. These Mouseketeers wore a simple T-shirt and, most important, Mickey Mouse ears. Kids actually wore those ears proudly!

The ears were molded to fit each kid's head. It was tough for some of the boys to wear those ears because most of them were wearing pompadours. The ears were supposed to be worn straight up, but the boys pushed them back as soon as the show started. If a Mouseketeer lost his or her ears, that child was fined twenty-five dollars, and when the Mouseketeers toured, fans were always trying to steal the ears.

The show was hosted by the freckle-faced Head Mouseketeer, Jimmie Dodd. The most loyal club viewers had a favorite Mouseketeer, the most popular being Annette Funicello and Darlene Gillespie.

The original Mickey Mouse club, with Head Mouseketeer Jimmy Dodd, ran for only four years in the 1950s. It was revived in the 1970s and again from 1989 to 1994.

From the Author's Collection

Among the other favorite Mousketeers were Doreen Tracy, Cubby O'Brien, Tommy Cole, and Cheryl Holdridge.

The show started in 1955 and, amazingly, was on the air for only four years. It was an incredibly short run for a show that has had the impact on the memories of so many people for so long. It was an hour show the first two seasons, but its final year was only a half-hour long.

The club was on five days a week and each day had a theme: Monday was Fun with Music, and Wednesday was Anything-Can-Happen Day. The Talent Round-Up was Friday. The serials were all original stories and had Disney production quality. The most popular was *Spin and Marty*, the adventures of two kids at a summer camp called the Triple R Ranch. There were three different serials, each of them consisting of twenty-five ten-minute segments.

The popularity of the show led to its being revived, the last time in 1989 as *The New Mickey Mouse Club*. What made that show so memorable was that the Mouseketeers included Britney Spears, Christina Aguilera, Justin Timberlake, Melissa Joan Hart, and Keri Russell. How about that for a talent discovery show?

And, finally, the never-to-be-forgotten ending of the original program, and this chapter:

Now it's time to say good-bye to all our company,

M-I-C . . . See you real soon!

K-E-Y . . . Why? Because we like you.

M-O-U-S-E.

Divorce Hearing was one of the first reality programs
. . . We would advertise in local newspapers for
couples who had filed for divorce and pay them
$150 to appear on the show. . . The stated goal was
to keep couples together. In reality we wanted them
to fight for the camera.

One couple I'll never forget was separating
because the husband was always drunk and his wife
was always complaining. The day of the show the
husband did a terrible thing—he came in sober. Our
producers took the guy to Diamond Jim's, the bar
next door, listening sympathetically as they bought
drinks for him. By the time the show started, the
guy was smashed. Seeing him like that, his wife
became irate. They started screaming at each other,
and the future was secure for all those shows that
exploit human relations.

—DAVID WOLPER, PRODUCER

A MERICAN IDOL, DANCING WITH THE STARS, THE WHOLE
Nickelodeon channel, *Law & Order, Deal or No Deal*—just
about all of the most popular programs on TV can trace their creative
roots back to the earliest days and nights of television.

By the mid-1950s there were three big networks—CBS, NBC, and, trailing behind, ABC. DuMont, the fourth network, closed down in 1956, keeping several independent stations and eventually changing its name to Metromedia. While the networks dominated television, a lot of independent stations desperately needed programming, so independent producers created all types of shows and sold them on a market-by-market basis. *TV Guide* explained the way the future would work: "[In 1949] actor Jon Hall got into his head that television was the coming thing and he better do something about it. The Columbia Picture star of *Ali Baba and the 40 Thieves* and *Arabian Nights* had been turning out three profitable pictures a year. When Columbia executives got wind of his defection they said to him, 'Television is for has-beens and never-will-bes. Why throw over a sure thing for what at best is a wild gamble?' The result is *Ramar of the Jungle* . . . It's a syndicated show. It sold in about seventy-five markets, and Hall made more money as Ramar than he ever did as a motion picture star. As he said, 'The pictures I made will never make another dime for me, but Ramar has the earmarks of being a gilt-edge annuity.'"

Both the independent producers as well as the networks churned out as much programming as fast as they could to fill the incredibly expanding TV world. When the networks started broadcasting from early morning until late night, the independent stations had to compete by also providing all-day programming. This was a great situation for people like me because I was young and had enough experience to do the job, whatever job it was that needed doing. These were generally shows that required few production elements, a small crew, and could be created very quickly. They were usually broadcast five days a week. A lot of these shows relied on the fact that ordinary people were desperate to be on TV. That was part of the magic of the camera; it could cause nice, even shy people to do things they would never do in their real lives. Or it could bring out a wonderful aspect of their personalities. The possibility that anything could happen was what made these shows so popular. And since human nature has not changed in the last sixty years, television producers today create the same sort of shows they did then.

One such kind of programming was that old entertainment staple the talent show, which had the tremendous advantage that *you didn't have to pay for the talent*! Talent shows offered the elusive hope to viewers that the next contestant might be a big future star. Talent shows also offered humor provided by the so-called talent of some of the contestants. And talent shows—especially local talent shows—offered the interest provided by contestants' family and friends rooting for the competition.

Years later I hosted one of the most successful of the pre-*American Idol* talent shows, the hour-long syndicated *Star Search*. Each week we had eight categories, and two people competed in each category, with the winner returning the following week. One thing I learned was how much undiscovered talent exists all over the country—and how badly people want to be discovered. Our first season on the air we auditioned twenty thousand acts and eventually had 170 people compete on the air. At our casting call in Minneapolis, seven thousand potential contestants stood in line for as long as a day; four thousand young people showed up in Los Angeles. If the *Star Search* bus on which we toured stopped at a traffic light, I would look out, and people on the sidewalk would start dancing. We discovered a gold mine of talent over the years—Rosie O'Donnell, Sinbad, Martin Lawrence, Drew Carey, LeAnn Rimes, Sam Harris, Kevin Meaney, Carrot Top, Lara Flynn Boyle, Dennis Miller, Keith Washington, Alanis Morissette, Aaliyah, Christina Aguilera, Jessica Simpson, Ray Romano, and Justin Timberlake. And the person who introduced our spokesmodel category was a young actress named Sharon Stone. At one point *Star Search* was syndicated to almost two hundred stations.

Courtesy of Stephen Cox Collection

As host of the talent show *Star Search*, I was joined (left) by my friend John Ritter and (right) by a celebrated discovery, Sinbad.

And all we really did was repackage one of the oldest formats in the entertainment business. *The Major Bowes Original Amateur Hour*, a half-hour program that went on the air in 1934, was one of radio's most popular shows. It featured all types of acts, from really talented young singers to a female violinist who clacked her false teeth to keep the rhythm for her music, and from Frank Sinatra to a contestant who made music by banging on his skull with a mallet. Listeners voted for their choice by postcard or a telephone call, and winners returned the following week to compete against another round of contestants. Almost three-quarters of a million acts auditioned for the *Amateur Hour*, and winners became part of several touring units that performed at county fairs, convention halls, and local theaters. At one point there were five units touring the country.

When Major Bowes died, Ted Mack, one of the talent scouts, took over on both radio and, starting in 1948, the DuMont Television

Network. *Ted Mack's Original Amateur Hour* stayed on the air until 1970, becoming one of very few shows to be broadcast on all four networks.

"My mother was a dance teacher in Brooklyn," Penny Marshall remembered, "and had this group I danced in, the Marshallettes. When we appeared on the *Amateur Hour*, it wasn't very glamorous. All I remember is that we did our number, then we sat down, and Pat Boone came in. Then people would call in and say, 'We're at a party and there are 120 people here and we all vote for the Marshallettes.' OK, that's 120 votes for the Marshallettes. It seemed like we were always competing against people with unusual acts, like a one-armed piano player. But that's how we became three-time winners." A typical show might have included a comedy impersonator, a Spanish dancer, a female saxophone player, a singer, a band, a baton twirler, and a tap dancer.

Among multiple winners on Ted Mack were ventriloquist Paul Winchell and singer Pat Boone. Boone caused just a little bit of a scandal when he appeared on a second talent show, *Arthur Godfrey's Talent Scouts*. *Talent Scouts* went on TV in 1948 and was different from *Ted Mack* in that contestants were discovered by talent scouts, and so many of them weren't amateurs, just unknowns. The studio audience voted for the winners by their applause, which was measured by the official applause meter. Boone was a winner on both shows, which meant that technically he wasn't an amateur.

Courtesy of Stephen Cox Collection

Ted Mack (right), here with famed quiz show host, sportscaster, and announcer Dennis James, hosted *The Original Amateur Hour* after the death of the show's creator, Major Bowes.

Godfrey's *Talent Scouts* helped introduce such great performers to the public as Tony Bennett, Connie Francis, Steve Lawrence, Lenny Bruce, Patsy Cline (who literally broke the applause meter), Al Martino (who also appeared on my show in Philly), Leslie Uggams, and Roy Clark. Of course, Arthur Godfrey's talent scouts missed a few too; they turned down Elvis Presley and Buddy Holly. And while the winner of *American Idol* gets a real shot at fortune and fame, Godfrey's winners won three guest appearances on his morning program!

The great announcer and *Price Is Right* host Bob Barker explained his start in talent shows: "In Los Angeles I did a talent show called *Your Big Moment*. No one came out of the show and went on to play Broadway or anything like that, but we had some talented people on that show. Sometimes, though, we weren't completely booked, and I remember the producer going around to bars in Hollywood looking for someone to fill in." Think about that one, a televised talent show in Hollywood that didn't have enough talent. If there is anything that accurately illustrates the perceived lack of importance of early TV, that is it.

In 1950 another well-known game show host, Robert Q. Lewis, opened CBS's talent show, *The Show Goes On*. One of the young talents he presented was comedian Nipsey Russell. Because there was still a lot of prejudice in TV and America in 1950, putting the African American Nipsey Russell on a show said a lot about Nipsey's talent—and about CBS.

Hollywood Screen Test, which went on the air in 1948, had relatively unknown young actors do scenes or read dialogue with established performers. That doesn't sound too impressive until you find out that Grace Kelly, Jack Klugman, Pernell Roberts, and Jack Lemmon all got their first breaks on this show. Within a year of his appearance on *Hollywood Screen Test*, Jack Lemmon was hosting his own variety-talent show, the *Toni Twin Time*.

Nineteen fifty-three's *Talent Patrol* was a military talent show hosted by Steve Allen, and it gave its winner a night out in Los Angeles with a pretty actress. *Chance of a Lifetime* was originally a quiz show, but when it failed, they simply bought an applause meter and transformed it into a talent show. Conversely, *Judge for Yourself* started as a talent show hosted by Fred Allen, on which an amateur panel and a show business panel judged acts. When it failed, it became a quiz show with Dennis James.

Dancing with the Stars is only the most recent of a long history of dance shows and traces its creative roots back to the 1956 *Step This Way*, a four-week contest in which couples competed for a trip to Bermuda. Dance shows were very popular with syndicators and local stations because they were inexpensive to produce, people liked to dance, they loved to dance with other people watching them, and these shows had strong local appeal.

The most successful such network show was *The Arthur Murray Party*, which was broadcast at different times by all four networks and ran for a decade beginning in 1950. It was basically an advertisement for the Arthur Murray chain of dance studios. Each week they would teach a celebrity a new dance step, and the first viewer to identify a secret dance won *two* lessons at the dance studio. Nanette Fabrey was on the show several times. "Arthur was very strange," she admits. "He sort of had the personality of a dry mop—and each show ended with him facing the camera, forcing a smile, and saying somewhat sheepishly, 'Kathryn [his wife] told me to smile.'"

There were many local versions of the Arthur Murray show, and just about every large city in the Midwest had a version of *Polka Party* and *Square Dancing Tonight!* Even in New York Frances Buss remembers directing an early 1940s show, *Country Dance Society of America*, hosted by May Gadd. "They would do rounds and squares to recorded music for an hour. It was pretty dull, I think."

The most popular of all dance shows, the show that ran for thirty years and influenced generations, the greatest rock-and-roll TV show of all time, was the one, the only, Dick Clark's *American Bandstand.* At least with my teenage daughter, Claudia, it was the one and only. *American Bandstand* was a phenomenon. It was the first TV show that every teenager in America had to see. It was sort of like America's high school, where everybody got involved with the lives of the regulars on the show, and a single appearance by a young singer could make him or her a star.

Bandstand wasn't the first dance show for teenagers. The first, *Soupy's Soda Shop,* began in Cincinnati in 1950 and was hosted by the young comedian Soupy Sales. The format immediately caught on. What could be more basic than kids and music and dancing, particularly that new music, rock and roll? *American Bandstand* was the Philadelphia version of Soupy's show and went on the air in 1952, hosted by two local disc jockeys. At first they just showed Snader Telescriptions, three-and-a-half-minute black-and-white minifilms of performers singing their songs that were made for sale to TV stations. Essentially, they were very early music videos. "The station bought these films," Dick Clark remembered, "and they didn't know what to do with them. So they brought in two local disc jockeys and told them to just play them. It was boring. So they let kids from the neighborhood come in. The kids watched for a while and then got up and started dancing. The director, Lee Davis, showed the kids dancing. They started getting telephone calls; kids wanted to see more of that. A lot of the films didn't work with the kids dancing, so eventually they dropped the films. There were no great minds behind any of what happened."

Dick Clark was working as a disc jockey on the radio version of *Bandstand,* and would occasionally fill in for the regular host of the TV show, Bob Horn. When Horn was arrested for drunk driving in

Courtesy of Library of Congress, New York World-Telegram and the Sun Newspaper Photography Collection

The man who launched 10,000 teenage romances, created America's greatest dance show, welcomed in countless New Years, produced numerous television shows—and arranged my first meeting with Johnny Carson—is my friend, the legendary Dick Clark. Here Clark (right) is twisting the afternoon away with rock legends Conway Twitty and Chubby Checker.

1956, Clark took over the TV show. It was still a local Philadelphia show, "But then we got a nine-week commitment from the local ABC affiliate," Clark remembered. "It was a nine-week test. Four weeks later, almost to the day, *American Bandstand* was the number one day-time show in the country. We had substantially fewer affiliates than either NBC or CBS, but we still beat them.

"In those days you learned about the music by the seat of your pants. We didn't have surveys; we didn't have electronic media. We talked on the phone to fellow disc jockeys. That's how we determined what was hot. I would get a call from a black friend of mine in Philadelphia, Georgie Woods. We'd talk three or four times a week, and he would tell me what the black kids liked. I thought, well, if the black kids like it, I know the white kids are going to like it. And it worked. *Bandstand* became a hit maker because radio disc jockeys and program directors listened to it. So simultaneously several hundred radio stations and the most important kids' television stations were all playing the same music."

Bandstand influenced American culture in many ways, but none more significant than in bringing black kids and white kids together on live TV. Clark explained that at first, "we had very few, very few blacks kids on the show. We lived in Philadelphia; it was a segregated community. There was no rule that they shouldn't come, no formal station policy, but if you were black in those days, you just didn't do that.

"But in 1957 or 1958 a guy named Tony Memoralla brought in some black kids. I can remember the very first time I talked to a black teenager on national television. It was on the rate-a-record portion of *Bandstand* in which kids listened to a record and gave it a rating. I talked to the black kid, the show ended, and for the first time in a hundred years, I got sweaty palms. Being on television doesn't make me very nervous. But that day I was sweating because I didn't know what the reaction would be with the southern affiliates. Sure enough, there wasn't a phone call; there wasn't a protest. From that day on we began to get more black kids in the studio. And when the show moved from Philadelphia to L.A. we had blacks, Mexicans, Chinese, every color of the rainbow, and the lovely part of it was we didn't do it because we were do-gooders. It was just a thing we ought to do, and it worked. And if the whole world could have done it that way, wouldn't it have been great? That was probably the show's greatest contribution, bringing blacks and whites together in a social atmosphere."

American Bandstand stayed on the air, mostly as a weekly show, for more than thirty years, one of the longest runs in TV history. "We went through the '60s protest era into the '70s disco era, and into the

1980s," Clark said. "Eventually we took it into cable television. In its last days it was done at Universal's amusement park, in a parking lot in daytime with no lights and bare sets. It was a tough grind. I looked at it one day and realized I really didn't want *American Bandstand* to be remembered that way. So it was my decision, or at least it was mutual, just to let it go. I'm sorry I did. If I just would have waited three more months, we would have been on the air in five different decades, from the 1950s to the '90s. That would have been wonderful."

While the girls were dancing, the boys were watching the numerous adventure shows, several of them set in outer space. These space heroes came from pulp magazines for boys, from comic books, from radio shows, and even from motion picture serials. The hero was almost always put in terrible jeopardy. For example, he and his entire crew might be knocked unconscious by an evil doctor and tied to the seats of their space rocket, which would be hurtling directly into the sun at supersonic speeds. The sun would grow bigger and bigger. There is no hope of survival until . . .

I'm sorry, but you will have to wait until my next book to learn if our hero survives.

The most popular space shows included *Buck Rogers, Flash Gordon, Tom Corbett—Space Cadet, Space Patrol,* and *Captain Video and his Video Rangers.* These shows were the forerunners of shows like *Star Trek, Lost in Space,* and *Battlestar Galactica. Captain Video,* whose mission was to stop the evil, hand-rubbing, crazed Dr. Pauli of the Astrodial Society from destroying the earth, was launched in 1949. It was TV's first science-fiction show and one of its first real hits. Among his crew were the teenaged Ranger and Tobor, the first space robot in a live series. For several years this show pretty much kept the entire DuMont network in business. It was done live, but sometime during each half hour, Captain Video would check his space scanner, which, no matter where they were in the solar system,

Courtesy of Stephen Cox Collection

One of the most popular early kids' shows, *Space Patrol*, featured the adventures of Commander Buzz Corey and the crew of the spaceship *Terra*. The show was on live five days a week and introduced props like space-o-phones and atom-o-lights—marking the beginning of TV merchandising—as well as ingenious special effects. For instance, firing a ray gun—get yours today kids!—resulted in a pre-planted charge exploding.

was incredibly and amazingly able to pick up from earth at least five minutes of an old western movie, which was described as the adventures of Captain Video's "undercover agents." *Captain Video* was also one of the first shows to be criticized for its excessive violence. But, gee willikers, if you can't use excessive violence to save the earth, when could you use it?

Like all the other children's shows, *Captain Video's* production values ranged between nonexistent and ridiculously cheap. The show was initially broadcast from a New York studio a couple of floors above Wanamaker's department store, and on occasion, when a prop was needed, a crew member would go downstairs and borrow it. To show the results of an explosion, the cameraman would jiggle the camera and production assistants would toss white powder on the set. But kids believed in the truth and virtue of Captain Video. In fact, once the actor who played the evil Dr. Pauli was pelted by stones when he stepped off the subway on his way home. Although the show was produced on the cheap, there was true gold among the scriptwriters: Arthur C. Clarke, Isaac Asimov, Cyril M. Kornbluth, Robert Sheckley, Damon Knight, and Jack Vance. This was the science-fiction version of Sid Caesar's comedy writers' room, but in the contributions they made to this world, the *Captain Video* writing staff was perhaps even more important. Captain Video was the first TV character to become a movie, actually a fifteen-part serial, *Captain Video, Master of the Stratosphere*, in which he traveled to the planet Atoma to battle the evil Vultura.

Space Patrol featured the thirtieth-century adventures of a United Planets of the Universe crew, under the leadership of Commander Buzz Corey, who roamed through space on his spaceship *Terra*, dispatching villains to the United Planets Medical Science Center, where evil was brainwashed out of their minds. *Space Patrol* was so popular that it was on locally—in Los Angeles—five days a week, nationally on ABC twice a week, and on radio twice a week. And then it became a comic book.

Although most of the costumes were recycled from old movie serials, and the female assistant chief of security's costume had been made by her mother, *Space Patrol* was one of the most financially successful TV shows in history. Let me write that again. *Space Patrol* was one of the most financially successful TV shows in history.

"Shootin' rockets," as Buzz might exclaim, "what in the universe are you talking about?" *Space Patrol's* sponsor was Ralston Purina, which had been radio's most successful supplier of premiums with its Tom Mix radio series, and it quickly turned *Space Patrol* into an out-of-this-world merchandise gold mine. For a few cereal box tops and some loose change, kids could buy a whole world of premiums, that world being the world of the spaceship *Terra*. Other shows had decoder rings and ray guns and space helmets, but Buzz Correy offered cardboard mock-ups of a space city or the rocket cockpit—with nine moving parts!—magnifying goggles, periscopes, microscopes, space phones, paralyzing ray guns that sent their victims into suspended animation, code belts, puzzles, space helmets, clothes, comic books, and a cosmic smoke gun that shot a cloud of sleep-inducing smoke that smelled suspiciously like talcum powder. "Just like Buzz Corey shoots people with, kids!" There were eighty different premiums. Many were sold in grocery stores and department stores or, always, by mail. In 1952 Ralston Purina estimated revenue from the sale of *Space Patrol* merchandise to be $40 million. That's $40 million in 1952 dollars! It was certainly more money than any other show of that time could generate. And more than most of today's shows as well, by the way.

Also in 1952 Ralston Purina ran the Name That Planet contest, one of the biggest promotions in the entire six-year history of network TV, and awarded the winner the grandest prize of all: a $30,000, thirty-five-foot-long, one-ton replica of the *Terra V*—which slept six—and the trailer on which it was mounted. Now, I know a thing or two about giveaways because for two decades I knocked on doors to tell people they had won the American Family Publisher's Sweepstakes. I saw reactions from complete disbelief—"Are you really Ed McMahon?"—to total euphoria. But I can't even imagine the reaction I would have received if I had shown up at a stranger's front door with a thirty-five-foot-long, one-ton replica of a rocket ship sitting in his driveway. At least, I hope the person who won it had a driveway. I don't know how someone would have gotten it into an apartment.

Before *Heroes*, it was a time for heroes. In addition to space heroes, kids' shows featured cowboy heroes, military heroes, and the greatest superhero of all, *Superman*—"Faster than a speeding bullet! More powerful than a locomotive! Able to leap tall buildings with a single bound. Look! Up in the sky! It's a bird. It's a plane! It's Superman!

"Yes, it's Superman . . . strange visitor from another planet, who came to the earth with powers far beyond those of mortal men! Superman, who can change the course of mighty rivers, bend steel in his bare hands, and who, disguised as Clark Kent, mild-mannered reporter for a great metropolitan newspaper, fights a never-ending battle for . . ."

Are you ready? Big finish here.

". . . Truth! Justice! And the American way."

Every kid knew Superman. He had sprung into existence as the subject of a comic book in 1938, then became a popular radio show, the star of feature-length cartoons, fifteen movie serials, and finally a feature film. Superman was perfect for television. National Comics produced the syndicated half-hour show beginning in 1951 starring B-movie actor George Reeves. The budget was very small, so the actors usually wore the same costume in every show so that footage from one show could be used in other shows. Sets were often whatever had been used in the last movie filmed on that particular soundstage, and special effects were not exactly special. Superman leaped in flight, for example, by jumping off a springboard. He landed by climbing the steps of a five-foot ladder out of camera range and jumping into the scene. He flew by lying on a table facing a fan as a rear-projection screen behind him seemed to show him in flight—although often it showed just clouds.

Courtesy of Photo/Ipol/Globe Photos, Inc.

Like so many B-movie actors, Reeves took the role for the salary, which was minimal, and he was only paid while the show was actually filming. The attitude in the film industry was still, "It's only TV; nobody's going to see it anyway."

Superman's extraordinary powers were demonstrated on TV by George Reeves. Co-starring with him was Noel Neill, who played *The Daily Planet* reporter Lois Lane, Superman's chief romantic interest.

Supposedly Reeves toasted the first show by telling a fellow actor, "We've now reached the bottom of the barrel."

Actually, it got a lot worse for him. The show was tremendously successful, and an epidemic of kids breaking their arms jumping off garage roofs to fly like Superman swept the country. Adults began using two of the most popular catchphrases from the series, *Daily Planet* editor Perry White's exclamation, "Great Caesar's ghost!" and his warning to cub reporter Jimmy Olson, "Don't call me Chief!" George Reeves became synonymous with Superman. Eventually he supplemented his growing salary with personal appearances, but kids always wanted to see if he really was the Man of Steel, and so they punched, poked, and kicked him. Maybe the low point of his career was when he participated in wrestling exhibitions wearing his costume.

Reeves was also the subject of one of television's great mysteries. In 1959, just before he was about to begin filming the next season, Reeves was found shot to death in his bedroom. It was ruled a suicide. Supposedly he was depressed because he had become typecast as Superman and couldn't find other roles, but a lot of people still believe he was murdered. In perfect entertainment-world harmony, many years later the Reeves murder became the subject of several TV shows.

Outer space shows were often described as "Westerns in space," meaning the good guys wore white space helmets, and the bad guys flew black rocket ships with evil-shaped wings, and the good guys always showed up at the last second to save the century. Well, Westerns were Westerns that took place in the Old West, and they were among the most popular children's shows on early TV. In movie theaters, Westerns were either Saturday morning serials or B movies, the second movie on a double bill. "What's a double bill?" you ask. A double bill meant the movie theaters showed two movies for one admission price. It's true. Once upon a time that did happen, and the second movie was usually quite forgettable.

Studios most people never knew existed turned out a roaring river of cowboy films with stars such as John Wayne, Randolph Scott, Alan Ladd, Gene Autry, and Roy Rogers. When the big studios refused to sell their pictures to television, the stations bought these B-films and serials, and the cowboy movie stars became even more popular as TV stars.

The first TV cowboy was Hopalong Cassidy played by William Boyd, who went on the air in 1949. The shows were actually cut-down versions of some of the sixty-six movies he had made beginning in 1935. The other movie cowboys watched with great interest to see if cowboys could ride the TV range. They figured out it was working when Hoppy showed up at a New Orleans department store to promote some of the forty Hopalong Cassidy products—and fifty

Courtesy of Stephen Cox Collection

Gene Autry, "The Singing Cowboy," starred in 91 episodes of *The Gene Autry Show* beginning in 1950. Although "That Silver-Haired Daddy of Mine" sold more than one million copies, Autry's biggest hit was "Rudolph the Red-nosed Reindeer."

thousand people showed up to meet him. Fifty thousand! In the first forty-five days the merchandise was on sale, it grossed more than one million dollars. Hoppy sold everything from roller skates to dinner plates, and in 1950 he became the first person to have his image on a lunch box. And six hundred thousand of them were sold! It didn't take much to realize that cowboys could be popular on TV.

And so, pardner, along came Gene Autry, and Roy Rogers, and the Lone Ranger, and about 117 other cowboys over the next decade. *The Lone Ranger* went on the air the same year as Hopalong Cassidy, after having been a popular radio program and comic book. The Lone Ranger was the only survivor of six Texas Rangers ambushed by an out-law gang led by Butch Cavendish. Although wounded, he was saved by a Native American who became his sidekick, Tonto. Tonto always called the Lone Ranger *Kemosabe*, which supposedly meant "trusty scout." The Lone Ranger wore a mask over his eyes so that Cavendish would not know that one of the Rangers had survived and was coming after him. The Lone Ranger was played for most of the series by Clayton Moore, although when he held out for more money, he was replaced by another actor. Imagine the genius of having your title character wear a mask so that any actor who worked cheap could play him.

The show's theme music, "The William Tell Overture" by Gioachino Rossini, sounded suspiciously like horses' hooves and became much better known for being associated with *The Lone Ranger* than as the overture to an opera. At the end of each show, the Lone Ranger left one silver bullet, his trademark, with the people he had helped. And inevitably, as he rode away, someone asked, "Who was the masked man?"

To which there was only one answer, said respectfully as he and Tonto rode into the dusty distance, "Why, that was the Lone Ranger," after which he was heard to shout, "Hi-yo Silver!"

Unlike Hoppy or the Lone Ranger, Gene Autry was a major star before making the transition to television. He was the first singer to sell a million copies of a record, "That Silver-Haired Daddy of Mine." He was the first performer to sell out Madison Square Garden for a live concert. And he was the first Hollywood star to make an original movie for television. *The Gene Autry Show* fit the cowboy formula: the Lone Ranger rode Silver, Hopalong rode Topper, Roy Rogers rode Trigger, and Gene Autry rode Champion. Rogers had comic sidekick, Pat Brady, the Lone Ranger had Tonto, and Autry had Pat Buttrum. The plot of Autry's first original cowboy half hour was pretty basic— a good ranch boss beats some bad cattle rustlers.

The Roy Rogers Show went on the air in 1951. Unlike Cassidy, Autry, and the Lone Ranger, Roy Rogers had a wife on the show, Dale Evans. Dale was also his wife off the show, and Trigger was his beloved horse. The plots on these cowboy shows were almost always the same— do whatever is necessary to sell branded merchandise. By the early 1950s stores were selling about forty million pieces a year, from toys to clothes, including more than five million repeating cap pistols.

There was money in them thar hills, Kemosabe, and Roy, Gene, Hoppy, and a lot of other cowboys and a few gals put on their spurs and rode out after it. *Wyatt Earp,* for example, became

Courtesy of Stephen Cox Collection

Clayton Moore played the Lone Ranger for eight years. The only survivor of six Texas Rangers, who were ambushed by Butch Cavendish's outlaw gang, the Lone Ranger and his sidekick, Tonto, roamed the southwest helping people who always asked at the end of each show, "Who was that masked man?"

the third most popular show on television, behind only *Ed Sullivan* and *I Love Lucy*. Among the many westerns aimed at least generally at kids were *Death Valley Days, Judge Roy Bean,* and *Tombstone Territory. The Adventures of Wild Bill Hickok* was on the air for seven years and much longer in reruns. His sidekick, Jingles Jones, played by Andy Devine, became better known for shouting his catchphrase as he desperately trailed his friend, "Wait for me, Wild Bill!" than for anything he had done in two decades of motion picture roles. *The Cisco Kid* roamed the Old West winning the day more by charming his opponents than killing them. His partner, Pancho, spoke his own kind of Spanglish. The most modern of the cowboys was *Sky King,* an Arizona rancher who roamed the skies with his niece Penny in his trusty white airplane, *Songbird*. Westerns became the most popular genre on TV. Most of them tried to attract an adult audience also, with the heavyweight among such shows being *Gunsmoke*, with James Arness, which went on the air in 1955 and lasted twenty years; in fact, it was on the air longer than it took to settle the real Old West.

WESTERNS ARE CERTAINLY NOT AS POPULAR TODAY AS THEY were when television was young, but creativity in educational programming still is.

At the very beginning of commercial television, a lot of people believed its success would be primarily as an educational medium and envisioned classrooms of kids being instructed by televised teachers. The FCC insisted that stations present a percentage of their broadcast time as public-interest programming.

Probably the most successful classroom TV show was CBS's *Sunrise Semester*, which offered New York University courses for credit and was broadcast practically at dawn for twenty-five years, although being "the most successful classroom TV show" meant that only forty-two of the two hundred CBS stations actually broadcast the show, and only forty-seven people were ever registered.

In 1948 *The Johns Hopkins Science Review* began a seven-year run on CBS that introduced real science to the country. It never found a large audience, but the *Science Review* did some remarkable things. When it was still prohibited to say the word *pregnant* on TV, it was the first show to broadcast a live birth.

Did I ever tell you how much I loved all these science and medical shows, but some of these doctors . . . A doctor on TV last week did a beautiful tonsillectomy, but the applause from the audience got him so excited he took out an appendix as an encore. And then . . .

Milton, that is not a true story and you know it. Actually, he took out a gallstone.

In 1953 *The Hopkins Review* taught women how to examine their breasts for cancer, and then showed a woman who had had a mastectomy playing the piano to demonstrate it was possible to live a complete life after that surgery. To prove that radioactive isotopes were not deadly, a Hopkins biologist drank a beaker of radioactive iodine and then traced its path through his body with a Geiger counter. To show how a fly drinks, they caught a fly and glued its wings to a stick, and lowered it over a dish of sugared water. They interviewed Nobel Prize winners. To show that insects can be a source of nutrition and eaten without harm, the host, Lynn Poole, ate a grasshopper. Poole also allowed himself to be whirled in a human centrifuge, although thankfully not on the same show on which he ate the grasshopper.

I have been on TV just about sixty years. I couldn't begin to estimate the number of hours I've been on the air. But in all those hours, I've never eaten a grasshopper, drunk a glass of radioactive iodine, glued a fly to a stick, or had a baby.

This is the do-it-yourself opening. You're playing the role of Detective Joe Friday, LAPD, investigating a crime:

You: My name is Friday. I'm a cop. I was working the day watch out of robbery when I got a call from the Acme School Bell Company. There had been a robbery.

Johnny Carson: There's been a robbery.

You: What was it?

Carson: My clappers. You know, those things inside the bell that make them clang.

You: The clangers?

Carson: We call them clappers in the business.

You: A clapper caper. Can I have the facts? What kind of clappers were stolen on this case?

Carson: They were copper clappers.

You: And where were they kept?

Carson: In the closet.

You: Uh-huh. Do you have any idea who might have taken the copper clappers from the closet?

Carson: Well, I fired a man, and he swore he would get even.

You: And what was his name?

Carson: Claude Cooper. That's right, I think Claude Cooper copped my copper clappers.

You: Do you know where this Claude Cooper is from?

Carson: Yep. Cleveland. And what makes it worse is
    that they were clean.

You: Why do you think Cleveland's Claude Cooper
    would cop your clean copper clappers kept in your
    closet?

Carson: One reason. He's a kleptomaniac.

You: Who first discovered the copper clappers were
    copped?

Carson: My cleaning woman, Clara Clifford.

You: Figures. Now let me see if I got the facts straight
    here. Cleaning woman Clara Clifford discovered
    that your clean copper clappers kept in a closet
    were copped by Claude Cooper, the kleptomaniac
    from Cleveland. That about it?

—JACK WEBB AND JOHNNY CARSON, *THE TONIGHT SHOW*

B Y THE MID-1950s TELEVISION WAS EVERYWHERE TO
stay. People were no longer watching the television set—the novelty was gone—because now viewers had choices. They could "vote
with their feet," as critics wrote, meaning if they were not satisfied, they
could get up from the couch and change the channel. Although today,
with remote controls, I guess people could vote with their fingers.
And as the mass audience was coming together, the kind of cultural
programming that had been an important part of early TV—symphony concerts, for example—began disappearing. Millions of people
began settling happily into what FCC chairman Newton Minnow
would describe only a few years later as a "vast wasteland."

Television producers discovered almost immediately that crime
pays, at least for television producers. In the first decade of tele-

vision, detective shows were second only to westerns in popularity. *Martin Kane, Private Eye* and Mike Barnett of *Man Against Crime,* TV's first hard-boiled private eyes, started to solve cases in 1949. Both shows were live, set in New York, and created and owned by tobacco companies, which, like most advertisers in the early 1950s, controlled the content of the shows. *Man Against Crime's* cigarette sponsor would not allow the writers to include fires or coughing in their scripts to avoid any negative associations. *Martin Kane's* sponsor made sure that their bow-tied, pipe-smoking private detective hung out at Happy McCann's Tobacco Shop, where he bought the sponsor's product on every show. Ralph Bellamy played Barnett, a tough and lean investigator whose gimmick was that he didn't carry a gun. Instead, he carried his fists.

Most of the early detective shows featured characters that had been created for another medium. *Ellery Queen*, which had started as a 1929 novel and was later a radio show, was the name of a mystery writer and amateur detective capable of solving crimes that baffled the often clueless police. It went on the air in 1950. *Dick Tracy*, which came from the comics and movie serials, went on the air in 1951. The masterful Sherlock Holmes, originally created by Arthur Conan Doyle for his novels, made his television debut in 1954. *Gangbusters*, which went on the air in 1951, was adapted directly from a very popular radio show that used stories based on real crimes. Each week the show ended with a "Still at Large" segment. The premise of the series was to illustrate scams so that you, the viewer, would not fall victim to con artists who, for instance, sell expensive patios and home-improvement packages and try to foreclose when you fail to make payments, or who impersonate lawyers to encourage estranged couples to get divorced and then charge exorbitant fees to help them go through with it. After the tough PIs came the amateur crime-solving combative comic couples in such series as *Mr. and Mrs. North, The Thin Man,* and *The Adventures of Boston Blackie.*

The most influential detective show in television history, the most realistic, compelling, gritty, and unpretenious show was—*dummm de-dum-dum—Dragnet.* "The story you are about to see is true," each show began. "Only the names have been changed to protect the innocent." Created by and starring Jack Webb as the no-nonsense, by-the-book LAPD Sergeant Joe Friday, *Dragnet* squeezed all the melodrama it could from the format and made the show about "Just the facts, ma'am," which quickly became a catchphrase that swept the country. Webb, a smart, funny guy, was a guest on *The Tonight Show* several times. In 1968 he and Johnny had the classic dialogue that opened this chapter. What made this skit so wonderful was that Jack Webb played it so straight.

Courtesy of Stephen Cox Collection

Jack Webb created the memorable detective Joe Friday, star of *Dragnet*, the most influential detective show in television history.

What set *Dragnet* apart from other detective shows was Webb's attention to detail and his demand for accuracy. To make sure that police officers were portrayed realistically, he would often visit Los Angeles police headquarters, spend time on patrol with cops, and attend classes at the police academy. And he succeeded so well that for a time the LAPD used episodes of *Dragnet* as training films in the academy.

Each show ended with the suspect that Friday and his partner, Sergeant Frank Smith, had arrested posing for his mug shot, and the announcer giving the verdict of the jury—which was always guilty—and the sentence he received. *Dragnet* and *I Love Lucy* were the first extremely successful programs to be filmed in Hollywood, so *Dragnet* had a practically unlimited supply of young film actors. Fess Parker remembers, "I was cast as a rookie policeman. And Jack Webb and his sidekick were both probably five foot seven. So I played my whole scene on my knees."

The realism of *Dragnet* eventually was replaced by fantasy PI shows in which an exotic location was often the most important aspect of the plot. It seemed that there was an incredible amount of crime being committed near beaches. The private investigators on *77 Sunset Strip*, which introduced the handsome teen idol and parking lot attendant Edd "Kookie" Byrnes, had their office next door to a glamorous Los Angeles restaurant where Kookie worked—although they did travel to other beautiful sites in search of truth, justice, and beautiful women in small bathing suits. *Bourbon Street Beat*, obviously, was set in New Orleans. *Surfside 6* took place in Miami Beach. New York was *The Naked City*. Bill Cosby and Robert Culp's *I Spy* was set in the great cities all over the world. *Route 66* followed the historic highway from Chicago to Los Angeles. Both *M Squad* and *Richard Diamond, Private Detective* took place in exotic Chicago. And, of course, *Hawaiian Eye*, and later *Hawaii Five-O* (the longest running crime series in TV history—"Book 'em, Dano!") were set in beautiful Memphis, Tennessee!

All right, you caught me. It wasn't actually Memphis. Have you ever thought about being a TV detective?

The most successful investigator of all time wasn't a detective or a private investigator or a newspaperman—it was a lawyer. *Perry Mason* never lost a case. He won 270 straight. In fact, the only person in the plot who could not possibly have committed the crime was Perry Mason's client. *Perry Mason* was the antithesis of *Dragnet*. Every suspect Sergeant Friday arrested was guilty; every suspect the

Courtesy of Stephen Cox Collection

Between 1957 and 1966, Raymond Burr created TV's greatest lawyer, Perry Mason. Assisted by his loyal and knowledgeable secretary, Della Street, played by Barbara Hale, he never lost a case—or a sponsor.

police arrested for a crime that Perry Mason defended was innocent. Earl Stanley Gardner had written a series of novels about Perry Mason, but for most people the character of Perry Mason was created not by Gardner, but by Raymond Burr. Burr's Mason had an extraordinary ability to wait until the real murderer was on the stand, testifying in the trial against his innocent client—which inevitably took place in the last five minutes of the show—before posing the key question that would cause the witness to unravel and confess that he or she had committed the crime.

"Is it not true," Mason might demand, "that you have eaten chocolate candy?"

That was all the witness needed to hear. "Yes, yes, I did it! I pushed him off the ski lift!" Then Perry's explanation detailing how he solved the case would follow, "I found a discarded candy wrapper in the corner of the ski lift chair that the police had overlooked!"

For more than nine years and many more years in reruns, *Perry Mason* made great television and spawned other lawyer shows such as Andy Griffith's *Matlock* and *The Defenders*, which started as a play on Studio One with William Shatner, who now plays lawyer Denny Crain on *Boston Legal,* and *Judd for the Defense.*

When asked why Perry Mason never lost a case, Raymond Burr replied that Mason had actually lost many cases, "But we only show the cases he won."

In addition to the courtroom dramas, fake-reality courtroom shows began in early television. The genre that created Judge Judy and Judge Joe Brown began with shows like *Traffic Court* on ABC, in which real cases from traffic courts were re-created. Other shows that faked courtroom reality included *Morning Court, Day in Court,* and *Night Court, Accused, They Stand Accused, The People's Court of Small Claims* and maybe the most successful, *The Verdict Is Yours,* hosted by Jim McKay.

Less than a decade after the FCC prohibited most violence on TV, the body count continued to rise steadily, and parents complained about too much violence on TV—complaints that have not ended. *The Untouchables,* the story of crime fighter Eliot Ness—played by Robert Stack—and his elite Justice Department squad of incorruptible agents who battled Al Capone and the Chicago mobs, went on the air in 1959 and almost immediately became one of TV's most popular—and most violent—shows. Quinn Martin, the producer, told his writers, "I wish you would come up with a different device than running a man down with a car, as we have done this on three different shows. I like the idea of sadism, but I hope we can come up with another approach to it."

The Untouchables' biggest controversy was caused not by its violence, but by the fact that most of the bad guys had Italian names. The Italian-American League to Combat Defamation started a campaign against the show. Longshoreman union boss "Tough Tony" Anastasia picketed ABC headquarters in New York and announced that his union would not handle the products of sponsor Liggett & Myers Tobacco Company if the situation didn't change. The situation changed. Liggett & Myers stopped sponsoring the show, and ABC agreed that Ness would pursue more criminals with non-Italian names and that the contributions of Justice Department officials who were Italian would be highlighted.

Courtesy of Stephen Cox Collection

The Untouchables, the legendary fearless and incorruptible Justice Department squad formed in Chicago in the 1930s to fight the mob, became one of TV's most popular shows in 1959, with Robert Stack as leader Eliot Ness and Neville Brand as his nemeses Al Capone.

The show continued to receive complaints, but maybe the strangest one came from the estate of convicted criminal Al Capone, who sued the producers for one million dollars—not for defamation or slander, but rather for using Capone's name and likeness without permission.

THE POPULARITY OF *DRAGNET* ENABLED IT TO BECOME THE first TV show to be made into a feature movie in 1954. The plot involved a mob killing, and Webb had some lines that would have made Clint Eastwood proud. When interviewing a mob guy who refused to answer questions, Webb warned him, "This badge pays $4.20 an hour. Sit back because I'm gonna blow about twenty bucks of it right now." And later Webb complained to the D.A., "Why does the law always work for the guilty?" to which the D.A. responded, "Because the innocent don't need it."

Only a few years earlier, movie studios had done anything they could to destroy TV. Paramount had even bought a sizable amount of DuMont stock and, by refusing to invest additional money, eventually contributed to the network's going out of business. Gradually, however, the barriers fell. When the Academy Awards ceremony was televised for the first time in 1953, NBC received the highest ratings in its history. But the making of the *Dragnet* film was significant because it meant the movie studios had finally accepted the inevitability of television and were working with it rather than trying to strangle it. And it was television that allowed some studios to stay in business.

The motion picture industry feared that television would take away its audience and had fought TV desperately by prohibiting stars from appearing on TV and refusing to sell stations the rights to broadcast movies. It also introduced gimmicks to draw people into theaters. In contrast to tiny black-and-white screens, more than half of all movies were made in color and new big-screen technologies like the giant wraparound Cinerama process, Cinemascope, Vista Vision, and Todd-AO were introduced. The movie studios tried to do anything that TV could not do, like make movies in 3-D and Smell-O-Vision. "Percepto" installed buzzers beneath every seat and shocked viewers at the height of scary scenes in *The Tingler*. "Emergo 3-D" included a skeleton on a wire that swept across the top of the theater when *House on Haunted Hill* was shown. Studios began making horror films so gory that they could not be shown on television at the time—and promoted them with warnings that "No one will be seated during the last ten minutes of this film," and "Due to the high level of tension, a doctor will be on the premises at all times." They even considered installing very large TV screens in theaters and broadcasting closed-circuit events and shows featuring the top entertainers that the networks couldn't afford.

But people just wanted to stay home and watch TV. For the first few years, the crossover for actors had been mostly one way—from TV to the movies. Charlton Heston was the first actor to star in television and move to motion pictures successfully, but Leslie Nielsen was close behind. Jack Lemmon hosted *Toni Twin Time* before working in pictures. Paul Newman and Joanne Woodward, Eli Wallach, and Anne Jackson all started in TV. The studios were very happy to reinforce the impression that television lacked the status of motion pictures by using TV actors.

But when established movie actors took jobs on TV, the studios got upset. Gene Autry was first, but gradually other semi-stars—particularly those who had been relegated to B pictures—made the move. Among the first was Ronald Reagan, an established minor motion picture star who began working in TV in 1952 and by 1954 was hosting and acting in a dramatic anthology series *G.E. Theater*, produced by Stan Rubin. "I don't think he was a great actor," Rubin said. "I think he was not incompetent. I used him as sparingly as possible, but enough so there wouldn't be an obvious complaint. Ronnie's powers grew as his contract was renewed, and by the fourth year he had the right to come in with stories and I would have to make them. I think he was guaranteed at least two half-hour segments. The material he brought in was always the same: I was a Communist for the FBI.

Courtesy of Stephen Cox Collection

B-movie actor and future president of the United States Ronald Reagan replaced "The Old Ranger" as host of *Death Valley Days*, an anthology of true stories from the old west. He also appeared in several episodes of the series as an actor.

"In 1963, the G.E. executives had meetings with the head of Universal. It turned out this would be the last year of the show, but nobody told me why. Years later I found out that the G.E. executives had asked Universal to replace Reagan as host of the show. He had become more reactionary and was going around the country making speeches as the host of *G.E. Theater* in which he attacked the Tennessee Valley Authority because he didn't believe the government should undertake public projects like that. But G.E. had a huge account selling turbines to the TVA. When Universal wouldn't replace Reagan, G.E. cancelled the show."

Richard Crenna remembered the Oscar-winning character actor Walter Brennan made the transition to TV, playing the role of Grandpa Amos on *The Real McCoys*. "Walter looked like a Boston banker and spoke like one until he went into character. He was always ready to go, always knew his lines, always the first one on the set and the last to leave. And I thought, this is what a professional does, this is what it means to be an actor. On the show Grandpa had a limp. People would often ask me, did Walter put something in his shoe? And I'd say, 'No, that's what we call acting.'"

One thing the movie studios did to limit the popularity of TV was simply to refuse to sell broadcasters any popular movies. If viewers wanted to see the great Hollywood stars, they would have to see them in the movie theater. But smaller, struggling studios like Republic and Monogram, the studios most affected by TV, happily sold their libraries to the networks—about four thousand B and even C movies. These were films that *Time* described as "the wilted coleslaw on television's bill of fare. The ancient cabbages that are rolled across the telescreen every night are Hollywood's curse on the upstart industry. Televiewers, sick of hoary Hoot Gibson oaters and ancient spook comedies wonder when, if ever, they will see fresh, first class Hollywood films."

When I went down into the vault of Philadelphia's WCAU to get a *Million Dollar Movie*, what I had to choose from were films that had been pretty much forgotten, with good reason. But the stations showed these films over and over and over.

Actually, it wasn't even Hollywood that sold the first major features to television. It was British producer Alexander Korda, who believed that movies and TV should be natural partners, and in 1954, to raise enough money to produce new films, he leased his old classics to major American stations. These were films with major stars, A-list movie stars like Vivian Leigh, Laurence Olivier, Charles Laughton, Merle Oberon, Elsa Lanchester, and Leslie Howard. When the studios realized how much money Korda was making from old films that had just been sitting in a vault somewhere, they began to think that maybe television wasn't exactly the enemy after all.

Howard Hughes owned RKO Studios, which he had pretty much destroyed to the point that it was not even making serious movies anymore, and he needed to raise some cash. So he licensed the entire

RKO library to a distributor for television. These were some of the greatest films in movie history, including *King Kong, Citizen Kane, The Hunchback of Notre Dame,* and *Top Hat.* That sale effectively ended the studios' boycott of television. In 1956 *The Wizard of Oz* was the first film to be shown in prime time. Distributors would sell a package of films to a station—sometimes with a hundred films in the package—but the station had to take the B films along with the classics. Agent Jerry Zeitman was at Universal-MCA for one of the bigger sales. "Lew Wasserman, the president of the company, was just years ahead of everyone else. We bought Paramount's entire library of pre-1948 films. I think we bought seven hundred films. Everybody wondered what we were going to do with those old films. What we did was make a fortune. Rather than making a deal with a distribution company, we started our own TV distribution business. We sold these films on a station-by-station basis, but we kept the remake rights."

Almost immediately movies began to dominate the TV schedule. Every station had an *Early Show,* a *Late Show,* a *Late-Late Show,* a *Million Dollar Movie,* an *Afternoon Movie,* a Not-So-Early-But-Not-Too-Late movie, a Medium-Late Show, a *Saturday Night at the Movies,* the *Sunday Matinee . . .* it was possible to turn on the TV at any time, day or night, and find a movie. New York stations were broadcasting more than one hundred black-and-white movies weekly.

Dragnet and *Lucy* played an important role in keeping the motion picture studios in business. These were the two most popular shows on television, and both were on film and produced on the West Coast. That was the beginning of the migration of the TV industry to Hollywood, and for the studios, it couldn't have come at a better time. The big studios were struggling financially. Paramount drained the huge water tank where so many ocean scenes had been filmed, laid off hundreds of workers, among them the gardening crew, and allowed secretaries to uproot plants and take them home. Twentieth

Century-Fox suspended production in England, shut down its Hollywood studio for a month, and laid off more than a third of its production people. Only Republic, which was basically out of the production business, was booming. "There's only one way to beat television," the studio's president said. "That's to get in it." Republic had rented its giant—and empty—soundstages to TV production companies to film shows like *Dragnet*. Business was so good, in fact, they built four new soundstages on the lot.

The battle between live TV and filmed shows was over. No contest. A CBS vice president explained, "We are primarily in the live TV business. We definitely wanted to shoot *I Love Lucy* live. But the sponsor made us go to film. You can say that we went into the film business at the whim of the sponsor."

It was not just the whim of a sponsor; it was the business savvy of the show's producer. Live shows were performed live only once. Kinescopes were generally of such poor quality they had little second-run value. But filmed shows could be run on the network and then sold to individual stations, or sold directly station by station. Film never got old, and Jack Webb and Lucille Ball had proved viewers didn't object at all. Within a couple of years, eight small movie studios were churning out TV shows almost exclusively. Hal Roach Studios produced filmed shows and sold them directly to sponsors, who would then buy time on independent stations to broadcast the shows, or sold them directly to the stations, which would then find sponsors for the shows. Roach made ninety-eight episodes of *Racket Squad* and sold them to a sponsor to cover his expenses. And then he sold the whole package to ABC for an additional million dollars. A whole new money-making model had come into being.

Eventually the big studios went into the television production business. The first TV show produced by Warner Bros. was appropriately named *Warner Bros. Presents* and went on the air in 1955. The competing *Twentieth Century-Fox Hour* and *MGM Parade* were on the air before the end of that season. And in 1956 all the studios officially discarded their rules that prohibited actors under contract from appearing on TV.

Once the studios got into business with the networks, they experimented with various kinds of marketing concepts. After Disney's *Davy Crockett,* black-and-white TV movies became a national craze. Disney sold more than one million coonskin caps and released a full-length motion picture called *Davy Crockett, King of the Wild Frontier,* in Technicolor. But that was taking advantage

Courtesy of Stephen Cox Collection

"King of the Wild Frontier" and future congressman Davy Crockett was played by Fess Parker (left), here with partner George Russel, played by Buddy Ebsen. The Disney show—and its merchandise—became a huge sensation, and could have been even bigger had the real Crockett not died defending the Alamo.

of a known commodity—and it worked. A movie named *Fire at One,* the story of an atomic submarine on a rescue mission at the North Pole, was shown on TV and then released in theaters—and was an immediate and complete failure. And in 1956 Laurence Olivier directed and starred in a three-hour-long British version of *Richard III,* for which he was nominated for a Best Actor Oscar. It was simultaneously shown on afternoon TV and released in the theaters. It was estimated more than twenty-five million viewers watched the movie on TV, more than the total number of people who had seen the play since its first performance 358 years earlier. However, it was a total failure at the box office. That should not have been a surprise. If more than twenty-five million people saw it for free on TV, why would people pay to see it in the theaters?

WITH THE EASY AVAILABILITY OF MOVIES, PROGRAMMING became more expensive, and advertisers began "participating," meaning they bought a "spot" on an existing show, with the cost of the spot based on the number of viewers. It was a fundamental structural change in the television world that several different people were credited for helping to create.

"Originally the sponsors owned and financed the whole show," said Herb Schlosser, who eventually became president of NBC. "It was all the eggs in one basket. If the show died, the entire investment was lost. That changed, I think, at least partially because of Pat Weaver, who created *The Today Show* and *The Tonight Show*. These were shows into which you could buy participations. You could buy a spot on the show. As programming became more expensive and programming development started to become much bigger at the networks, the concept of buying into participations became much more prevalent. It didn't happen overnight, but it happened."

About three hundred years before television came along, Dr. Samuel Johnson wrote in his magazine, *The Idler*, "Promise, large promise, is the soul of advertisement . . . The trade of advertising is now so near to perfection that it is not easy to propose any improvement." Ah yes, the good doctor was perhaps having his folly with us—but little did he know that advertising would become the root of all entertainment.

At first, there was some question about whether it was worth it to advertise on TV. Was anybody going to buy the products they saw advertised? The value of television advertising was proved in

1947 when Kraft promoted its new product, McLaren's Imperial Cheese, on its dramatic show *Kraft Television Theatre*. This cheese was expensive and not selling very well. Kraft did not want to use a celebrity, fearing the celebrity might detract attention from the product, so they simply shot a woman's hands preparing a variety of dishes using the cheese, while the announcer, Ed Herlihy, gave the recipe to viewers. Within a few weeks every package of McLaren's Imperial Cheese was sold—and it had not been advertised anywhere except television. A poll showed that *Kraft Television Theatre* had the highest sponsor identification in television. So take that, Dr. Johnson.

Kraft was a well-known company, and everybody liked cheese. But the power of TV to create a market for a brand-new product was demonstrated in 1950 when a former Atlantic City boardwalk pitchman named Leonard Rosen, his brother, and one other man developed a hair tonic that they named Charles Antell's Formula 9. Believe me, there were no formulas 1 through 8. I spent several years working that same boardwalk, selling Morris metric slicers. People had been selling hair tonics out of the backs of wagons for a hundred years. Television was simply the new covered wagon. The Formula 9 factory was in Leonard Rosen's basement. In a barter deal with WOR, an independent station in New York, Rosen paid a fee to a film distributor and showed his fifteen-minute-long "educational program on hair care by the founder of the Charles Antell Cosmetics firm." The spot consisted of a pitchman standing in front of a camera demonstrating the product, which was described as "healthy for your hair" because it contained lanolin. Lanolin, he explained, comes from the skin and wool of sheep, "and you've never seen a bald sheep." This amounted to the first infomercial, and it was a big success. Charles Antell's Formula 9 became one of the best-selling hair products in the country.

A couple of years later, a small, completely unknown company in Holyoke, Massachusetts, produced a commercial at a cost of about five thousand dollars to demonstrate the first liquid cleaner, Lestoil, and showed it in one market. After that proved successful, the company moved to other markets and within four years was grossing twenty-five million dollars annually. To get a piece of that action, Procter & Gamble created Mr. Clean, and Colgate began marketing Ajax and White Tornado, and in nine months sold thirty-five million bottles of liquid cleaner. Television had helped create a huge market for an entirely new product line.

Television advertising was demonstrated to be effective, and at the beginning it was the advertisers who controlled programming. As MCA agent Jerry Zeitman said, "We didn't sell shows to the networks. We would sell them to the advertisers. We sold *The George Burns and Gracie Allen Show* to Carnation Milk who then bought time on CBS. We did a show called *The Bob Cummings Show* that we sold to R. J. Reynolds, and they used it to introduce Winston cigarettes. We did something interesting with *Mr. Ed*, the talking horse. We syndicated the show, but we had a national sponsor, Studebaker. We sold it to individual stations but Studebaker was always the sponsor.

"It was pretty simple. General Foods, not CBS, programmed CBS Monday night at eight o'clock. General Foods owned it, and they would program anything they wanted to put in at that time. That wasn't true of every time period. But it began changing when Jim Aubrey became president of CBS. He said, 'I program the network. If you want to buy Monday night at eight o'clock, you'll buy what I put there.' That was a major upheaval. That was a big change."

Whether a show had an individual sponsor—as in the earlier years—or a group of participating sponsors, when the advertisers paid the bills, they wanted to exercise control over their shows. Herb Schlosser remembered "a meeting we had with John DeLorean, who was the president of the Chevrolet Divison of General Motors. Chevy was a major advertiser and sponsored *Bonanza*, one of our most popular shows. We would show him our merchandise before it was revealed to the world. We would do that for all our major advertisers. DeLorean came in and told us what he liked and didn't like. And we listened to him because we knew how much money he controlled. A guy like DeLorean would have an impact on where his program was scheduled. He would be very interested in the show in front and behind. Could he exercise his power over the schedule? Of course."

Advertisers approved the scripts and the actors, and they even changed words in the script. On *Make Room for Daddy*, Danny Thomas referred to Sir Winston Churchill as a member of the British House of Commons rather than a member of Parliament because his cigarette sponsor did not want to plug a competing brand. *Playhouse 90* was sponsored by an instant-coffee maker who objected to a British sailor asking for a pot of tea. During the brilliant *Playhouse 90* production of "Judgment at Nuremberg," American judge Claude Rains asked a convicted Nazi to explain the crematoriums—and the sponsor, the American Gas Association, refused to allow him to use the words *gas oven*. The judge's lips moved, but his words were edited out.

Performers would try to find ways of sneaking words into scripts, but no one ever matched the great Mr. W. C. Fields, who figured out a way to get around his American Tobacco sponsors. Whenever he didn't get something he wanted, he would taunt his sponsor by talking about his beloved son, Chester. "Ah yes, I was talking to son Chester, a fine young man . . ." Think about it—W. C. Fields' son Chester.

Sponsors changed the whole script when they felt it was necessary. Twice Rod Serling wrote scripts vaguely paralleling the story of fourteen-year-old Emmett Till, an African American from Chicago who was beaten and then shot to death in the Mississippi Delta after supposedly whistling at a white woman. The two obvious suspects were tried and acquitted. In Serling's first effort, sponsored by U.S. Steel, "Every word of dialogue that might be remotely Southern in context was deleted or altered," he explained. "A geographical change was made to a New England town. When the show was ultimately produced, its thesis had been diluted, and my characters had mounted a soapbox to shout something that had become too vague to warrant any shouting."

His next attempt to tell the story a year later for *Playhouse 90* had several sponsors, and all of them requested changes. Rather than taking place in Mississippi in 1955, the locale became "a small Southwestern town in the 1870s." In this version Emmett Till was a romantic young Mexican who admired the woman "with his eyes." An ad agency for one of the sponsors vetoed use of the phrase "twenty men in hoods," suggesting it be changed to "wearing home-made masks." A black character named Clemson had his name changed because Clemson University in South Carolina was, at that time, all white. The agency for Allstate Insurance would not permit the script to include a suicide. It was like a Mel Brooks plot. Any term that offended anyone was removed from the script. The producer, Marty Manulis, said after the broadcast—who knows how seriously—"It's a great tribute to the ad agencies that they ever let this show go on the air."

Before July 1, 1941, advertisers did not approve television scripts and actors because before that date the FCC did not permit any commercial advertising on TV. In 1930 an experimental station, W1XAV in Boston, ran an advertising spot for the fur industry and was fined for doing so.

After World War II, most commercials were done live, and accidents and mistakes were quite common—and some even became legendary. In early commercials for Pan American airlines, a model of the famed Pan Am Clipper was suspended in front of a globe about the size of a soccer ball that slowly rotated on a waist-high pillar. To provide a sense of movement, the commercial was shot by a single camera with a manually operated zoom lens, and as the announcer read his lines, the camera would slowly zoom in. One night the cameraman had forgotten to pull the lens back before the commercial started, so it was already fully extended. The director still wanted movement and ordered the cameraman to slowly move the dolly in closer to the model. The cameraman moved his big camera forward, not noticing that the large base of the camera was pushing against the pillar with the globe on it. Finally, the camera knocked over the pillar and, on camera, the earth just dropped right out of the frame and crashed onto the concrete floor. Unfortunately, the motor that turned the globe shorted out when it hit the floor, and a cloud of black smoke enveloped the Clipper. The cameraman tried to help and let his camera tilt, making it appear like the plane was caught in black smoke turbulence. Meanwhile, people were running all over the studio, shouting instructions, which did not faze the announcer, who continued to remind viewers that Pan Am was "the world's most experienced airline." Finally the director was smart enough to cut away.

One of the famous live commercials was the Timex torture tests in which newsman John Cameron Swazye demonstrated the durability of a Timex watch by attaching it to the leg of a racehorse or the bow of a water ski boat or Mickey Mantle's bat or a lobster claw or dropping it over the Grand Coulee Dam—have you ever thought about a group of advertising people sitting around thinking up these tests?—or some other demonstration that was going to spin, bang, crush, whirl, drop, bake, and somehow batter the watch. Then Swayze would hold it up proudly and announce, "Takes a lickin', but keeps on tickin'." Except for the night he attached it to an outboard motor propeller in a water tank. When the propeller stopped spinning, the watch had completely disappeared. Swayze dug into the tank searching frantically for the watch, which apparently had been smashed into smithereens, all the while assuring viewers that the demonstration had worked perfectly in rehearsals—and the watch had kept on tickin'.

In 1953 an actor named Ian Keith starred in a TV version of *Dark Victory* on *Broadway Television Theatre*. At that time actors also often did commercials, which Keith did not want to do. He said flatly that Nash automobiles, the sponsor, were not very good at all. Then he turned and thumbed his nose at the director, successfully ending his career on that show.

Arthur Godfrey's great announcer, Durwood Kirby, was doing a coffee commercial during which he was supposed to say, as the camera moved in, "Pure. Nothing added." Unfortunately as the camera held on a close-up of the coffee can, he said smoothly, "Pure. Nothing."

Often commercials were introduced with a brief lead-in, just a few lines by the star or host to set up the spot, such as "And now a word from our sponsor." One night bandleader Spade Cooley gave the lead-in for a baby food commercial, telling viewers, "Mothers, if you're having trouble with your kids, listen to this message." The problem was that instead of the baby food commercial, someone in the control room ran one for an insect spray: "Feed 'em Snairol. It'll kill the little pests."

Early in his career, producer Woody Fraser worked on a children's show sponsored by a hamburger chain. One morning the host announced excitedly that every kid in the audience was going to get a coupon for a free hamburger! He then asked one of the kids what he thought about that—to which the kid replied, "My mother won't let me eat those things." The host recovered to tell the audience that "nine out of ten people liked them."

The use of basically unprovable comparison statistics probably reached the low point when Camel boasted in 1952, "A nationwide

survey showed that more doctors smoke Camels than any other cigarette. A few years ago, 113,597 doctors in every branch of the medical profession were asked, 'What cigarette do you smoke, doctor?'
The brand named most was Camel."

It's easy to make fun of cigarette commercials now, but being a
spokesman for a cigarette brand was considered one of the best jobs
an announcer could have. I never got one, although I came very
close. I heard Old Gold was going to replace its announcer, and I
auditioned for it. The problem was that I didn't smoke, but I knew I
would have to learn. I practiced everywhere. I practiced on the train
between New York and Philadelphia. I practiced at home. I went
through all the auditions and was very close to getting the job, but
then was asked to meet the account supervisor at the ad agency. The
woman who had selected me picked me up in a limo, and we were
on our way up to the agency when I casually took out an Old Gold
and started smoking. The woman looked at me and asked, "So how
long have you been smoking, Ed?"

What was I going to say? This woman was a casting director who
had used me before and, I hoped, would use me in the future. So I
was honest with her and said, "Three weeks." She smiled and then
told the driver, "Turn the car around." To do a cigarette commercial,
she explained, you have to smoke cigarettes.

A lot of actors and TV personalities hated having to do commercials, but they figured that was the price they had to pay to work on
television. Others enjoyed it. Mike Wallace wore a straw hat and carried a cane for Peter Pan Peanut Butter on *Super Circus*. Dick Clark's
first network job was doing Tootsie Roll commercials for Paul
Whiteman's *TV Teen Club* on the ABC network—all five stations in
the network. Marilyn Monroe began her career doing a TV commercial for an oil company. Dean Martin and Jerry Lewis did live commercials, and Jerry remembers, "When we worked for Kellogg's, I'd

go out to Lansing to visit the sponsor or go to Jersey when it was Colgate-Palmolive, 'who makes some of the best products for your home, especially when you get up in the morning and grab a tube of Colgate and the freshness you feel in your mouth carries you through the entire day.' We did the commercials straight. They wouldn't let us screw with them. I would have, believe me. I would have squeezed it and had the toothpaste come out the wrong end. But you didn't fool around with the sponsor."

The smart young New York performers understood that and appreciated the opportunity to earn extra money. James Garner explained, "There was a progression. There was the stage. Then if you went from the stage to the movies, that's a step down. If you went from movies to television, another step down. If you went from television to commercials, another step down. Everybody looked down on television and commercials. But an actor is an actor, and you can be just as good at a commercial as you can on a feature.

"Once in a commercial for Winston cigarettes, a girl and I were playing Scrabble, and I said something like, 'Look, honey, we win,' and then I lit up a cigarette and said, 'It tastes good, like a cigarette should.' I think I was the guy who made the grammatical error, using 'like' instead of 'as.' A year or so later Winston had a whole ad campaign in which it crossed out the 'like' and wrote 'as' under it. If a commercial paid five dollars, it was good to me, but I think I made something like two thousand dollars over the years on that commercial. I felt I had hit the jackpot."

I agreed with James Garner and enjoyed making commercials because I loved selling. The first TV commercial I ever did was for a pants presser, a metal frame you stuck inside the legs of your pants, and it stretched out the wrinkles. I sold Dole Pineapple Juice. I even sold rubber duckies. Absolutely true. It was a kids' bathtub toy that I sold on *Strictly for the Girls*, and every mother wanted one. I did several gas station commercials with a young actress named Barbara Walters. We drove around in a convertible from station to station filming them. If something could be sold on TV, I wanted to be the one to sell it.

One difference between radio and TV was that on television, the commercials themselves became entertainment. That had not happened on radio. In 1948 Milton Berle's *Texaco Star Theater* featured four service station attendants singing, "Oh, we're the men of Texaco, we work from Maine to Mexico . . . " Texaco had America singing the first great TV jingle from coast to coast. That same year the first identifiable animated characters appeared: the Ajax pixies, who interacted with actors to sell "the foaming cleanser." The admittedly somewhat bizarre, human-sized Old Gold cigarette packs with long, attractive legs appearing out of them tap-danced in front of a curtain. Originally the dancing cigarette packs were accompanied by a dancing matchbook, while an announcer boasted that Old Golds were "made by tobacco men, not medicine men." I like to think that if I had been a smoker, I could have been that announcer.

One thing for sure, as far as the audience was concerned, I always left them laughing. If they didn't laugh, I would leave. You see, I come from a long line of comedians—and that line was usually in front of the unemployment office. Why my Uncle Max, he . . .

That will be enough for this chapter, Milton.

Cigarette manufacturers often insisted that the hosts of shows they sponsored smoke during the broadcast. At times that got a little strange—as on the sitcom *Topper* when Topper's two ghostly friends, George and Marion Kirby, joined him for a smoke break in the middle of the show or, most bizarre of all, when at the conclusion of

The Flintstones in 1960, Fred and Wilma would relax with a Winston. Because they were good parents, Fred and Wilma stopped doing smoking commercials when Wilma got pregnant.

The commercials I loved the most, ones featuring the Anheuser-Busch Clydesdale horses, made their debut in 1951. Once, I was doing a spot with the Captain, one of those beautiful, very big horses. I held a microphone in one hand and a cup of Budweiser in my other hand. I spoke about the great tradition and quality and the ingredients, and then I said, "It's nice to know that people still value quality. Isn't that right, Captain?" Captain had been trained to nod his head, agreeing with me. Instead, he leaned forward and took a sip of the beer right out of my mug. It was the single best ad-lib I had ever seen—and it was done by a horse. Budweiser ran that commercial for several months, but eventually the company received too many complaints about horse abuse and had to take it off the air.

Eventually commercial characters such as Sharpie, the Gillette parrot, and Kellogg's Tony the Tiger started to become popular. In 1952 Bordon's Elsie the Cow actually beat out one of the nation's leading politicans, Senator Robert Taft, as well as movie star Van Johnson, in polls of America's most identifiable icons.

One thing ad agencies didn't like in commercials was humor because advertisers did not believe viewers should laugh at their products. The animated characters Bert and Harry Piel, the Piel Brothers, for Piels Beer in New York, gained some recognition, but it was thought that the problem was that people tried the beer because of the commercials, and didn't like it. By 1963 the company was sold.

It was thought that if viewers were too busy laughing at the cleverness of some art director's work, they wouldn't remember the product. Comedian Stan Freberg changed that. Freberg came along at the perfect time. Because more advertisers were buying a single commercial on a show that was already popular instead of risking money in developing new shows, there was more opportunity to sell single spots.

In 1956 a small California tomato paste company, Contadina, was losing its market share to giant Hunts. The owner of Contadina had heard Stan Freberg's comedy records and thought a humorous approach to the company's advertising might create attention. Freberg came up with the campaign, "Who put eight great tomatoes in that little-bitty can?" It won advertising awards, but more importantly, it enabled Contadina to increase its sales.

That was the beginning of Freberg's career—and funny advertising. In a spot for Chun King chow mein, he claimed, "Nine out of ten doctors prefer Chun King chow mein," and then showed his ten doctors—

One of TV's first successful commercial characters was "Speedy" Alka-Seltzer, who co-starred in this spot with legendary comedian Buster Keaton.

nine of whom were Chinese. For Sunsweet prunes he wrote the line, "Today the pits, tomorrow the wrinkles."

From there it was only a matter of time—and good taste—until "Mamma mia, that's-a one spicy meatball-a!" was used to promote Alka-Seltzer.

Q: What is the importance of this question? Name the kings of Denmark, Norway, Sweden, Jordan, Iraq, and Belgium.

A: This was the question Charles van Doren supposedly missed and cost him the championship on the rigged quiz show 21. The correct answer in 1957 was Frederick (Denmark), Haakon (Norway), Gustave (Sweden), Hussein (Jordan), Baudouin (Belgium), and Faisal (Iraq). Van Doren incorrectly named Leopold as the king of Belgium.

M Y REAL TALENT HAS ALWAYS BEEN THAT I CAN TALK. I can tell a story, I can tell a joke, I can read copy, and I can ad-lib. I'm an announcer, and that's how I earned my living. So I loved doing commercials, I loved working with talented stars like Johnny on *The Tonight Show* and Jerry Lewis on decades of telethons, and I loved hosting my own shows. And probably the type of show I hosted most often was quiz shows because the popularity of quiz shows offered the most opportunity for announcers. I could talk. I could ask questions. Let me give you an example: What was the first quiz show on television?

See how easy it is.

Do you have any idea how many different formats of quiz shows there have been?

I don't know either. My job is to ask the questions; your job is to answer them.

All I know is that there have been hundreds and hundreds of different game shows and quiz shows. *Professor Quiz*, which is credited with being broadcasting's first quiz show, debuted on radio in 1936. Contestants asked Professor Quiz questions, and if they stumped him, they received twenty-five dollars. That was the gimmick—the contestants asked the host the questions.

Don't get any ideas. I ask the questions in this book.

Within two years there were more than two hundred quiz shows on radio. It was as if radio gold had been discovered. So naturally the quiz show was one of the first formats producers adapted for TV. On the first day of commercially licensed television in 1941, *Truth or Consequences*, hosted by Ralph Edwards, was broadcast by NBC's New York City station. The "truth" was generally a question that couldn't be answered. As the great announcer Bob Barker, who hosted the show for decades, explained, "You are asked a question, and if you don't tell the truth, you must pay the consequences. Of course, these were fun questions, but the consequence was the important thing . . . I would ask a question and occasionally the contestant would answer it. I had picked this contestant, and I didn't want to lose him, so suddenly it became a two-part question. I did the show for eighteen years, and once I had a fellow answer two questions—but would you believe it? That was a three-part question."

The program was known for opening with the audience in hysterics. They were laughing because they were watching two men from the audience competing to put on women's clothing as fast as they could. Hooking the bra always got the biggest laugh.

There was a writing staff that did nothing but think up wild stunts—the consequences. Barker remembered one of his favorites, "We once had a fellow row from Los Angeles to New York. How were we going to do that? We had a boat on top of a truck. He had to row all the way to New York to win his prize. Every contestant got a bottle of Jungle Gardenia perfume for appearing on the show. I gave away gallons of it."

Of course perfume was a much better prize than Tennessee Ernie Ford gave away on *Whole Hog or None* in which contestants could win ham, bacon, or the whole hog. And Allan Sherman, the great song parodist, hosted a show in which he gave away weird prizes including real garbage. One of the prizes was a garbage disposal and a year's worth of garbage.

Quiz shows were popular in the early years of television because they were inexpensive to produce—prizes were generally a small amount of money or an appliance, often a television set—and always included local residents as contestants. People from the neighborhood could go down to the studio and get on the show. And, as I learned with *Star Search*, it's amazing how many people want to be on TV.

One quiz show format viewers particularly loved was stunt shows, and the more embarrassing the stunts, the more viewers loved them. On Bud Collyer's *Beat the Clock,* contestants had to complete a made-for-TV stunt within a specific period of time to win. Among the writers who created the stunts was Neil Simon, and one of the "stunt testers" who made sure it could be done was James Dean. The stunts almost always involved balancing or piling or throwing common household items, often blindfolded, without using hands or feet. Usually whipped cream or other messy stuff was somehow involved. On *Dollar a Second*, hosted by comedian Jan Murray, contestants had to complete stunts before a certain event took place. The gimmick was that no one really knew how long the event would take. The event might be the length of time it took for one hundred cars to go through New York's Lincoln Tunnel or when the eighth plane landed at LaGuardia Airport or how long it would take for a runner to complete two laps around a track. When the stunt was completed, the contestant could quit and would win a dollar for every second he had been on the air, but if he failed to complete the stunt or the certain event was completed before he finished, he would lose everything he had earned.

Other quiz show formats got quite creative. Robert Q. Lewis, who often substituted for Arthur Godfrey, hosted several shows, including *Masquerade Party*, in which a panel had to figure out what celebrity was in disguise by asking simple questions, and *The Name's the Same*, in which panelists had to figure out a contestant's unusual name— Ima Hogg, for example, or Fillmore Johns—or the name they shared with a celebrity, such as Abraham Lincoln or Joe DiMaggio. *It's News to Me* was at first hosted by John Daly, who asked questions about current events. John Reed King hosted shows on both radio and TV, including both the radio and TV versions of *Missus Goes A-Shopping*,

Courtesy of Stephen Cox Collection

Famed game show host John Reed King emceed more than a dozen shows between 1944 and 1955, among them *Chance of A Lifetime*, seen here.

the 1946 TV quiz show *It's a Gift, Chance of a Lifetime, Give and Take, Battle of the Ages*, and *Why?*

By 1951 the prizes started getting bigger. *The Big Payoff*, hosted by Randy Merriman and former Miss America Bess Myerson, went on the air in 1951. This was a question-and-answer format in which men could win prizes for their ladies. Four correct answers—which wasn't easy—won a mink coat and a trip to France. *The Big Payoff* eventually became the top-rated network daytime show in the country—not just the top-rated quiz show, but the top-rated show of any type.

The two most popular panel shows were *What's My Line?*, hosted by tuxedo-clad newsman John Daly, and *I've Got A Secret*, which was hosted by all-around popular guy Garry Moore. On *What's My Line?*, based loosely on the old game of Twenty Questions, the panel tried to guess a contestant's line, or profession. When an attractive blonde professional wrestler was the guest, panelist Groucho Marx asked if her profession involved being blonde. When she said it didn't, Groucho pointed out, "A woman can't make a living being a blonde? I've known some who do."

Bow tie–wearing Garry Moore, one of television's most popular personalities, had his own daytime and nighttime variety shows—he's credited with discovering Carol Burnett and Alan King—and was host of *I've Got A Secret*. Like other popular TV personalities such as Art Linkletter, Bill Cullen, Henry Morgan, Robert Q. Lewis, Bud Collyer, Bob Barker, and Ralph Edwards, Garry Moore didn't sing or dance or tell jokes or balance plates on poles or do ventriloquism. He just made the audience feel comfortable, as if they were with an old friend. Garry Moore smiled easily and often and knew the broadcaster's secret that the better your guests and costars look, the better you look. His announcer was the long and lean Durwood Kirby, later made even more famous on *Rocky and Bullwinkle* as the character Kirwood Derby.

I've Got a Secret, which was produced by the legendary Mark Goodson and Bill Todman, was created by Allan Sherman and for a time held the record as TV's longest-running network game show, running fifteen years before going into syndication. The format was as simple as the title. The show's panel had to guess the secret of the guest contestant. On the first show, celebrity guest Boris Karloff, known for playing very scary roles, admitted that he was afraid of mice. Paul Newman's secret was that while studying acting he had worked in the Brooklyn Dodgers' Ebbets Field and had served a hot dog to panelist Henry Morgan. A ninety-six-year-old guest was the last living person who had been inside Ford's Theater the night Abraham Lincoln was assassinated. The biggest prize a contestant could win was eighty dollars, but everyone went home with a carton of Winston cigarettes.

OK, it's time for our next challenge. What is the retail price of this book? Don't look at the cover; just try to remember exactly how much it is, whether you paid that much or not. Now let's see which of our readers came closest to the actual retail price of this book without going over. And that is pretty much the entire premise of *The Price Is Right*.

Courtesy of Stephen Cox Collection

In 1950 CBS changed the name of Goodson and Todman's first TV game show, *Occupation Unknown* to *What's My Line?* hosted by John Charles Daly (bottom, center) surrounded by panelists Arlene Frances (left), Bennett Cerf (top) and Dorothy Kilgallen (right). The show ran for 18 years in primetime and seven more years in syndication.

The Price Is Right, which premiered in 1956, and was hosted by Bill Cullen, is the longest-running—and according to *TV Guide*, the greatest—game show in TV history. The original show, in which four contestants competed to guess the retail price of various items without going over, ran nine years. The format was revised in 1972 so that one contestant would play various pricing games to win some pretty big prizes. That new *The Price Is Right* is the longest-running game show in TV history, hosted for thirty-five years by Bob Barker.

By the way, the shortest-running game show was Jackie Gleason's *You're in the Picture*. Contestants poked their heads through a large picture and had to figure out what it depicted. It lasted exactly one week. The following week Gleason appeared on stage, sitting in a chair sipping an unknown liquid from a coffee cup, and discussed the magnitude of "that bomb."

Only one game show other than *The Price Is Right* has been broadcast in every decade since the 1950s: *To Tell the Truth*. Three contestants would each claim to be an unrecognizable person who had accomplished something special or had something to make him interesting: "I am the world's only snake milker," "I graduated from college in three weeks," "I am the world's greatest liar." Announcer Johnny Olson would start the show by asking, "*What* is your name, please?"

My name is *David Fisher*.

My name is David Fisher.

My *name* is David Fisher.

The panel would then ask questions and have to determine which one of the three contestants was telling the truth about having worked with Ed McMahon to write the book you are now reading, *When Television Was Young*, and his 1998 biography, *For Laughing Out Loud*, for example. Johnny Olson would then say his next memorable line, "Will the real David Fisher please stand up."

Through the years, *To Tell the Truth* had a number of hosts, including Bud Collyer, Garry Moore, and Bill Cullen. Among the many panelists was the real Johnny Carson. Johnny Olson, one of the finest announcers in television, was the announcer for thirty-two different game shows including *To Tell the Truth*, *The Price Is Right*, *I've Got a Secret*, and *Snap Judgment*, "with your host Ed McMahon!"

Now I have another little game for you. Try to create the worst possible format for a quiz or game show, something so incredible that the audience would watch it with their mouths open in disbelief. One such show might be one in which sick contestants reveal their symptoms to a panel of doctors, who try to guess their diseases. Contestants who fool the panel win a free week at the famed Mayo Clinic. Just such a show aired. But even that doesn't begin to qualify as the worst quiz or game show ever. How about a show in which the winner is the person who has suffered the worst tragedy? A show in which a contestant who has absolutely nothing loses to someone who has even less?

Strike It Rich was adapted from radio in 1951 and ran on television through 1958. It was a quiz show for really poor people who desperately needed money. Contestants would explain why they needed money for an operation or to keep their farm or to be able to get the old car fixed so they could get to the hospital for kidney dialysis. They would then have to answer a few relatively simple questions and win prizes like a new refrigerator or a trip to Bermuda. But if they didn't win, they had one final hope—the Heart Line. Host Warren Hull would urge people to phone in with cash or gifts for this poor family. This wasn't simply a tearjerker; it was a tear yanker, a tear factory. Warren Hull defended the show: "We don't force people to appear on our show or say anything they don't want to say, but the people who have been criticizing us should read some of the mail from people whose lives have been saved. Mothers and fathers have been reunited with children. Doctors and nurses have finished their training." The show received an estimated three thousand requests a week to appear as a contestant.

TV Guide described *Strike It Rich* as "a despicable travesty of the very nature of charity." The Family Service Association of America said, "Victims of poverty, illness, and everyday misfortune should not be made a public spectacle or seemingly be put in a position of begging for charity." Finally, the government tried to ban *Strike It Rich* and all giveaway shows in a case that was argued in front of the Supreme Court. Justice Felix Frankfurter commented that people watched these shows because of a "vacuity of mind." But that action went nowhere, and about twenty-five million people a week continued to watch the show.

The worst thing about *Strike It Rich* is that it wasn't even the worst show. The worst game show of all was *Queen for a Day*. Four contestants appeared each day and told their terrible stories, and then the audience voted by applauding with the result registered on an applause meter. The stories these people told were just terrible. A woman who was the fourteenth of seventeen children won by asking for furniture and appliances for her parents. In addition to furniture, she won a stay at the Hollywood Knickerbocker Hotel, a makeup session, and a hair-styling session. A pregnant woman with nine children whose husband had died in an accident wanted paint and materials to repair her home. A woman with a premature baby asked for a nipple, bottle warmer, and sterilizer. A woman in a hospital in an iron lung—a large metal chamber that helped a person breathe and was used mostly to help victims of polio—asked for her own iron lung so she could go home. Although she won and host Jack Bailey went to the hospital to crown her and hand her roses, she actually received a washing machine. The publicity she received on the show caused the state to take away her four children. The show was popular on radio

...a word from JACK BAILEY:

"TAKE MY ADVICE...YOUR OPPORTUNITY WILL BE BETTER IF YOU READ THIS!"

We're looking for unusual and interesting wishes . . . and the reason for these wishes.

1. WISH FOR SOMETHING FOR YOURSELF OR YOUR FAMILY. DON'T WISH FOR MONEY. <u>WISH FOR THE THING YOU WANT THE MONEY FOR.</u>

2. We cannot accept wishes for operations or medical care.

3. Make your wish and the reason for your wish complete and honest. Do not attach anything to your ticket.

4. To be a candidate you must be 18 or over unless married.

DOORS CLOSE 12:15 P.M. • JULY 17, 1959

Queen For A Day was one of several shows that exploited misery, with the winner being the neediest person. Unanswered was the question of how bad a loser felt when she realized her life wasn't bad enough to win. This is a ticket for the show.

for twelve years and on television for a decade. It was so popular, in fact, that NBC lengthened it from thirty to forty-five minutes.

I hosted several quiz shows, most of them in later years: *Snap Judgment, Missing Links, Whodunnit?,* and for brief time I hosted a terrific show called *Concentration*, in which there was a prize behind each number on a board. Contestants who matched the same prize behind two numbers uncovered pieces of a rebus. The first person to figure out the puzzle got to keep all the prizes they had matched. It was a good show.

The first network job I had was hosting *Bride and Groom*. The show had already been cancelled when I was hired, but someone was needed to announce the show for the final six weeks. I would ask the bride and groom how they met, how the groom proposed, where they intended to live, and then watched as they were married on the show. The couple received various inexpensive prizes donated by the manufacturers in return for the product plug—including the opportunity to drive a new car all the way to the airport! We did give away honeymoon trips, sometimes as far as Hawaii. But when one contestant learned he and his bride would be going all the way to Princeton, New Jersey, he started arguing with the crew, which caused a fight with his bride, who then cancelled the wedding and walked out on him. That night he broke into her house and was arrested. That was not exactly the result he had in mind when he agreed to get married on television. Another couple was given a Hawaiian honeymoon—and had filed for divorce before the kinescope was broadcast there.

Several game shows tested contestants' knowledge of music. The best was *Name That Tune*, in which opponents competed to see who could identify a song from the fewest notes. The syndicated show *Tuno* was played at home. Viewers picked up *Tuno* cards, which were basically bingo cards, and checked off numbers on the card corresponding to songs played on the show that they could identify. The first ten winners to call a sponsoring store in each market won small prizes. However, when a main sponsor decided it wanted to offer bigger prizes to all winners, somebody made a slight mistake that enabled 250 winners to show up—and to receive more than fifty thousand dollars in prizes, quite a bit more than the sponsor had budgeted.

Some shows existed primarily as platforms for their very clever hosts and talented young announcers. The best known was Groucho Marx's *You Bet Your Life*, announced by Groucho's foil, George Fenneman. It started as a radio show and went on television in 1950. Originally the sponsor expected Groucho to wear the black frock coat and painted-on mustache familiar to movie fans, but he refused, saying, "If I can't be funny on television without funny clothes and makeup, the hell with it." A pair of contestants wagered a few bucks that they could answer some questions, but while doing so, as Groucho explained, "Say the secret word, and a duck will come

The great Groucho Marx— here with announcer George Fenneman—starred in the quiz show *You Bet Your Life*, which served as an excuse for him to talk to guests. Typical of the questions he asked contestants was "What's a paradox?" The answer: "Two doctors."

Courtesy of Stephen Cox Collection

down and give you fifty dollars." The duck—with Groucho's signature mustache, eyeglasses, and a cigar in its mouth—was as much the star of the show as Groucho. If the contestant did say that word— and there were times Groucho led them to it—the duck descended from the ceiling carrying the cash.

The format allowed Groucho to interview the contestants, which was really what the show was all about. Supposedly spontaneous, some of the show was scripted. Everything was set up for Groucho simply to be Groucho, "Where are you from?" he asked one typically attractive young woman. She replied that she was from Ralph's Grocery store. "You were born in a supermarket? I thought supermarkets didn't make deliveries anymore."

Another young mother told him she and her husband were educating their children at home, teaching them the "three R's." "The three R's!" Groucho said. "I remember them from vaudeville. They were awful." The woman explained she actually meant reading, writing, and arithmetic, to which Groucho pointed out, "Well, now only one of those begins with the letter *R*. Do you have an explanation for that?"

If the contestants didn't win any money, Groucho asked them a twenty-five-dollar consolation-prize question such as, "Who's buried in Grant's tomb?" "How long do you cook a three-minute egg?" "What color is an orange?" or "When did the War of 1812 start?" The show lasted an amazing fourteen years. And since it was one of the very few game shows done on film—to allow Groucho's ad-libs to be edited—it became the first game show to be rebroadcast in syndication.

Another show that existed almost entirely to showcase the talents of its brilliant host was *Who Do You Trust?* starring the young comedian Johnny Carson and his faithful sidekick—me. Johnny and I first worked together on this show, a partnership that lasted more than three decades. The connection between Johnny and Groucho was strong. In fact, our first night on *The Tonight Show,* Groucho introduced Johnny, almost as if he was handing him the comedic crown.

Before becoming host of *Who Do You Trust?* in 1957, Johnny had done another quiz show, *Earn Your Vacation. Trust* was a new version of a prime-time quiz show entitled *Do You Trust Your Wife?* hosted by ventriloquist Edgar Bergen and his dummy. When they moved the show to daytime, Bergen did not want to participate and Johnny was hired. Johnny would ask questions to a couple, and the husband had to decide if he or his wife would answer them. The couple who answered the most questions correctly got to play for the grand prize, which, truthfully, was not so grand.

But it was all a set-up for Johnny. We had unusual guests—for example, a woman who wanted to teach Johnny how to breathe through his toes or a pharmacist who sold voodoo supplies—and Johnny participated in all kinds of demonstrations, from riding a motorized soap box derby car—and crashing it into the set—to putting on scuba gear and falling into a giant fish tank that happened to appear onstage.

The best *Who Do You Trust?* shows were the Monday shows. Generally we did one show a day live, but on Fridays we did two shows: one in the morning, and we taped the show for the following Monday much later in the afternoon. Between shows Johnny and I would spend several hours at Hurley's bar on the corner of Forty-ninth Street and Sixth Avenue, which is why the Monday shows were always the most entertaining.

Johnny did one other thing every day—he set fire to my script. That was our joke. Well, actually, it was his joke. At the beginning of the show, I would have to billboard our six sponsors for that day, and while I was doing that, Johnny would snap open his lighter and set fire to my script. Admittedly there were days I did speed up, but somehow I would get it done. There was pride involved. I was an announcer!

Courtesy of Stephen Cox Collection

On October 1, 1962, when Groucho Marx introduced Johnny Carson to the nation's late-night television audience as the new host of *The Tonight Show*, he passed his creative torch to the new young comedian from *Who Do You Trust?*

We did that show for five years on ABC until NBC hired Johnny and he asked me to come with him. ABC tried to continue *Who Do You Trust?* without him, but it failed after one season. Johnny was the show. Johnny was always the show.

By 1958 there were twenty-two quiz shows on the air, and the competition had caused a major change—the shows were offering big prizes. *The Big Payoff* in 1951 was peanuts compared to what contestants could win just four years later. In 1955 CBS launched *The $64,000 Question,* hosted by an actor named Hal March and based on the radio show *Take It or Leave It* with its famous sixty-four-dollar question. Contestants answered progressively more difficult questions, doubling their winnings with each correct answer until they reached $64,000. They could quit at any point and take their winnings, and if they had reached the eight-thousand-dollar level and failed to answer a question after that, they left with a new Cadillac. Contestants could choose their own category in which they had some expertise. After winning eight thousand dollars, they returned each week to tell America if they were going to go on or take it and leave; if they continued, they stepped into an "isolation booth" and put on a pair of headphones so they could not hear the audience.

The $64,000 prize was by far the most money ever made available on a quiz show, and it reinforced the idea that television was bigger and better than radio—in this case, one thousand times better. But it was the contestants who eventually captured America's interest. There was an older woman named Myrtle Powers who was an expert on baseball; a Bronx shoemaker, Gino Prato, who, with his heavy Italian accent, seemed to know everything about opera; and psychologist Joyce Brothers who was an expert on boxing.

Do you think you could have done well? The subject is Shakespeare. For sixteen thousand dollars, give the full names of the two publishers of the first folio of Shakespeare's plays and the year it was published . . .

Um, what have you got for a dollar-fifty? The correct answer is Isaac Jaggard and Edward Blount, 1623. OK, I had to look it up.

The first contestant to go for the big prize was retired marine captain Richard McCutchen, whose subject was cooking. The first $64,000 question was, "Identify five dishes and two wines on the now famous menu of the royal banquet given in 1939 by King George VI for French President Albert Lebrun." McCutchen answered it correctly: Consommé quenelles, filet de truite saumonòe, petits pois à la françhaise, sauce maltaise, corbeille, château yquem, Madeira sercial. And he became an American hero. He was invited to appear on other TV shows, to make personal appearances, and to write cookbooks.

Within weeks of its debut, *The $64,000 Question* had become one of the most successful TV shows in history. Fifty-five million people watched McCutchen win the jackpot. For more than a year it was the number one program on television. Other networks almost immediately introduced competing big-prize shows, including CBS's *The Big Surprise* with a $100,000 first prize and *Tic-Tac-Dough*. NBC countered with *The $64,000 Challenge*, which featured the contestants America had come to love on *The $64,000 Question*.

The only show to compete successfully with *The $64,000 Question* was *Twenty-One,* in which two contestants in isolation booths struggled to answer questions of progressive difficulty until one of them accumulated twenty-one points. The added wrinkle of contestants competing against each other made the show popular and eventually turned cleancut, handsome Columbia college professor Charles Van Doren—whose father was the renowned poet Mark Van Doren—into a national icon.

The show was created by Dan Enright, who had created and produced several other game shows, including *Juvenile Jury* and *Life Begins at 80,* which consisted of a panel of eighty-plus-year-olds answering questions. It created a minor scandal when it turned out one of the panel members was actually only in his midsixties. The clever Enright sheepishly admitted the deception, and then conducted a national poll asking whether or not this young whippersnapper should be permitted to stay on the show. The nation voted overwhelmingly that he should stay. It was a silly mistake made by Enright, soon forgotten, but a brightly flashing sign of things to come.

Charles Van Doren won his *Twenty-One* championship by defeating the rather ordinary-looking and noncharismatic Herbert Stempel. Asked, "Which film won the Academy Award in 1955?" Stempel incorrectly answered *On the Waterfront*. And this was 1956—just one year later! The correct answer was *Marty*, one of Stempel's favorite movies.

Unlike *The $64,000 Question*, contestants on *Twenty-One* could continue to play the game until they were defeated. Like an intellectual warrior, Van Doren slayed his opponents week after week until he had won $129,000. It seemed as if the entire nation sweated with him in that confined isolation booth as he desperately searched for the correct answer and, somehow, incredibly, managed to find it

Courtesy of Stephen Cox Collection

The most popular quiz show contestant in TV history was Charles van Doren (left), here with the host of *21*, Jack Barry. Television's Golden Age ended with the revelation that major quiz shows were fixed—and that van Doren had been fed the answers.

somewhere in his mind at the last possible second. He appeared on the cover of *Time* and was a regular guest on *Today*. The great drama made *Twenty-One* the most popular show on TV, even beating *I Love Lucy* in the ratings.

The problem was that the show was rigged. Fixed. Practically scripted. Every bit of it. Stempel not only had been told to give the wrong answer, but he had been provided the wrong answer to give. For a minute he considered being honest, which would have destroyed the show, but he went along with the scam. But months later, when he failed to get a job as a panelist on a future quiz show as Enright had promised, he went public, attempting to inform investigators that the show was hooey. But nobody paid any attention to him, a disgruntled loser—until a notebook was found in which the correct answer to each question asked on the daytime game show *Dotto* was discovered. It turned out that *Dotto* was rigged too. Contestants on *Twenty-One* were in effect nothing more than actors. They were told how to dress, what to say, and how long to wait before responding to a question. And what question to miss. To make contestants sweat inside the isolation booth, the air-conditioning was turned off. The whole thing was a great con, a scam. And it worked . . . until the day Van Doren admitted it while testifying under oath in the House of Representatives.

Within a few months most quiz shows were off the air. Only some of the small-prize game shows survived. This was the first and still remains the biggest scandal in television history. *Twenty-One* was also one of the biggest cons successfully—almost—played on the entire nation. As it turned out, although *The $64,000 Question* wasn't rigged, the producers did manipulate the show by giving harder questions to contestants they wanted to get rid of quickly.

POPULAR BROADCAST TELEVISION, WITH TV SETS IN America's homes, was only one decade old when the scandal erupted.

In that short period of time television had spread successfully from coast to coast, and a lot of it was broadcast in color! The networks had become powerful entertainment corporations, far more important than the movie studios. Movie stars who only a few years earlier would not appear on TV were now practically begging to promote their new movies and other products on television. The short-lived era of live television was over, replaced by film and videotape, which opened up the syndication market and made local stations far more valuable. The industry was moving from New York to the giant sound stages and great weather of Hollywood.

Me? I had come all the way from Philadelphia to New York, and within another decade would be moving to California, too, with Johnny Carson, Doc Severinson, and the whole crew of *The Tonight Show*.

But we had been there at the beginning, right at the beginning, back when television was young. In our own way, we had all made a small contribution to its growth. We had walked the streets of Philadelphia and New York, listening to people tell us it would never work and that we should get into radio, struggling with very long hours and very short pay.

So when I think back on that time . . .

"Think back? Did I ever tell you the one about the agent and the blonde? No? Well, it turned out this blonde walked into the agent's office wearing her personality and . . ."

Milton! Please!

INDEX